IMAGES
of America

CASWELL COUNTY

I0805875

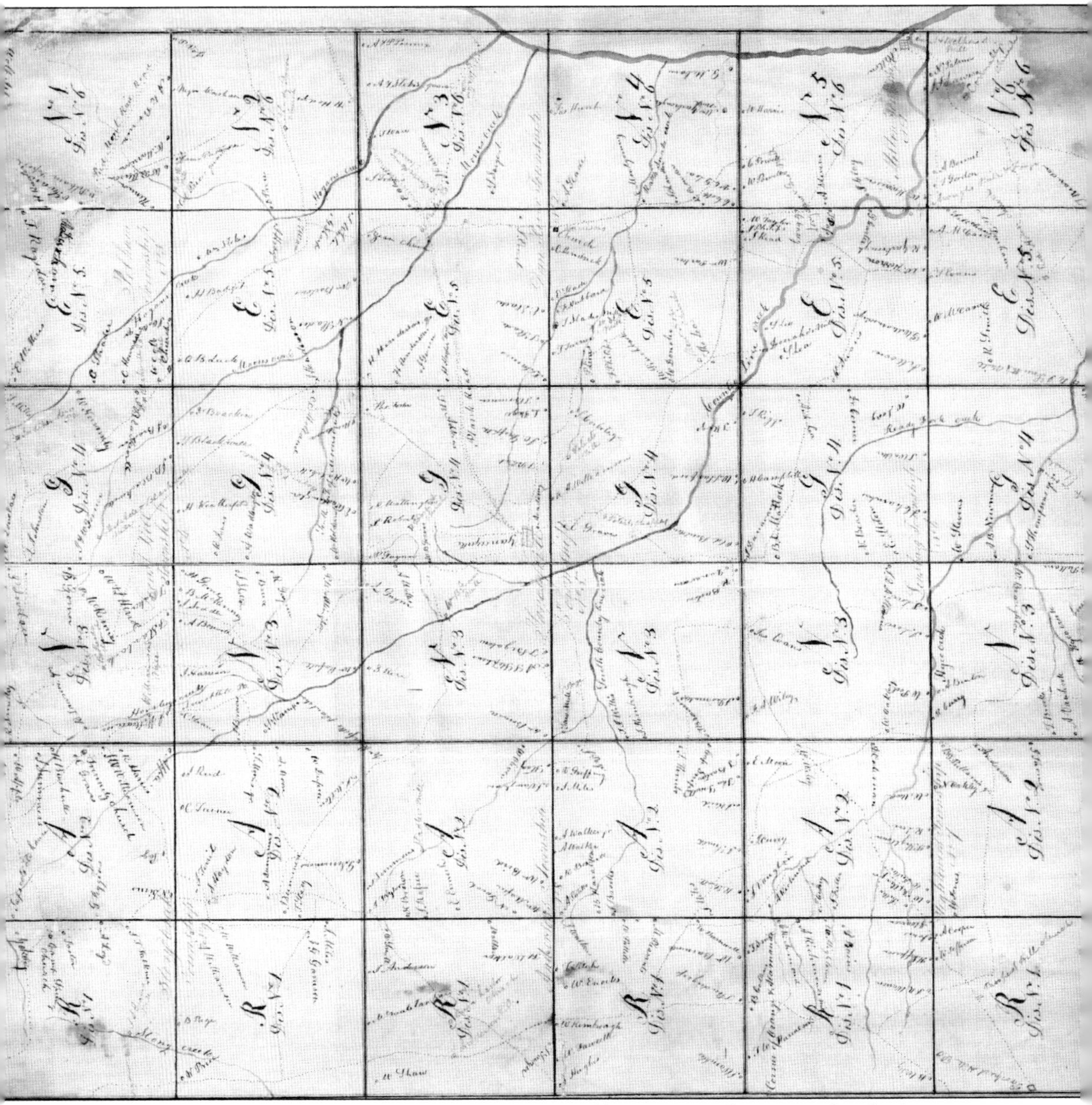

As required by North Carolina law, in 1868 Caswell County took steps to divide the county into townships and school districts. To accomplish this, Samuel Lyle Venable was appointed county surveyor and instructed to conduct the appropriate survey and to prepare maps showing the nine townships and 66 school districts. For the maps, Venable was paid $50. Here is one of the three full-size maps Venable created. A larger version of the map can be found at http://nccha.org/map.jpg. (Courtesy Caswell County Historical Association Photograph Archives.)

ON THE COVER: Caswell County farmers assess the functionality of a Fordson tractor during a demonstration day in the 1920s. The multipurpose tractor was a favorite with Caswell's small farmers as it could be used for many crops, including tobacco. A new Fordson tractor sold for around $400 delivered, which caused mules to remain in use on some farms well into the 1950s. (Courtesy John O. Gunn Estate.)

IMAGES
of America

CASWELL COUNTY

Caswell County Historical Association

ARCADIA
PUBLISHING

ISBN 978-0-7385-6782-2

Published by Arcadia Publishing
Charleston, South Carolina

Printed in the United States of America

Library of Congress Control Number: 2009921905

For all general information contact Arcadia Publishing at:
Telephone 843-853-2070
Fax 843-853-0044
E-mail sales@arcadiapublishing.com
For customer service and orders:
Toll-Free 1-888-313-2665

Visit us on the Internet at www.arcadiapublishing.com

Caswell County has been a special place for over 230 years, and this book is dedicated to the many people who made it so. However, an additional tribute is owed to those who have helped preserve Caswell's history: Sallie Pridgen Anderson, John Oliver Gunn (1892–1992), Annie Yancey Gwyn (1891–1985), Dr. Houston G. Jones; Katharine Kerr Kendall (1921–1997), Ruth Little; Kathy Simmons McPherson, Thomas Richmond McPherson Jr., Millard Quentin Plumblee (1906–1987), William S. Powell, Mary McAden Satterfield (1911–2003), Jeannine Dare Whitlow (1930–2004), and Tony P. Wrenn.

Contents

Acknowledgments

The Caswell County Historical Association (CCHA), organized in 1956, is fortunate to have extensive photograph archives, and many of those images are shared in this book. These photographs have been donated over the years by the wonderful people of Caswell County and those with ancestors from the area. Many photographs never seen by the public were made available for sharing here, and thanks go to all those named as contributors of individual photographs.

Special thanks go to Ann Gunn Everitt, who contributed many photographs, provided editorial and composition advice, and scanned many of this book's photographs.

The CCHA also is indebted to Dr. Houston G. Jones, who contributed many old photographs and wrote the introduction, which provides a historical context for the images of Caswell County.

Thanks go also to Karen Wade Avants, Chris Holaday, Yancey Moorefield Smith, Martha Bradsher Spencer, and James B. Upchurch Jr., who assisted with photograph collection and authorizations.

CCHA archivist and webmaster Richmond S. Frederick Jr. coordinated the project. Without his efforts, this book could not have been published.

—Karen Oestreicher
President
Caswell County Historical Association, Inc.

Several abbreviations and abbreviated phrases are used in the photograph captions. "CCHA Photograph Archives" indicates that an image is owned by the CCHA. "North Carolina Collection" is the North Carolina Collection, University of North Carolina Library at Chapel Hill. "NCSHPO" is the North Carolina State Historic Preservation Office.

Other than Leasburg, Milton, and Yanceyville, Caswell County generally is rural. References to those three communities will be without designating the county and state.

For additional information on the history of Caswell County and the genealogy of its people see the Web sites listed on page 127.

Introduction

by Dr. Houston G. Jones

East met west in Caswell County. By the 1750s, when Robert Kilgore on Hyco Creek and Thomas Hart on Hostler Branch took up land just south of the Virginia border, the territory then in Orange but destined to become Caswell was no longer a mystery to westward-moving Europeans. Nor had it been a mystery to small bands of ancient Asiatic stock who for centuries had camped and hunted along the same streams. Abandoning the land to the strangely clad invaders bearing magic weapons, these darker-skinned itinerants, as they retreated westward, left behind little more than stone implements. As in all of what was to become the United States of America, our ancestors occupied someone else's land. For nearly three more centuries, their descendants would also depend heavily upon someone else's labor. With several costly interruptions, the new settlers and their descendants—joined by arrivals representing much more diverse origins in both Europe and Africa—felled the trees, tilled the soil, built permanent residences, and established laws that eventually sought to atone for that initial inhumanity. That is the history of Caswell County—and of the United States.

These lands leaned northeasterly, drained by creeks like Hyco, Country Line, Rattlesnake, Moon, and Hogan. Only one stream was dignified as a river—the Dan—and it wiggled across the border only far enough to isolate a virtual no-man's land, its future residents feeling more Virginian than Carolinian. Caswell's terrain was too irregular for the Great Wagon Road from Pennsylvania and the Great Trading Path from coastal Virginia, the first of which passed to the west, the latter to the southeast. Nature was to dictate the future of the region.

These few hundred transplanted easterners soon complained about the distance across many streams to the county courthouse in far-off Hillsborough. The "Inhabitants of the North side of Orange County" submitted a mild appeal to Royal Governor William Tryon, but they soon had an even greater complaint—corrupt county officials. Landholders voted for only delegates to the Colonial Assembly, which, in cahoots with the governor, appointed all local officials. The most mistrusted of these officers were the county sheriff, who collected taxes, and the county clerk, who pocketed fees levied on all legal transactions. Distant settlers joined with more substantial farmers in vocal protests, which, when no relief was offered, led to isolated acts of violence. The response was a requisition for steers and flour for the use of brightly dressed soldiers that marched from New Bern to put down the "rebellion." It will never be known how many frontiersmen from northern Orange took up arms in the Regulator War that ended disastrously in the Battle of Alamance in 1771, but within a few years they rose to challenge an even greater eminence, the Crown of Great Britain. The American Revolution did not always pit neighbor against neighbor in battle, but the years of requisitioning livestock, wagons, and foodstuffs for the troops strained relations and created suspicions of disloyalty. Scattered forces passed through, but the northern swath of Orange escaped major depredation.

As created in 1777, Caswell County stretched along the Virginia line between Granville and Guilford (after 1785, Rockingham), with the county seat in the vicinity of present-day Leasburg. The population of the county increased rapidly—it reached 10,000 by 1790—and the eastern part was carved off as Person. The downsized county's new and more centrally located seat was initially called simply Caswell Court House. Thus, as the 19th century approached, Caswell took on its present configuration of about 435 square miles. By 1810, its population reached the figure contained in the larger boundaries 20 years earlier. Its most distinguished visitor, Pres. George Washington, spent a short night at "one Gatewoods" during his southern tour in 1791. A highway historical marker commemorates the visit near the Virginia border.

Far from centers of commerce and without a stable currency, early settlers sought self-sufficiency, raising livestock and growing foodstuffs from the soil. Gristmills, indispensable institutions, sprang up along streams to turn grain into food for man and beast; they also served as community centers for the spreading of news, sharing of common concerns, and conduct of elections. Distilleries, turning grain into hard drink, were ubiquitous, and sawmills provided planks that gradually replaced logs for construction. Most clothing, including footwear, was made locally.

Despite its backwoodsness, Caswell was not without promise. A native son, Archibald DeBow Murphey, moved off to Hillsborough for a distinguished career as attorney and educator, but not before one of his students, Bartlett Yancey, emerged as the brightest star in Caswell. Then only 25, Yancey in 1810 penned a brief but revealing description of his fellow residents: "Caswell is not distinguished for men of talents: We have no men of the first rate talents; but a great number entitled to the rank of mediocrity, and some above it." Religion had taken hold: there were a dozen or more churches, mostly Baptist, Methodist, and Presbyterian; five physicians; three lawyers; and several private schools teaching reading, writing, and ciphering "as far as the rule of three." The best land could be bought for $5 to $10 per acre. Yancey, for whose family the courthouse village was named, went on to become judge, congressman, and speaker of the state senate before dying at the age of 43. By that time other Caswellians—such as Bedford Brown, United States senator; Romulus M. Saunders, minister to Spain; and Calvin Graves, speaker of the state senate—were emerging in leadership roles.

Caswell's economic sun rose during the four decades preceding the Civil War and set with the collapse of the Confederacy in 1865. Tobacco transformed subsistence living to money-crop agriculture. While lowlands continued to grow foodstuffs, the gently rolling highlands produced tobacco, which, with innovations in curing processes (such as demonstrated on Abisha Slade's farm near Purley), increased the popularity of tobacco smoking. The size of farms increased; slavery became more prevalent; tobacco reigned as king of crops; and wealthier farmers fashioned themselves planters. It was during this period that the county's architecturally important courthouse and some of its most impressive homes were built. But as the era of relative prosperity became threatened by the antislavery movement, political views hardened. When war came in 1861, some of Caswell's young men rushed to volunteer; others waited for conscription. Many returned maimed, if they returned at all. During the four war years, women, old men, and black slaves of both sexes carried much of the burden on the home front.

The federal census of 1860 showed that enslaved blacks outnumbered whites 9,355 to 6,578. There were also 282 free persons of color, one of whom, Thomas Day, was a talented furniture-maker who owned six slaves. Five years later, nearly 6 out of 10 persons found themselves "free" but propertyless; many of the others—even whites owning property—were also destitute because of the collapse of the Confederate economy and currency. Well-meaning but naïve Republican efforts to assist the freed people were largely ineffective because even the extension of suffrage to black men was insufficient to counter the devices of the Democratic Party, which soon reestablished white supremacy. In the Caswell County Courthouse in 1870, the bloody murder of state senator John W. Stephens by members of the Ku Klux Klan presaged three decades of racial strife, economic decline, and political intolerance that culminated eventually in the virtual elimination of black suffrage throughout the South. In contrast to the considerable prosperity enjoyed in the antebellum era, Caswell County during the post–Civil War decades became a region of struggling farms and widespread tenancy, including sharecropping, the economic cellar into which many blacks and whites fell.

It was well into the 20th century before Caswell began its recovery from the Civil War and its aftermath. Public education, which became a passion in North Carolina after 1900, was the key. The dual system taxed scarce resources for both black and white schools—the system was never racially equal—but illiteracy gradually gave way to a reading public, and, with the advent of the radio in the 1920s, to a listening public. For whites, community schools yielded to larger consolidated buildings reached by buses driven by students. However, until after World War II, black grammar-grade children walked to dozens of small local schools. Black high school students were, however, bussed to Yanceyville's Caswell County Training School, whose principal, Nicholas Longworth Dillard, was a highly respected educator.

From Colonial times, residents were responsible for roads in their community, but state assistance beginning in the 1920s led to improved roads that lessened the isolation of farm families and broadened the sense of community. From the standpoint of the county's economy, however, the ease of travel produced a detrimental effect, for trade tended to be transacted at Reidsville, Danville, Roxboro, or Burlington, depriving the county of needed revenue. Even Milton's tobacco market and mills were phased out.

Although tobacco returned as the county's money crop in the early part of the new century, overproduction resulted in low prices, and the repeated use of the same fields led to widespread soil erosion. By the 1930s, the term "Thank God for Anson" reflected Caswell County's rating as the second most-eroded county in the state. Consequently, one of the beneficial roles of "New Deal" policies in the 1930s was the introduction of improved farming practices, especially through the Civilian Conservation Corps (CCC), which gave employment to thousands of young men during the Great Depression. Caswell's CCC camp, located near the old county home, assisted farmers in terracing fields and planting soil-saving vegetation (including pestiferous kudzu). Another innovation of the Roosevelt administration was the introduction of a tobacco-growing quota system under which farmers contracted to limit production in return for guaranteed price supports. Citizens of the county shared the pain of the Great Depression, but they proudly pointed out that of the heads of families who accepted federal relief funds, nearly three out of four continued to work, mostly on the land.

About 200 county residents served in the armed forces in World War I, many more in World War II, and graves of Caswell's young men dot foreign countries. A consequence of the latter war—a heightened sensitivity to racial segregation and discrimination—led to tense relations between whites and blacks during the ensuing 50-year civil rights era. It is to the credit of the level-headedness of both races that the county adjusted to revolutionary changes with only a few confrontations. In January 1963, several black students were admitted to previously all-white schools, thus beginning the process of racially integrating the county's public schools. Extension of electricity to rural areas had a direct influence on education and literacy; according to the federal census, illiteracy during the century from 1870 to 1970 decreased from 7,847 to 475. The countywide Gunn Memorial Public Library was opened in Yanceyville in 1966, further stimulating education among the adult population. Many families subscribe to national magazines and daily newspapers, and the telephone, radio, and television now connect citizens throughout the county. Caswell is no longer isolated.

As the 21st century begins, Caswell remains rural—only Milton (with one of the county's few traffic stoplights) and Yanceyville are incorporated. However, except for producing foodstuffs, fewer residents are practicing farmers. Mules and horses have been replaced by mechanization, and much of the county's tobacco acreage quota is controlled by absentee purchasers. There is little industry but many locally owed small businesses; hundreds drive to work in surrounding counties.

The county's history has been modest but—as reflected by frequent genealogical inquiries to the Caswell County Historical Association—is a subject of intense interest to descendants scattered across the country, many of whom chuckle over the quaint community names such as Hell's Half Acre, Kill Quick, Pea Ridge, Purley, Rabbit Shuffle, Buzzards' Roost, Stickridge, and Topnot. Three previous hard-cover publications have helped record that history: William S. Powell (with enormous assistance from M. Q. Plumblee and John O. Gunn), *When the Past*

Refused to Die: A History of Caswell County, 1777–1977 (1977); Jeannine D. Whitlow (editor), *The Heritage of Caswell County* (1985); and Ruth Little-Stokes (compiler), *An Inventory of Historic Architecture, Caswell County, North Carolina* (1979).

Now the Caswell County Historical Association, in association with Arcadia's Images of America series, will preserve a selection of views of the county's people, institutions, activities, and places—images that might otherwise have remained hidden among old papers. If previous publications serve as a guide, these views will reawaken interest and lead to the discovery of additional images that illustrate Caswell's interesting past.

—Houston G. Jones
Cobb Memorial High School Class of 1941

Dr. Houston G. Jones, a native of Caswell County's Locust Hill Township and a navy sonarman in World War II, earned his Ph.D. from Duke University and served as state archivist (1956–1968) and director of the North Carolina Department of Archives and History (1968–1974). For the next 20 years, he was curator of the North Carolina Collection and adjunct professor of history at the University of North Carolina at Chapel Hill, where, at 85, he continues as part-time Davis Research Historian. Among national offices, Dr. Jones has served as president of the Society of American Archivists and secretary of the American Association for State and Local History. In 1975, he founded the North Caroliniana Society and remains its secretary and editor. His books include *For History's Sake*, *The Records of a Nation*, and *North Carolina Illustrated*.

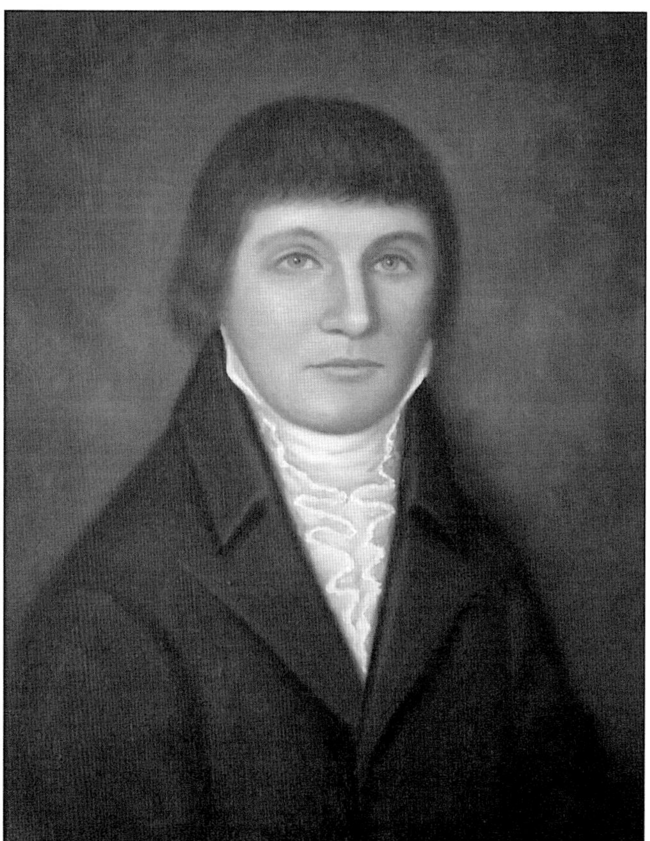

Caswell County is named for Richard Caswell (1729–1789), Revolutionary War hero and the first governor of North Carolina. In 1774, Caswell was elected to represent North Carolina at the Continental Congresses held in Philadelphia. John Adams stated: "We always looked to Richard Caswell from North Carolina. He was a model man and true patriot." (Likeness courtesy Grand Lodge of Ancient, Free, and Accepted Masons of North Carolina.)

One

Caswell's People

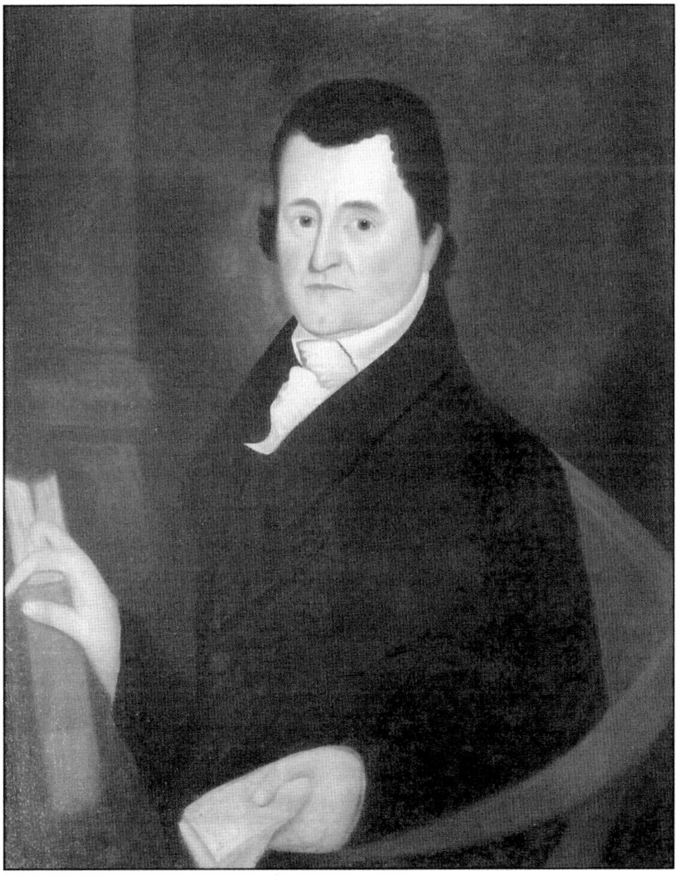

Bartlett Yancey Jr. was born 1785 in Caswell County, where the county seat was named Yanceyville in his honor. Yancey attended the University of North Carolina, became a lawyer, and served in the North Carolina House of Commons, in the U.S. Congress, and in the North Carolina Senate (he was elected speaker seven terms). He died in 1828 and was buried in the family cemetery in Yanceyville. (CCHA Photograph Archives.)

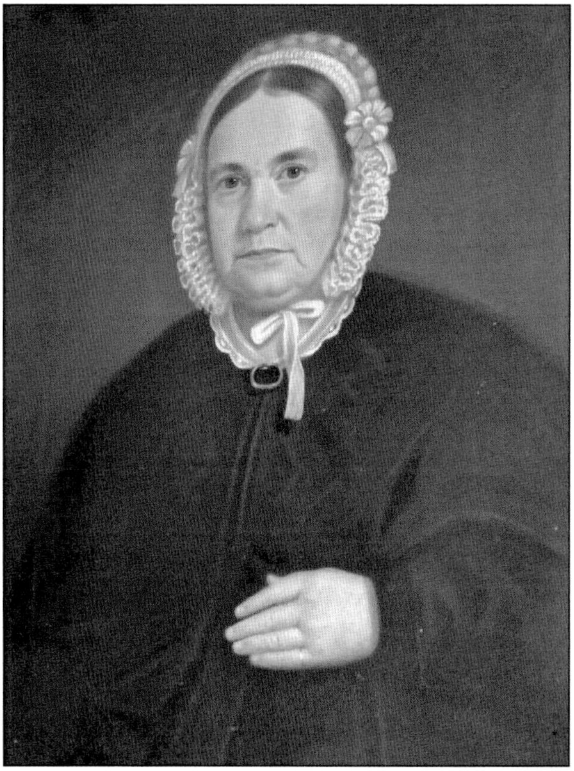

Nancy (Ann) Graves Yancey (1786–1855) was the daughter of Revolutionary War veteran Capt. John Herndon Graves (1746–1829) and Nancy Slade Graves (1749–1807). In 1808, she married her first cousin Bartlett Yancey Jr. (1785–1828). This relationship created the oddity of the mother and wife of Bartlett Yancey Jr. having the same name, Nancy (Ann) Graves Yancey. (CCHA Photograph Archives.)

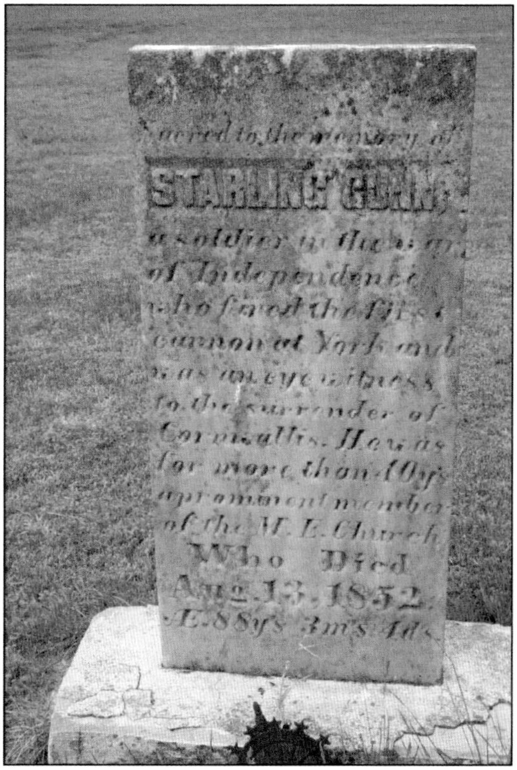

The inscription on the Yanceyville gravestone of Starling Gunn (1764–1852) reads, "Sacred to the memory of Starling Gunn a soldier in the war of Independence who fired the first cannon at York and was an eye witness to the surrender of Cornwallis. He was for more than 40 yrs a prominent member of the M. E. Church. Who Died Aug. 13, 1852. AE. 88y's 3 m's 4d's." (CCHA Photograph Archives.)

Archibald DeBow Murphey (1777–1832), attorney, legislator, and jurist, was born in Caswell County's Red House Community. He was a member of the North Carolina State Senate (1812–1818), where he proposed education and internal improvement programs. His efforts led to the State Literary Fund and the state's first public school act. Murphey died at age 55 and was buried at the Old Town Cemetery in Hillsborough, North Carolina. (CCHA Photograph Archives.)

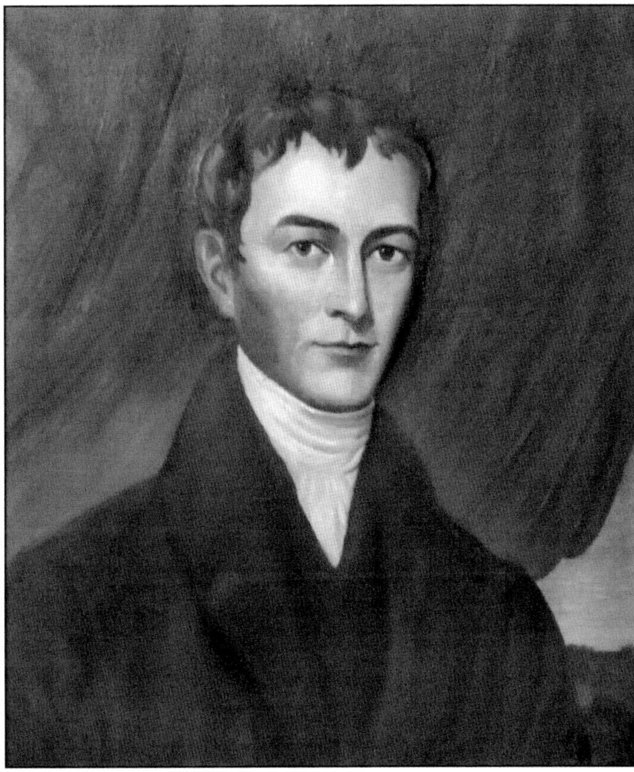

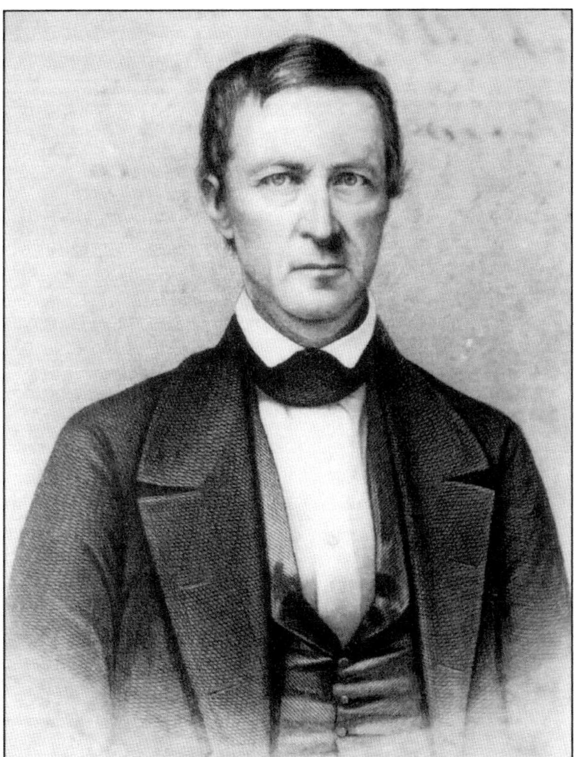

Calvin Graves (1804–1877) was a planter, lawyer, member of the North Carolina House (speaker in 1842), and member of the North Carolina Senate (speaker in 1848–1849). His statesmanship was shown by his tie-breaking vote in 1849 as Speaker of the Senate that authorized an east-west railroad for North Carolina instead of a north-south route that would have run through Caswell County. He never again held political office. (CCHA Photograph Archives.)

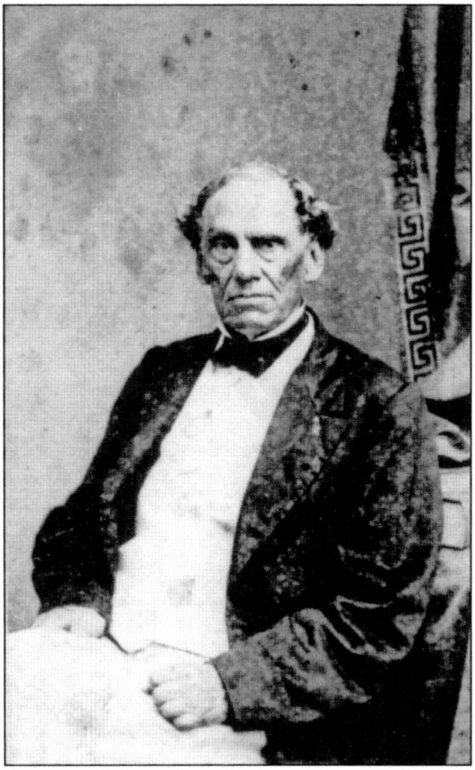

Bedford Brown (1795–1870) was born and died in Caswell County. This photograph was taken by Mathew Brady after the Civil War. Brown served in the North Carolina House of Commons, the North Carolina Senate, and the U.S. Senate. Highly respected, Bedford Brown was one of the leaders of the Democratic Party in the South. His home, Rose Hill, can be seen in Chapter 4. (Courtesy Houston G. Jones.)

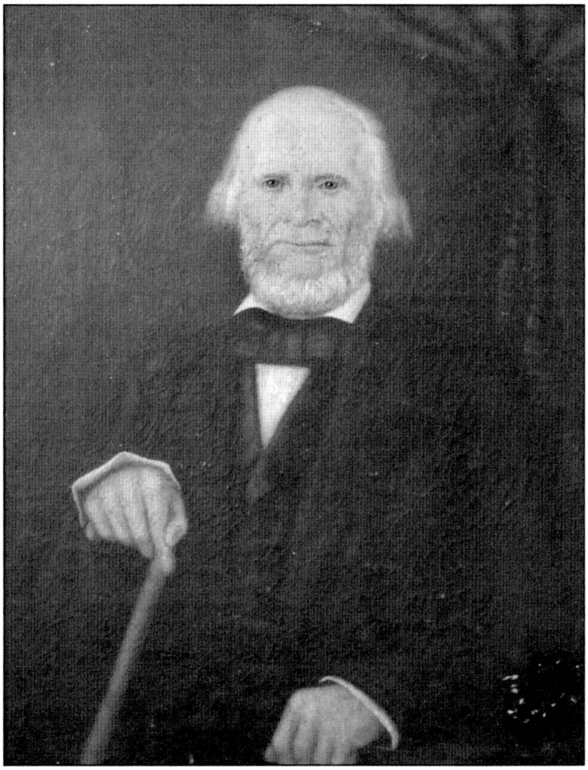

The portrait of Jeremiah Graves (1786–1868) hangs in the Richmond-Miles History Museum in Yanceyville. Graves was a wealthy tobacco planter who owned extensive acreage in Caswell County and many slaves. In the 1830s, he built Dongola, which is described by architectural historian Ruth Little as the "most architecturally pretentious house in Caswell County." A photograph of the house is in Chapter 4. (CCHA Photograph Archives.)

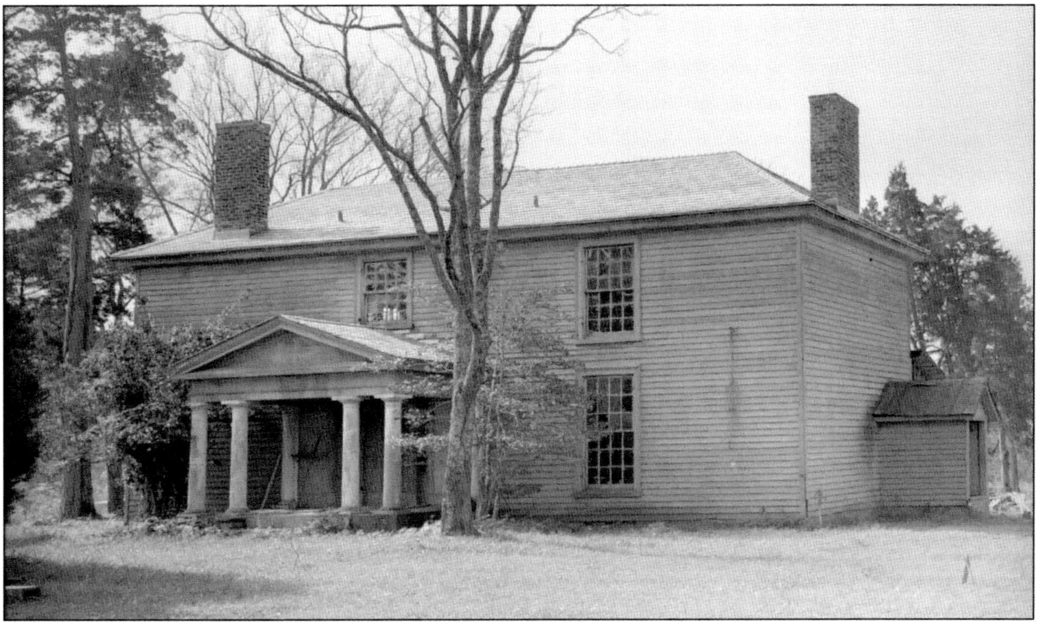

Longwood, near Milton, was the Caswell County home of Romulus Mitchell Saunders (1791–1867), lawyer, judge, member of North Carolina House of Commons (including Speaker of the House in 1819 and 1820), U.S. Congressman, North Carolina Attorney General, unsuccessful North Carolina gubernatorial candidate, and U.S. minister to Spain. He is buried in an imposing vault in Raleigh's old City Cemetery. The house is on the National Register of Historic Places. (NCSHPO.)

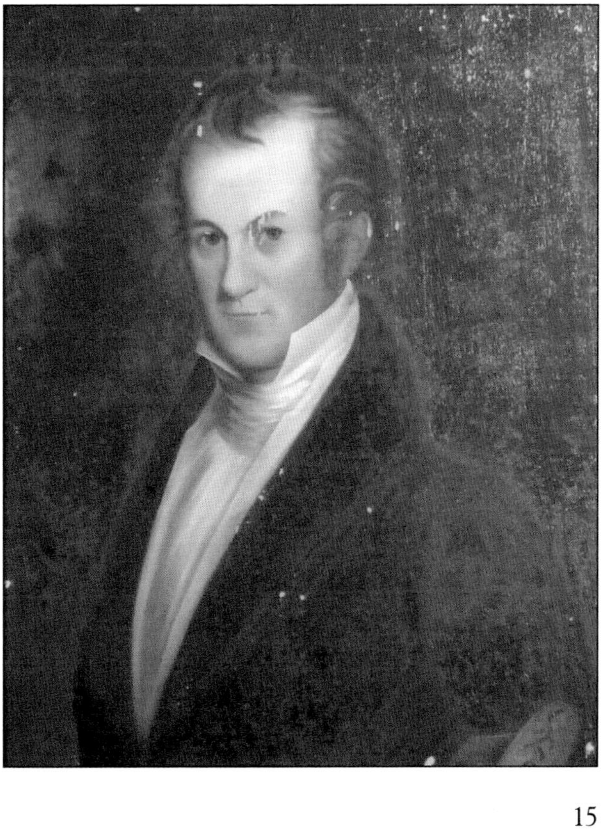

Caswell County native Gen. Azariah Graves (1768–1850) was in command of the 16th Brigade, 3rd Division, of the North Carolina State Militia during the War of 1812. He was a member of the North Carolina State Senate from 1805 to 1811. His portrait hangs in the Richmond-Miles History Museum in Yanceyville, and he is buried in a family cemetery in western Caswell County. (CCHA Photograph Archives.)

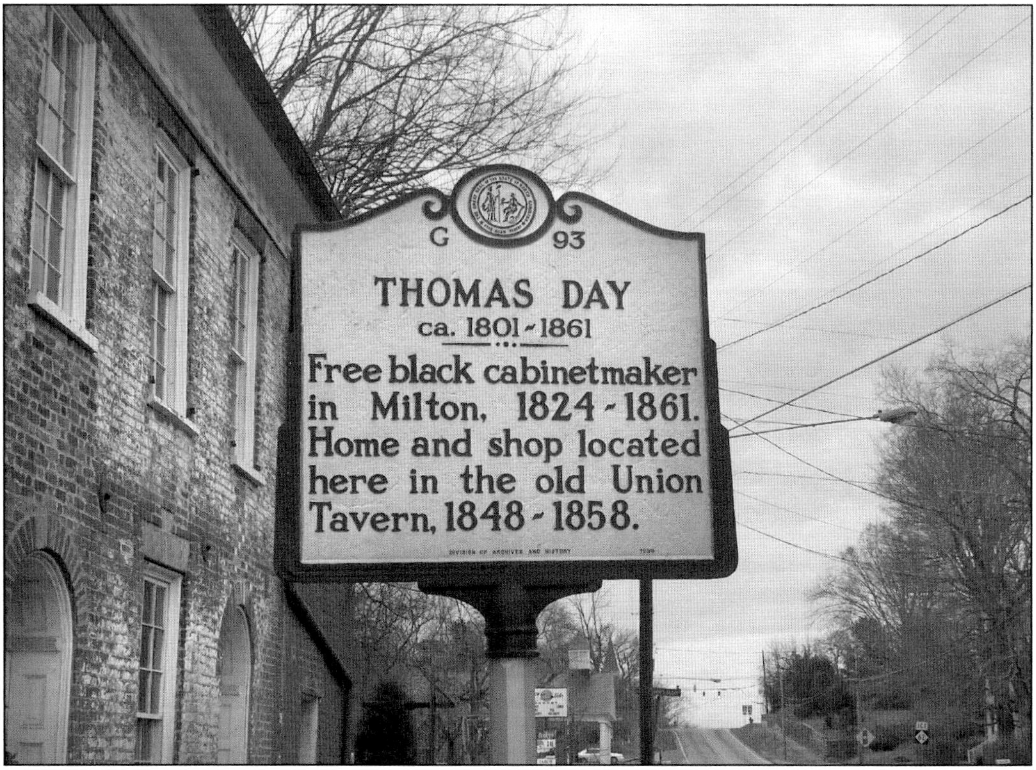

The furniture of free black master craftsman Thomas Day (1801–*c.* 1861) featured expertly crafted beds, rockers, bureaus, sideboards, and tables. He also specialized in interior trim such as mantels and staircases. Before the Civil War, Day owned one of the state's largest furniture workshops (in which he purportedly used slave labor). Day is buried on private property outside Milton. (CCHA Photograph Archives.)

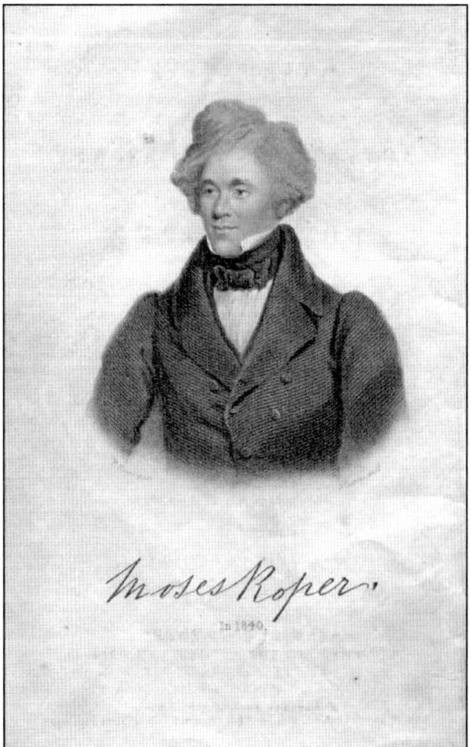

Slave Moses Roper was born in Caswell County around 1815, the son of Henry H. Roper and his mulatto slave Nancy. Escaping after separation from his family, Moses returned to Caswell and found his mother but was discovered and held in the Red House Tavern and at the Caswell County Courthouse. After his final escape he went to England, where he lectured and wrote his autobiography. (North Carolina Collection.)

Paul Anderson Haralson (1798–1852) was born in Yanceyville and served as clerk of court from 1821 to 1841, a position that had been held earlier by his father, Herndon Haralson (1757–1847). In 1836, Paul Haralson built the large house just southeast of the Caswell County Courthouse that is called the "Clerk's House." Because of his wife's poor health, Haralson moved his family to Georgia, where he died in 1852. (Courtesy Tommy Booker.)

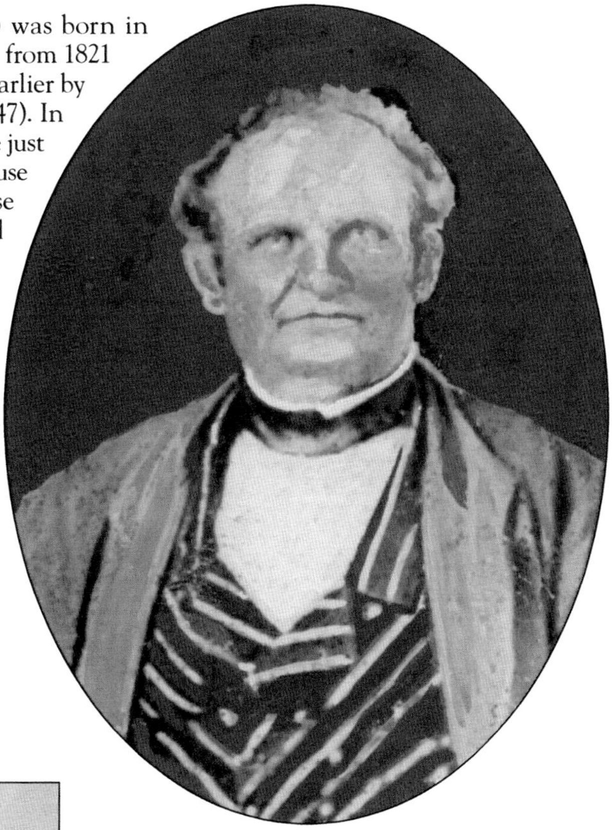

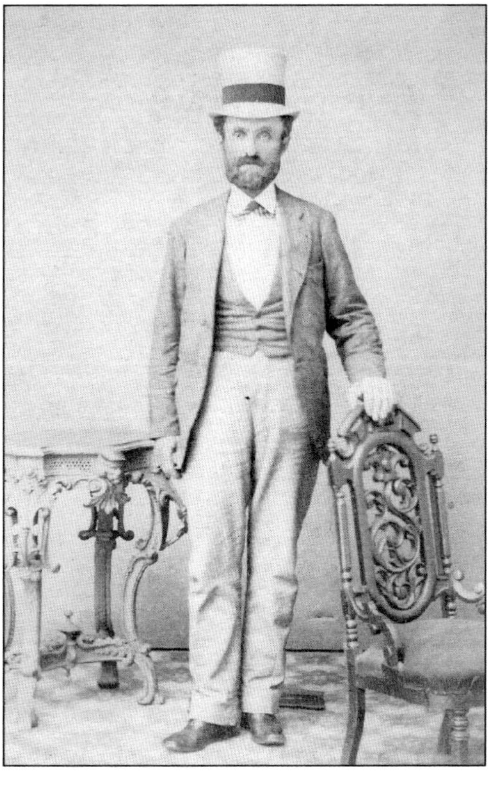

One night in mid-September 1838, Samuel Satterwhite Harrison (1818–1885) rode all night from school in Tennessee to marry his first cousin Louisa Matilda McDaniel (1820–1889). Tradition has it that the house of Samuel Satterwhite Harrison gave the Caswell community of Purley its name. His house, built before 1846 atop a hill, was painted a gleaming white. From a distance it appeared to be a pearly white house. (Courtesy Roger Anderson.)

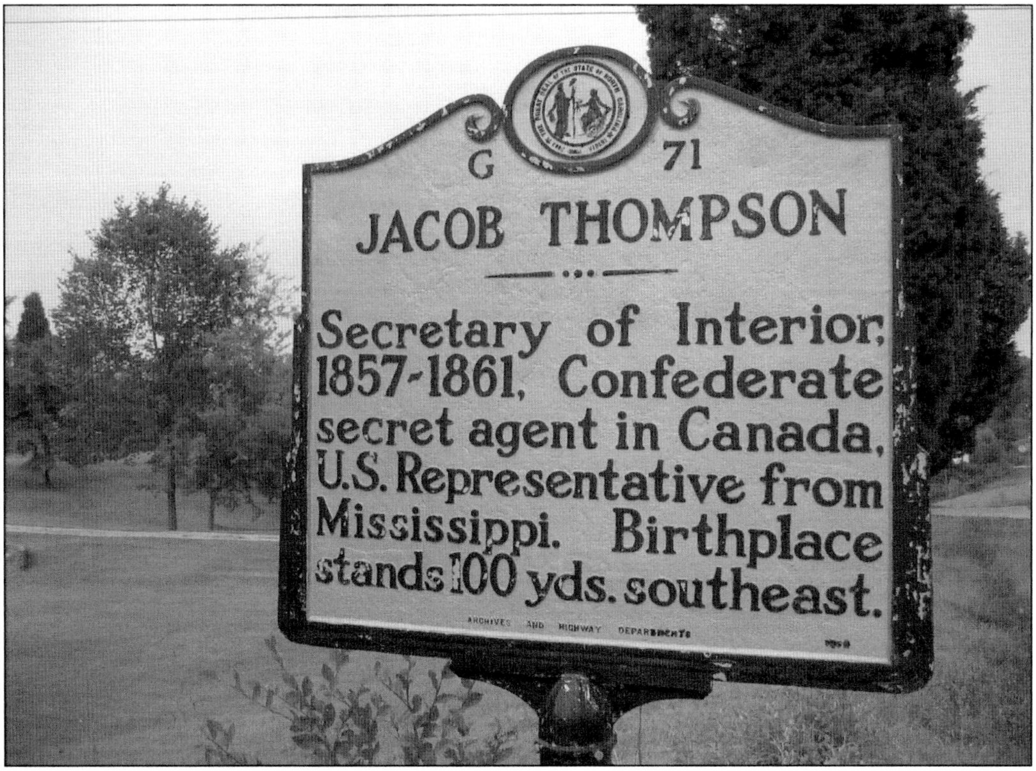

Jacob Thompson (1810–1885) was born in Leasburg, graduated from the University of North Carolina, practiced law in Mississippi, was a U.S. Congressman from Mississippi, and was Secretary of the Interior under President Buchanan. During the Civil War, Thompson served as inspector-general of the Confederate army, as governor of Mississippi, and as a Confederate confidential agent. He died in Memphis, Tennessee, in 1885. (CCHA Photograph Archives.)

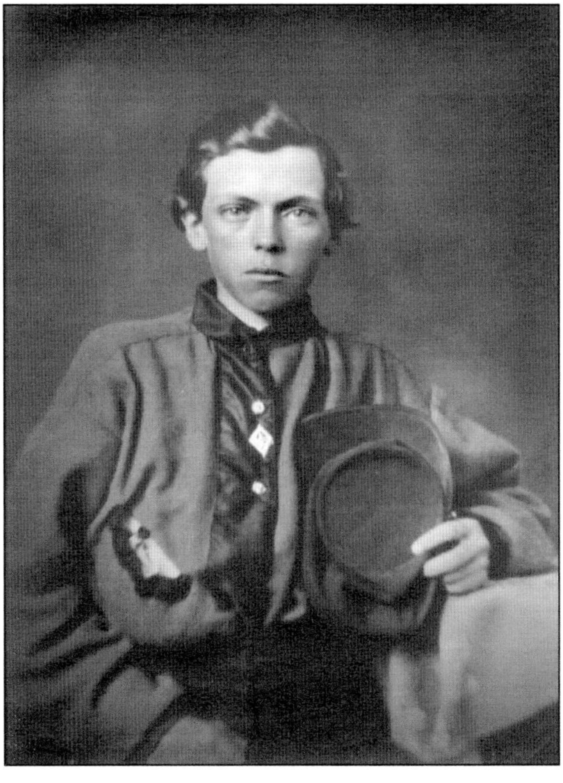

The most lasting contribution made by any soldier during the Civil War may have come from John Baptist Smith, born in 1843 at Hycotee, Caswell County. He invented a system of lanterns with sliding doors used by Confederate blockade-running ships to signal their position as the coast was approached without informing the enemy. Smith died in 1923 and is buried at Caswell's Red House Presbyterian Church. (Courtesy John Storey.)

During the Civil War, Lt. Willie Person Mangum Robertson (1842–1862) served the South as part of the Yanceyville Grays. His Yanceyville gravestone reads: "Lt. Willie P. Robertson, Killed at Gaines Mill, June 27, 1862, Nobly He Fell While Fighting for Liberty." His sister Sallie wrote in her diary: "My 'dearest brother' Willie is no more Oh! How my heart grieves for him." (Courtesy Karen Wade Avants.)

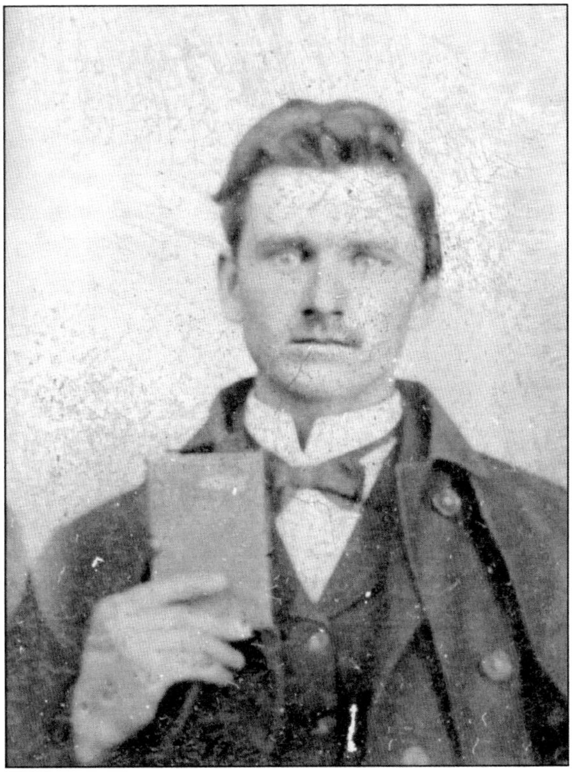

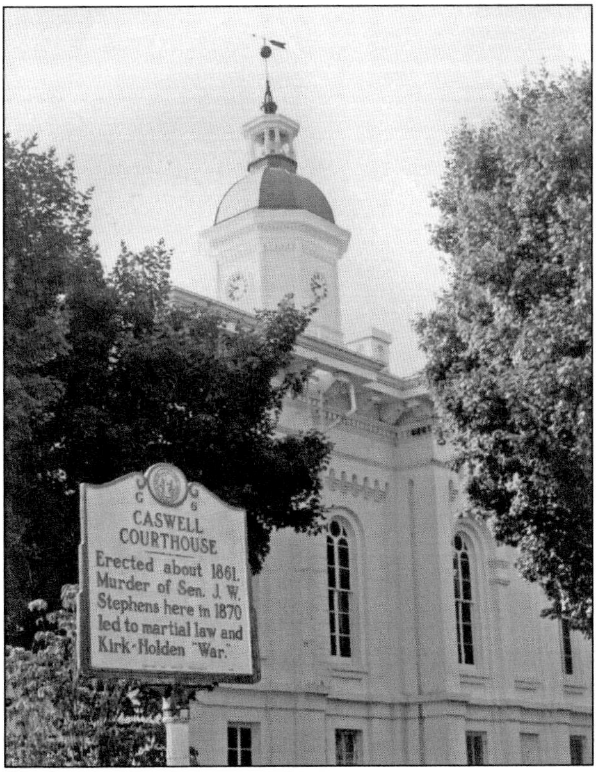

In 1940, the historical marker in front of the Caswell County Courthouse referred to the "alleged" Ku Klux Klan murder of Sen. John Walter Stephens (1834–1870). The language later was changed to confirm that in 1870, North Carolina state senator Stephens indeed was murdered in the courthouse by the KKK. Stephens was unpopular with the white community because of his relationship with the recently freed slaves. (Courtesy Susan Lassiter.)

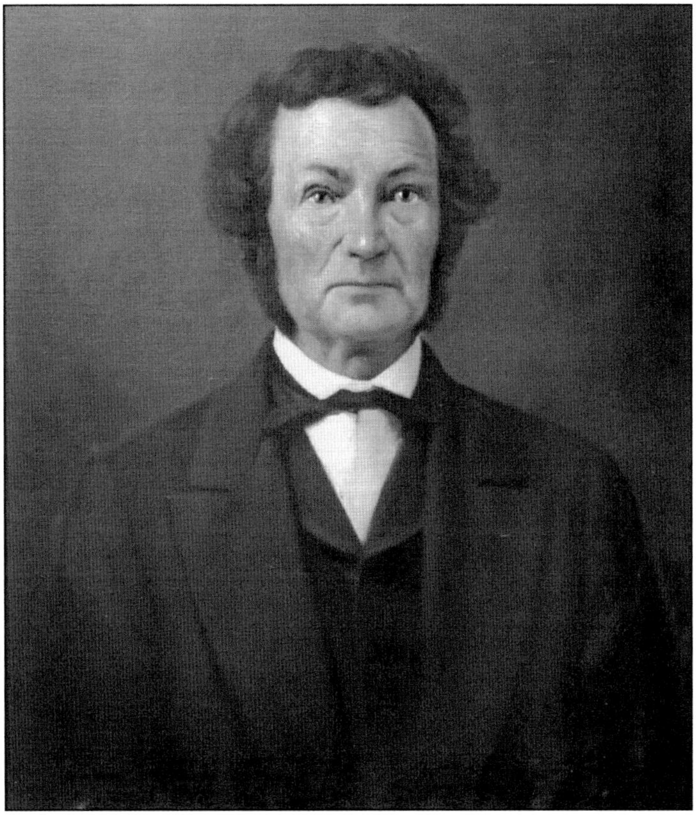

Born in Leasburg, Rev. Solomon Lea (1807–1897) was an educator of some renown. A graduate of the University of North Carolina and a Methodist minister, he taught at the prestigious Warrenton Academy and at Randolph Macon College, was the first president of Greensboro College (Greensboro, North Carolina), and founded the successful Somerville Female Institute in Leasburg (which he operated for 44 years). (Courtesy Brock Historical Museum of Greensboro College.)

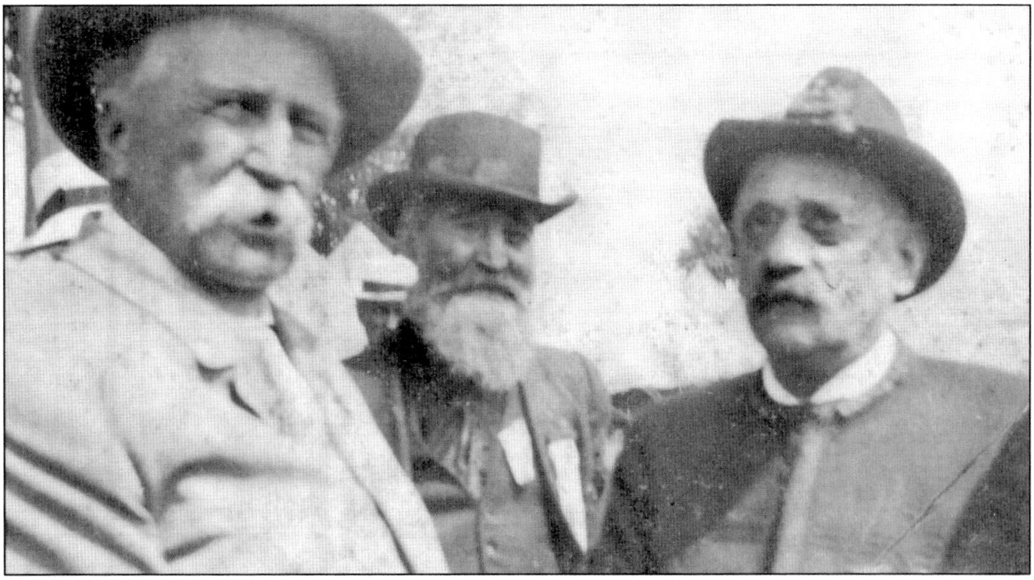

John Hosea McNeil Kerr (1844–1924), on the left, was a lieutenant in the Confederate army and lost a leg in fighting around Winchester, Virginia. He was Caswell County's clerk of court from 1874 to 1882 and purchased the historic brick building in Yanceyville that became the Kerr Hotel. The identity of the other men at this Civil War reunion is not known. (Courtesy Karen Wade Avants.)

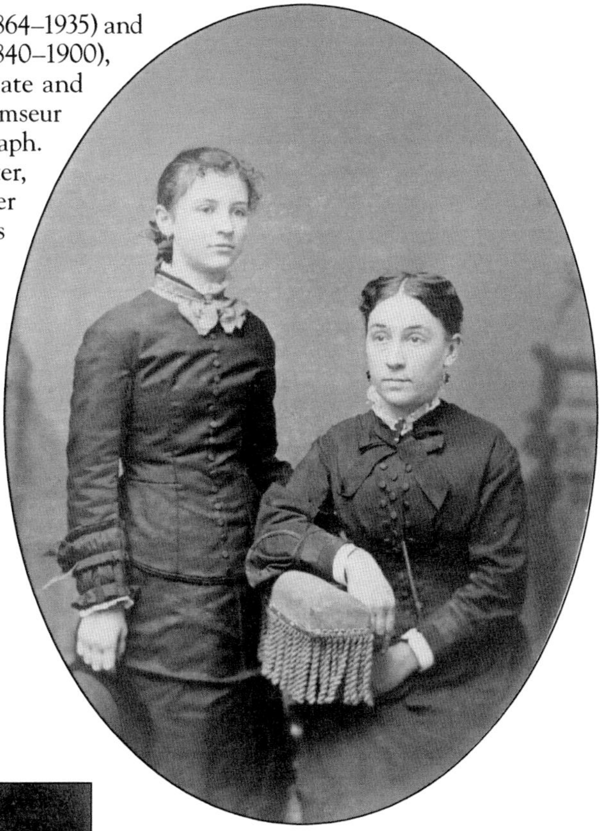

Twelve-year-old Mary Dodson Ramseur (1864–1935) and her mother, Ellen Richmond Ramseur (1840–1900), daughter and wife of West Point graduate and Confederate general Stephen Dodson Ramseur (1837–1864), appear in this 1876 photograph. General Ramseur never saw his daughter, as he was killed in battle soon after her birth. At his side when he died was his friend from West Point, Union general George Armstrong Custer. (CCHA Photograph Archives.)

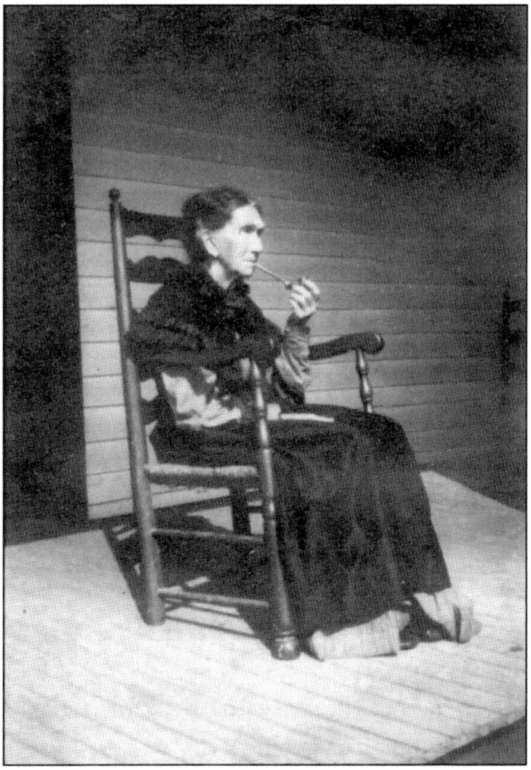

Martha Collins Harrelson (1822–1916) of southern Caswell enjoyed smoking a pipe. She was the second wife of Thomas Williamson Harrelson (1805–1876), and the couple had 12 children. Her older sister Euphrasia was the first wife of Thomas Williamson Harrelson. The photograph dates from the 1890s. (Courtesy Nelson and Cindi Straughn.)

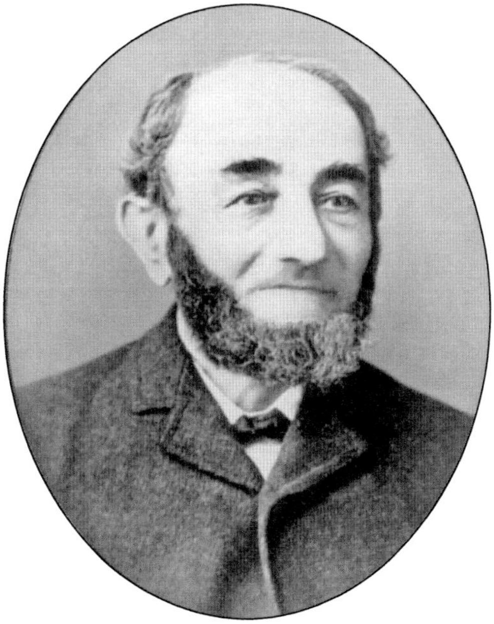

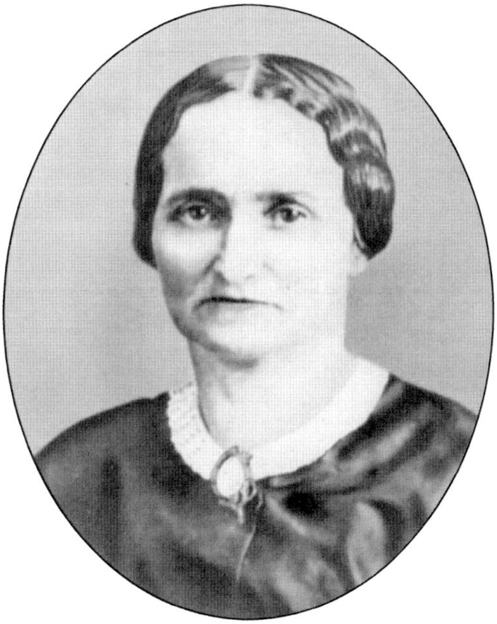

Lazarus Fels (1815–1894) and Susanna Freiberg Fels (*c.* 1818–1876) emigrated from Bavaria to the United States in 1848. In 1855, Fels moved his family to Yanceyville, where he was the town's leading merchant. Fels was Yanceyville's postmaster during the Civil War. In 1866, he moved the family to Baltimore and later to Philadelphia. The family is best known for Fels Naptha Soap, which provided great wealth. (Courtesy Samuel S. Fels Fund.)

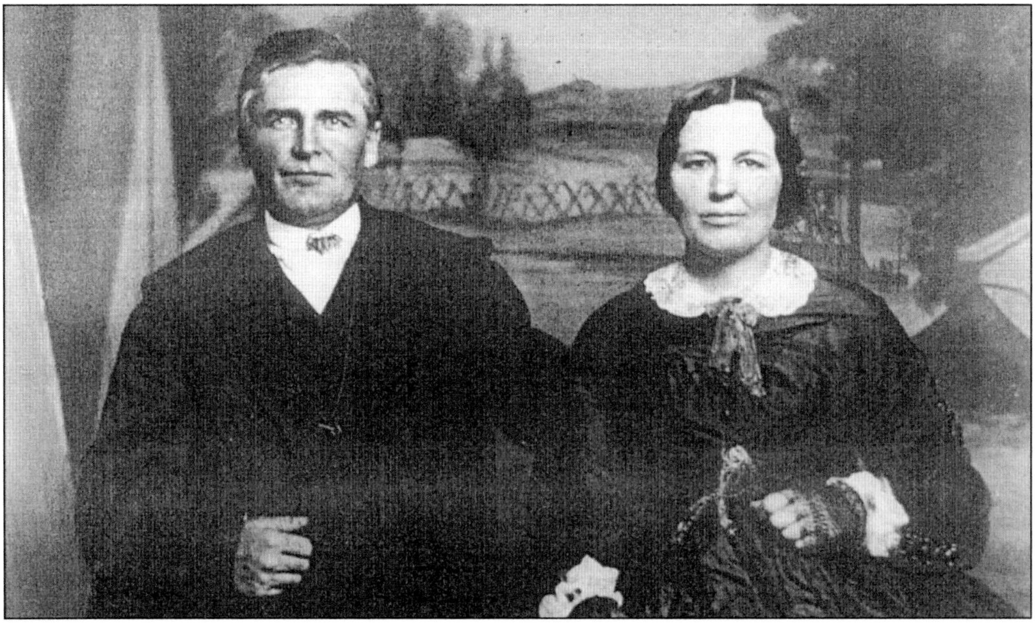

In 1890, Dr. Josiah Asbury Stanfield, M.D., (1829–1896) and wife Agnes Sargent Stanfield (1832–1916) lived in a substantial house in Leasburg. Dr. Stanfield graduated from the Philadelphia Medical College. His descendants have his Civil War pardon from President Johnson (in its metal container) and his medical diplomas. A pardon petition was necessary because of Dr. Stanfield's wealth and slave ownership. (Courtesy Betty Fitzgerald.)

According to Caswell historian M. Q. Plumblee, Thornton Yancey Baynes (1829–1894) moved to Caswell County from adjoining Person County and was among the most popular and useful men of South Caswell. Baynes was buried at the family cemetery in Anderson Township. However, on September 29, 1982, the remains from this cemetery were disinterred and moved to the nearby Baynes Baptist Church cemetery. (Courtesy Nelson and Cindi Straughn.)

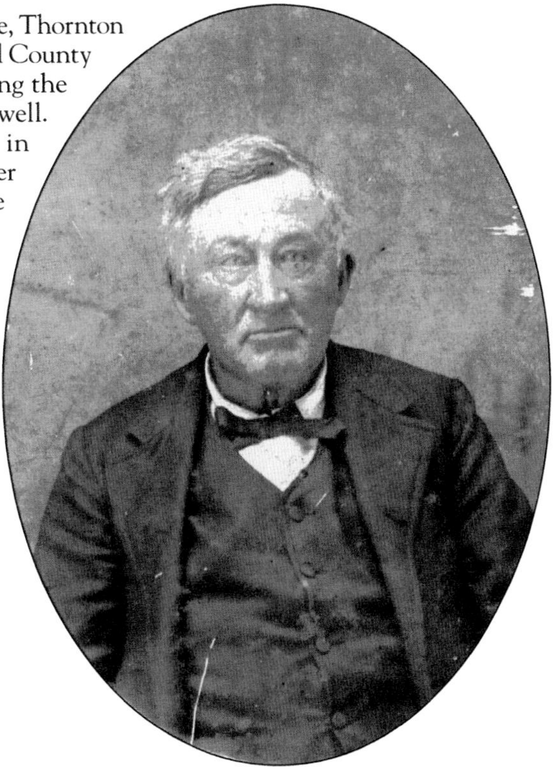

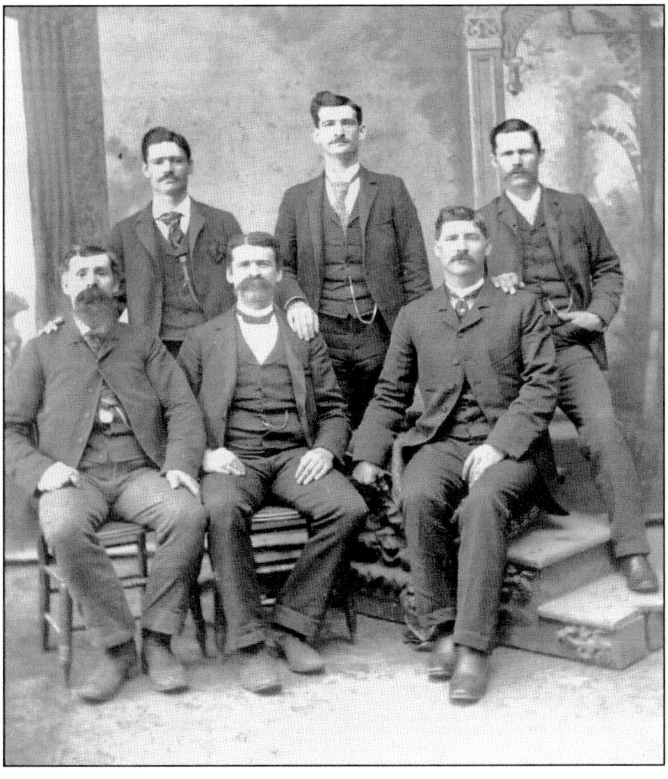

John Bunyan Stanfield (1819–1886) and Silvera Ellison Stanfield (born 1826) had six sons. All six are in this 1897 photograph of the "Singing Stanfield Brothers." From left to right are (seated) John Erasmus Stanfield, Stephen Marmaduke Stanfield, and Robert William Stanfield; (standing) Eugene Stanfield, Thomas Alvis Stanfield, and James Benjamin Stanfield. (Courtesy Nelson and Cindi Straughn.)

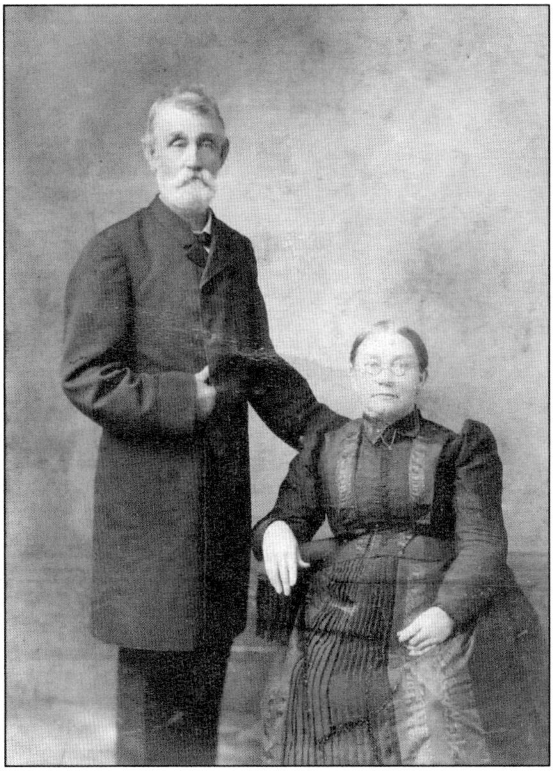

Dr. John Quinton Anderson, M.D., (1820–1899) and Minerva Isabella Rice Anderson (1836–1903) of Caswell's Anderson Township are in this 1880s photograph. Dr. Anderson was a much-loved country doctor. He graduated from the University of Pennsylvania Medical College and practiced medicine from his home for over 50 years, riding horseback over the red hills of Caswell County. (Courtesy Roger Anderson.)

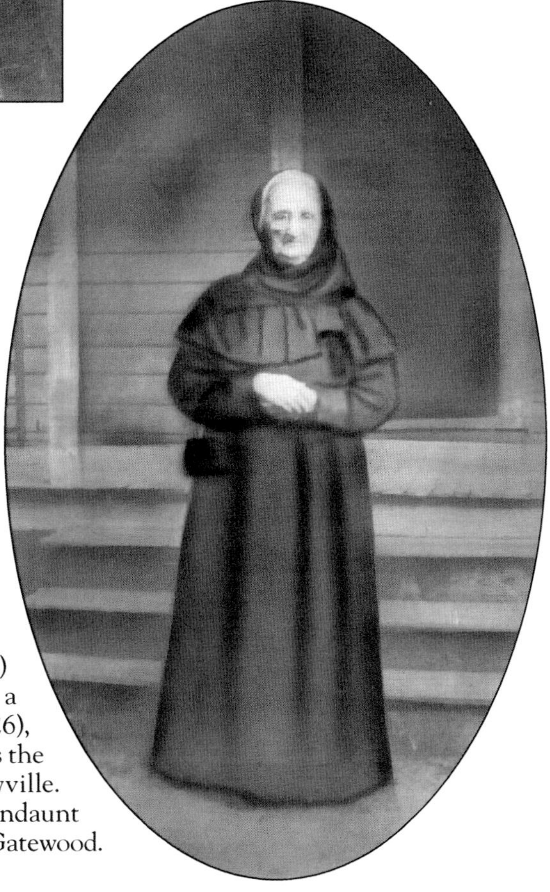

Mildred Ann Florance Kimbro (1847–1928) was a daughter of Empson Florance (1820–1888) and Eliza Boswell Florance (1823–1877) and a sister of Thomas Jefferson Florance (1858–1926), who once owned the house that now contains the Richmond-Miles History Museum in Yanceyville. Mildred Ann Florance Kimbro was the grandaunt of famous Yanceyville artist Maud Florance Gatewood. (Courtesy Phyllis Dawson.)

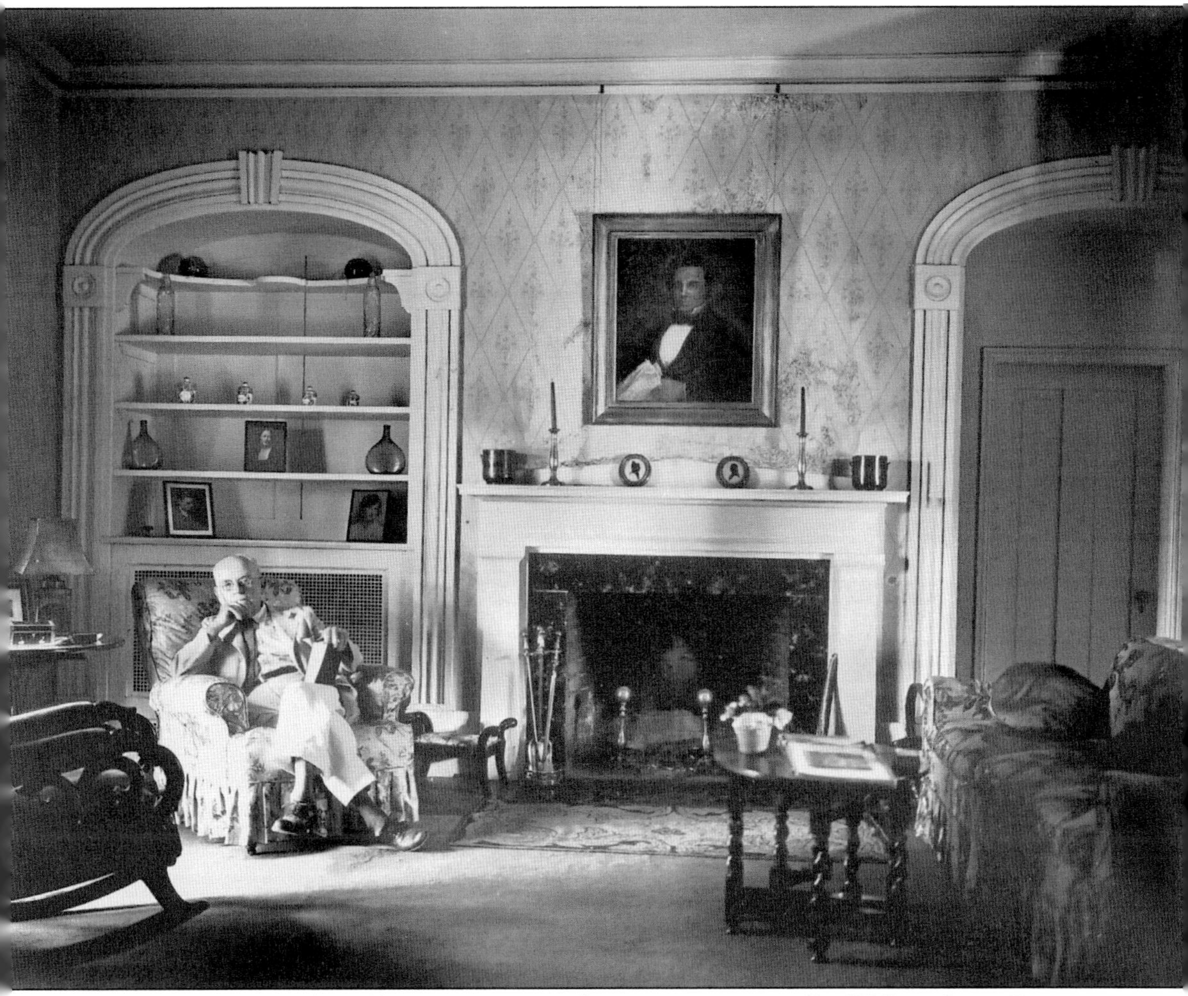

Seen reading in the parlor of his Forest Home plantation in 1929 is Dr. William Louis Poteat (1856–1938). This was the place of his birth, and over the mantel hangs a portrait of his father, Capt. James Poteat (1807–1889). Forest Home was built around 1855 and anchored a major plantation. Dr. Poteat graduated from Wake Forest College and obtained advanced degrees from several universities. He married Emma James Purefoy in 1881 and had three children. Dr. Poteat played a prominent role in the development of Wake Forest College (now University), serving on the faculty (1878–1905) and as the institution's longest serving president (1905–1927). Dr. Poteat was active in the affairs of North Carolina Baptists and was a popular lecturer on religion, science, temperance, and education. He was a member of North Carolina Conference for Social Service (president), North Carolina Anti-Saloon League (president), Southern Baptist Education Association (president), Council of Church Schools of the South (president), North Carolina Reconstruction Commission, North Carolina Academy of Sciences (president), and many other movements of his day. (NCSHPO.)

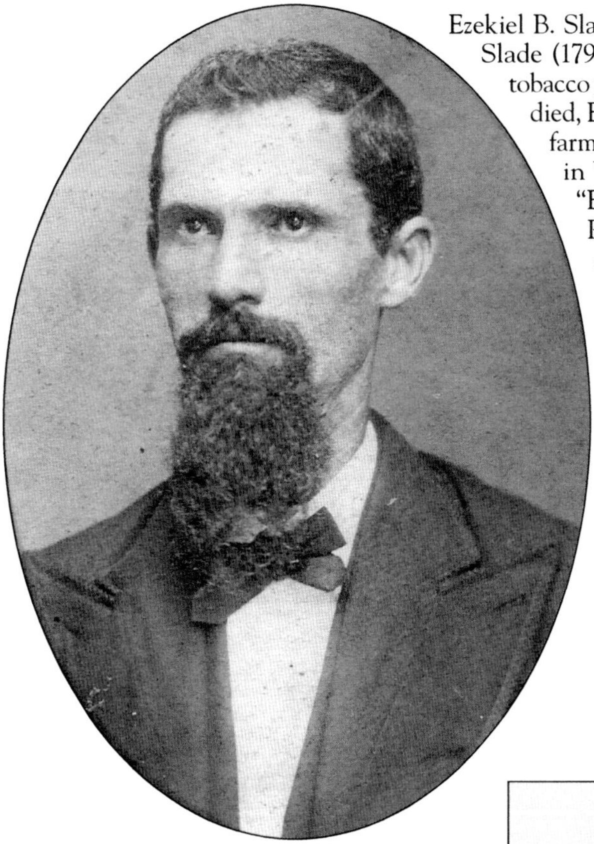

Ezekiel B. Slade (1838–1914) was a nephew of Abisha Slade (1799–1869), on whose farm the bright-leaf tobacco process was discovered. After Abisha Slade died, Ezekiel B. Slade moved his family from the farm to the imposing Abisha Slade brick house in Yanceyville. A Slade descendant relates: "Ezekiel Slade moved to this house from Purley with one wagon load of furniture and two wagon loads of kids." (Courtesy Roger Anderson.)

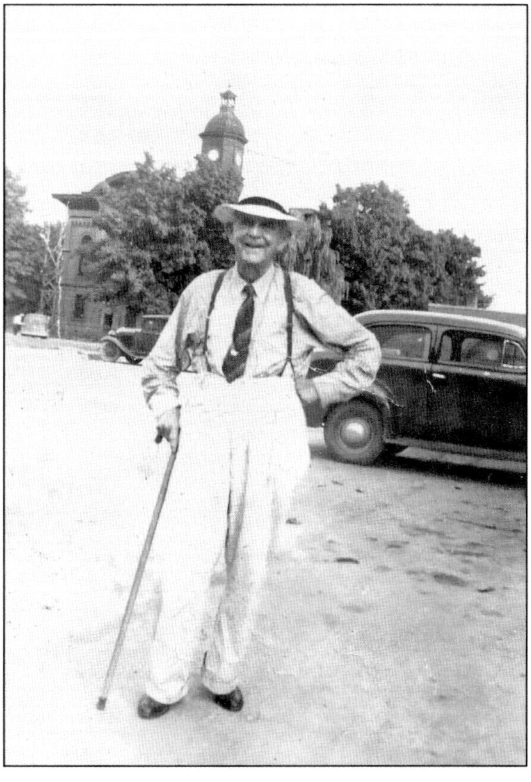

Strolling on the square in Yanceyville in the early 1940s is George Andrew Anderson (1869–1945). He was Caswell County superintendent of schools for 17 years, a newspaper editor, and clerk of Superior Court for eight years. His published books include a history of Caswell County in World War I and biographies of Caswell County statesmen Bartlett Yancey and Bedford Brown. Anderson School was named for him. (Courtesy Roger Anderson.)

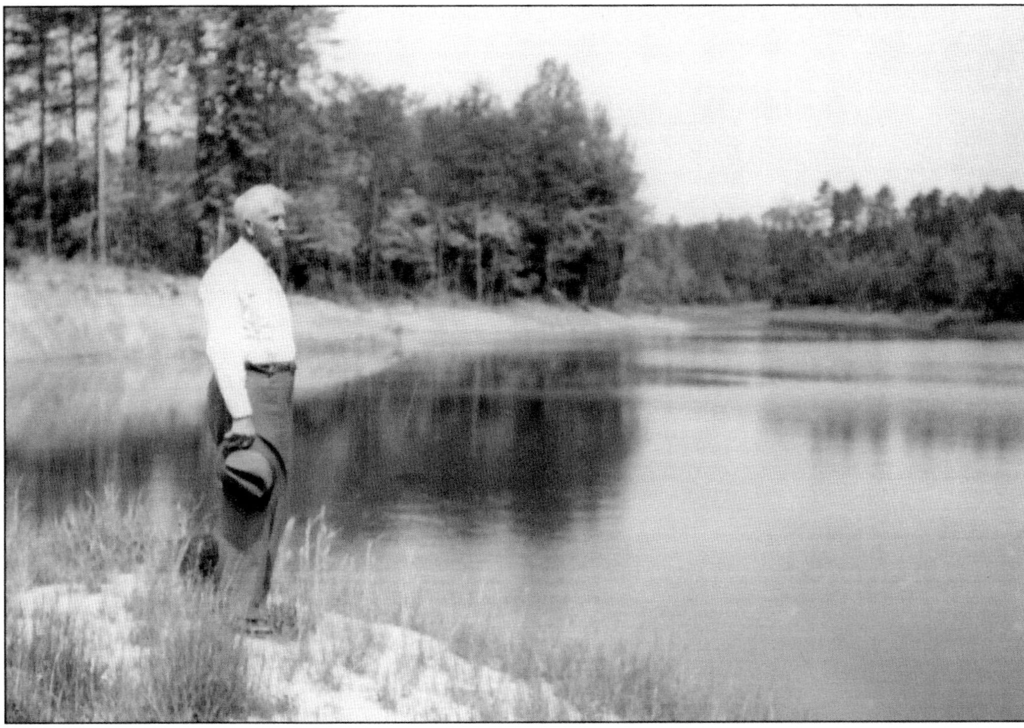

John Henry Gunn (1882–1962) views the newly constructed Yanceyville reservoir in 1953. He was Caswell County sheriff for 22 years (1920–1929, 1936–1950), having been elected to that office eight times. His Ford automobile, the "Red Horse," was one of the first motor vehicles in the county. Gunn's great-great-grandfather was Revolutionary War veteran Starling Gunn. (Courtesy Ann Gunn Everitt.)

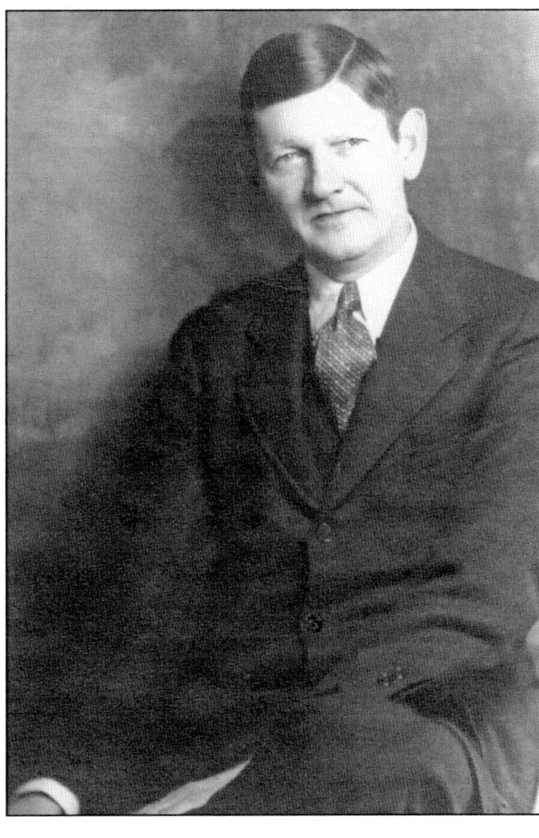

At age 13, Thomas Johnston Henderson (1883–1959), a self-described "scribbler," began a newspaper in Yanceyville called the *Little News*. In 1908, he launched the *Sentinel*, a weekly newspaper that was published in Yanceyville and covered Caswell County. Henderson went on to be a regional writer of some fame, publishing a series of small booklets in the 1940s. (Courtesy Thomas Farrar Wilkerson.)

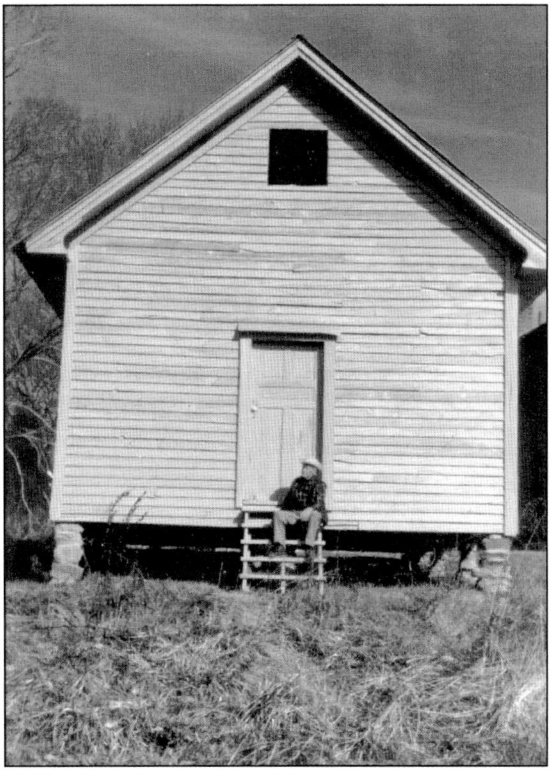

Judson Grear Holt (1905–1997) is seated on the steps of the restored Poteat one-room school, relocated to the Yanceyville Historic District. Holt, a forestry consultant, farmer, and expert on Caswell's fields and woodlands, has a trail named for him at the Boy Scout camp in Caswell County. The monument to him on the trail reads, "Dedicated to Those That Love The Out Of Doors." (Courtesy Laura Holt Collie.)

At the square in 1948 with the fire truck behind them is the Yanceyville Volunteer Fire Department. From left to right are Robert Ham, Bill Murphy, Dorsey Bradner, Dallas Briggs, Wallace Burke, Tom Poteat, Earl Watlington, Billy Oakley, Rigby Green, Robert Brooks, and Johnny Harwood. The fire truck was housed in a structure attached to the Caswell County Courthouse. Volunteers responded to the fire siren located on the Yanceyville water tower. (CCHA Photograph Archives.)

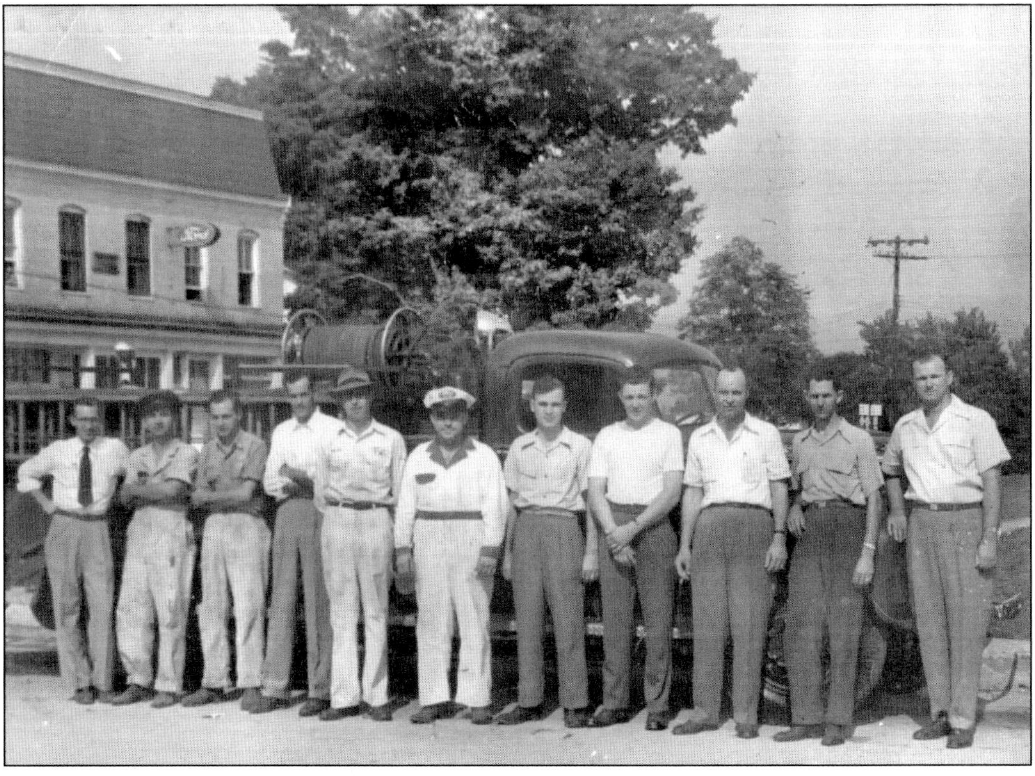

Ida Isabella Poteat (1858–1940), artist, teacher, and patron of art, was born at Forest Home near Yanceyville, the daughter of James and Julia A. McNeill Poteat. She was an art instructor at Oxford Seminary in Oxford, North Carolina, but with the opening in 1899 of Meredith College in Raleigh, she joined the faculty as professor of art (heading the department), a position she held for 40 years. (Courtesy Meredith College Archives.)

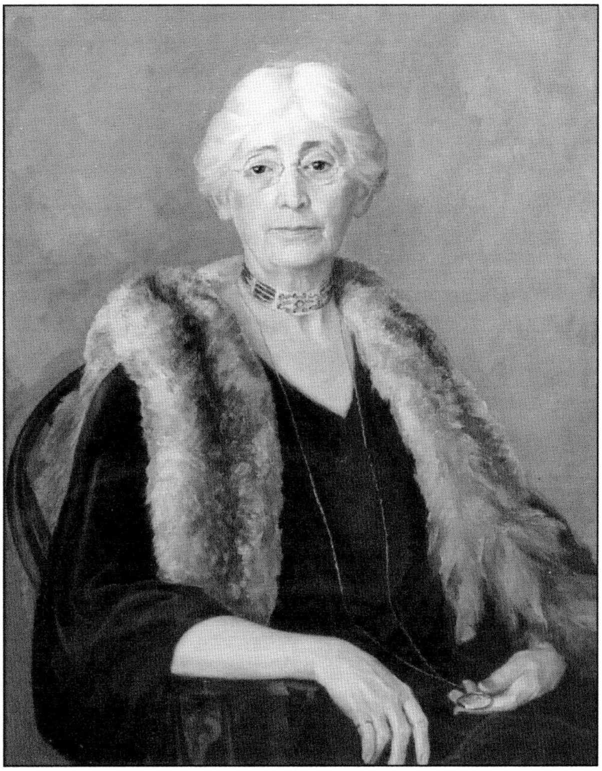

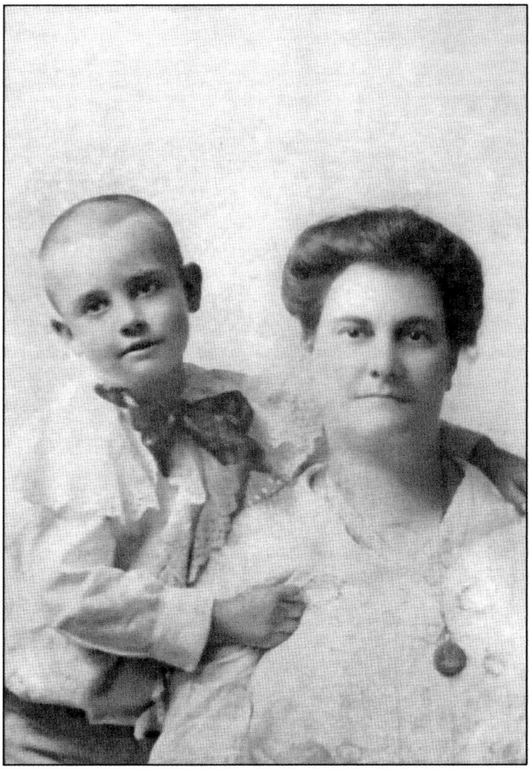

In the early 1900s, Montrose Staton Angle (1900–1984) poses with his mother, Eva Margaret Staton Angle (1869–1949). The family lived in the historic Glenburnie house near Milton, and Montrose would become Milton's mayor. During his years in office, many improvements were made, including the municipal water system, upgraded telephone service, and planning for a new bridge across the Dan River. (Courtesy Lois Angle Love.)

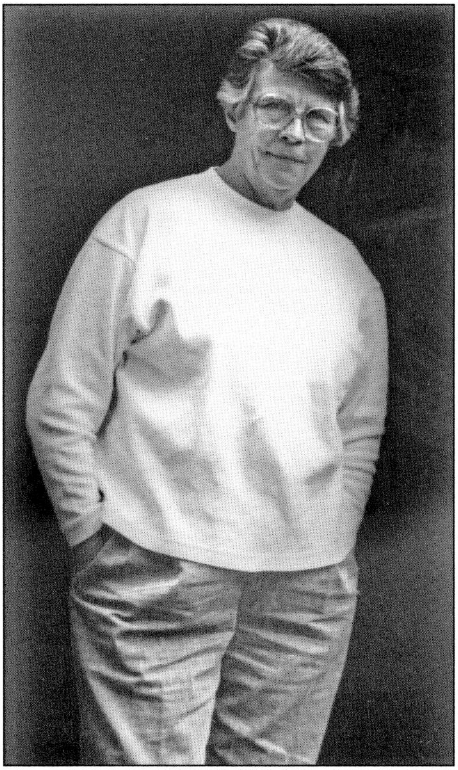

Caswell native Maud Florance Gatewood (1934–2004) arguably was the most important North Carolina painter during her lifetime and is considered by art historians, curators, museum directors, and collectors as one of the most important painters in North Carolina history. Her work is familiar to museumgoers throughout the South. Maud was a prominent figure in the southeastern United States during her 55-year career and served as Caswell's first female commissioner. (CCHA Photograph Archives.)

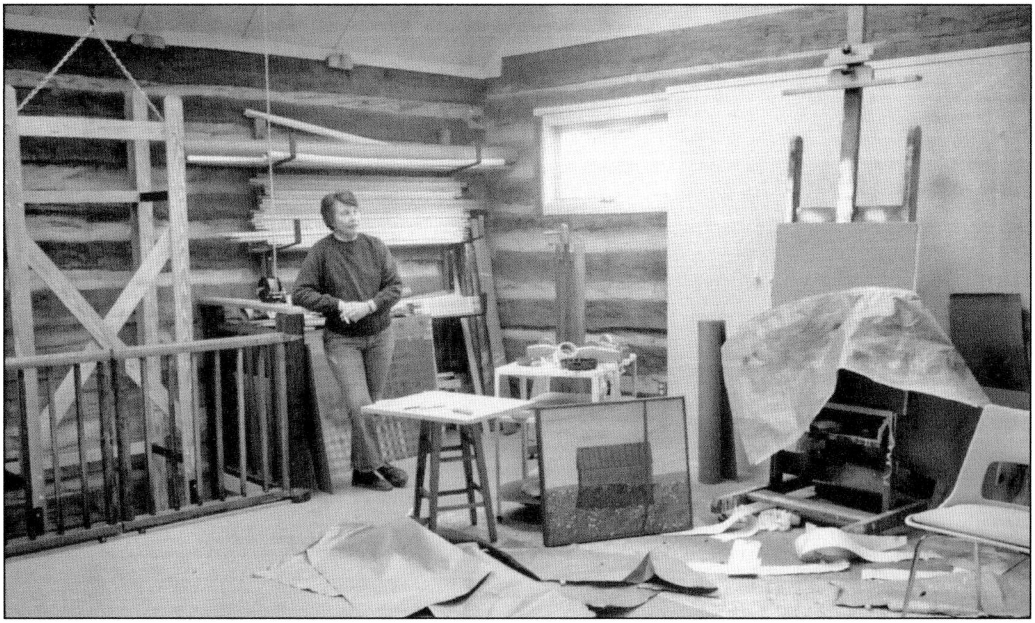

Maud Florance Gatewood and a friend purchased and restored historic Longwood, just outside Milton. Maud converted an old barn on the property into her studio, complete with an "elevator" for moving painting materials and finished works between the floors. Skylights and an array of gable-end windows provided natural illumination. From here, Maud's art was inspired by her beloved Caswell County. (Courtesy Ryland Lee Farmer.)

Glen Garland Donoho (1867–1945) of Milton, affectionately known as "Mr. Doney," was a son of Thomas A. Donoho (1827–1887) and Isabella Glenn Garland (1832–1886). The Donoho family was in Caswell County (then Orange County) before the Revolutionary War and participated in that conflict. However, Donoho is one of the once-prevalent surnames that have disappeared from Caswell County. (Courtesy Lois Angle Love.)

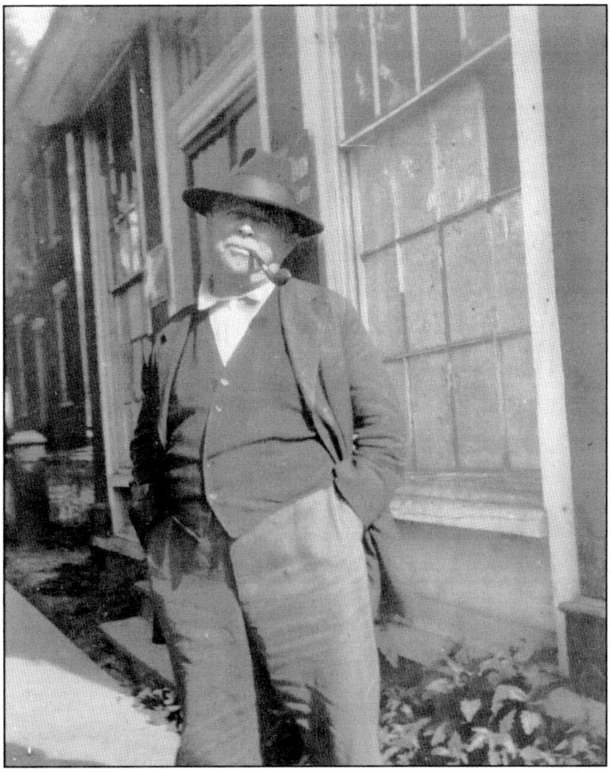

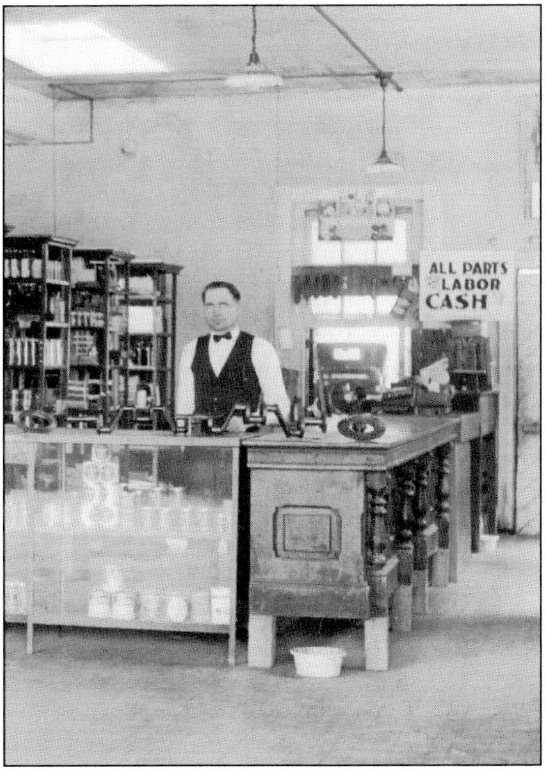

In 1927, Hubert Hodnett Page (1897–1974) was employed at Crowell Auto Co. in Yanceyville as the parts manager. He later founded Caswell Hardware and Implement Co., which was an authorized outlet for Pontiac cars, Farmall tractors, and International Harvester trucks. Page was a descendant of Revolutionary War soldier Starling Gunn. Note the crankshaft on the parts counter and the service area through the open window. (Courtesy John O. Gunn Estate.)

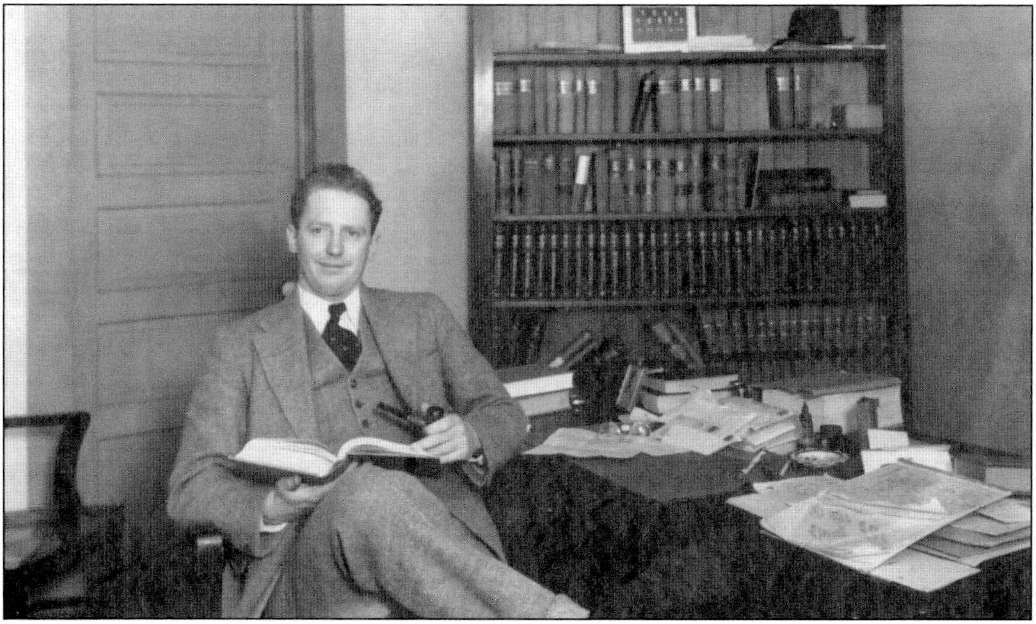

Working at his Yanceyville office in the 1940s is Clarence Lilly Pemberton Jr. (1908–1995). Born in Fayetteville, North Carolina, Clarence Pemberton (affectionately called "Pem") began his Yanceyville law practice in 1935. He was a local judge, University of North Carolina trustee, and the first American sailor to set foot ashore in Manila in 1945 when General MacArthur made his promised return. (Courtesy Pemberton family archives.)

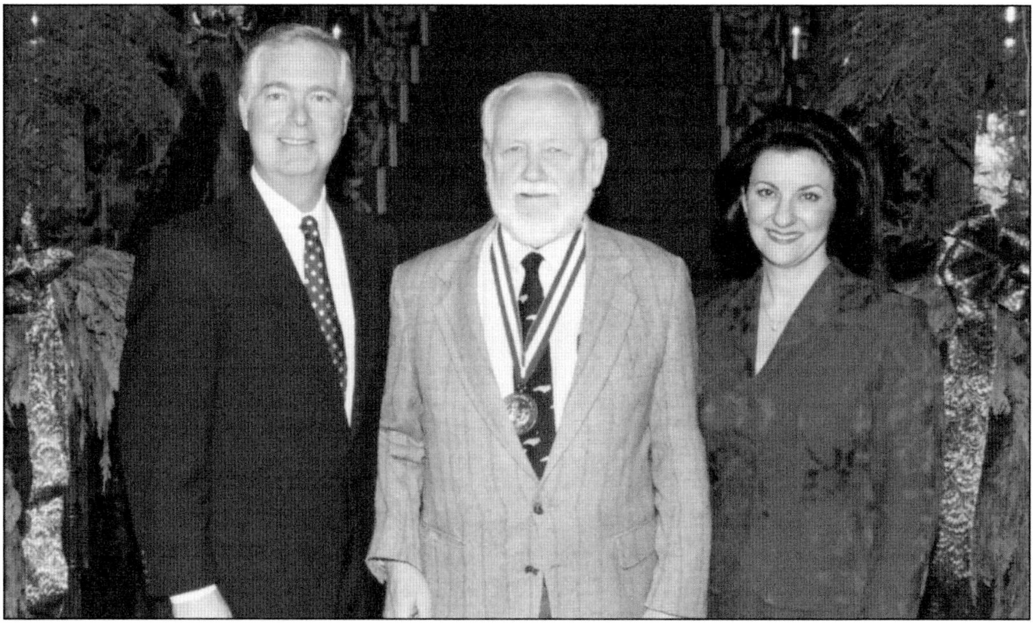

Dr. Houston G. Jones was the first from Caswell County to receive the state's highest civilian honor, the North Carolina Award. Here Jones (center) is receiving the award in 2002 from Gov. Mike and First Lady Mary Easley. Jones was North Carolina state archivist, director of the North Carolina Department of Archives and History, and professor at the University of North Carolina, and is a prolific author. (Courtesy North Carolina Department of Cultural Resources.)

Two

Churches and Schools

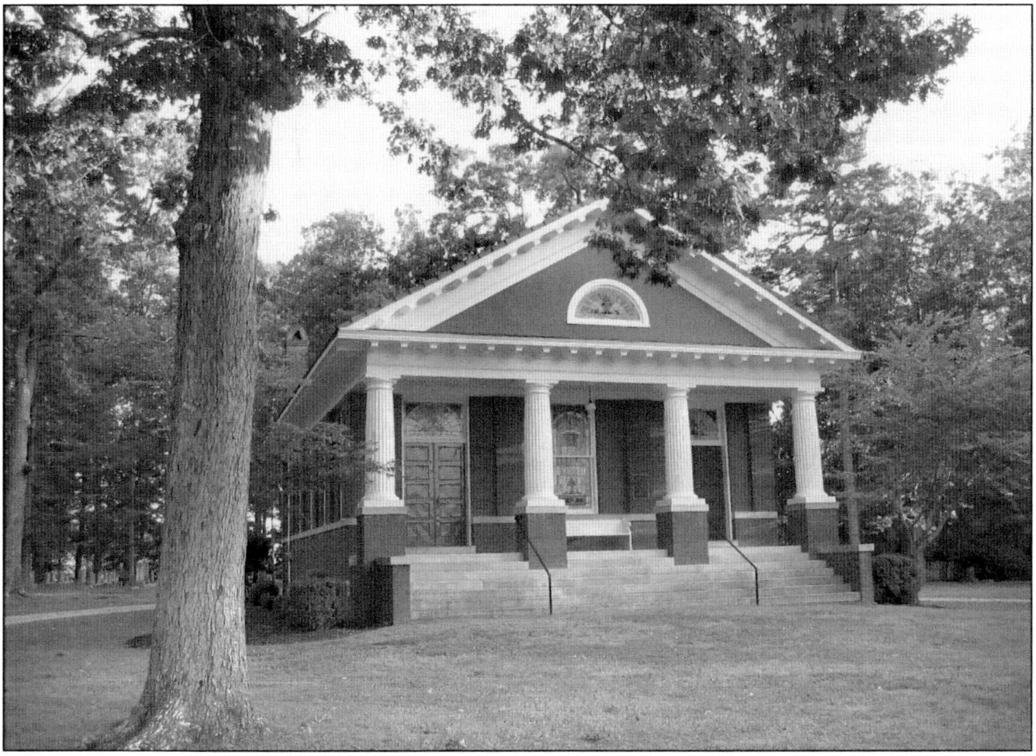

The current Red House Presbyterian Church building was constructed in 1913. However, the congregation dates back to 1755. Rev. Hugh McAden (c. 1730–1781), a pioneer missionary from Pennsylvania, preached at a chapel on this site in 1755, served the church from 1768 to 1781, and is buried in the church cemetery. McAden's grave purportedly was disturbed by British soldiers during the Revolutionary War due to his political views. (CCHA Photograph Archives.)

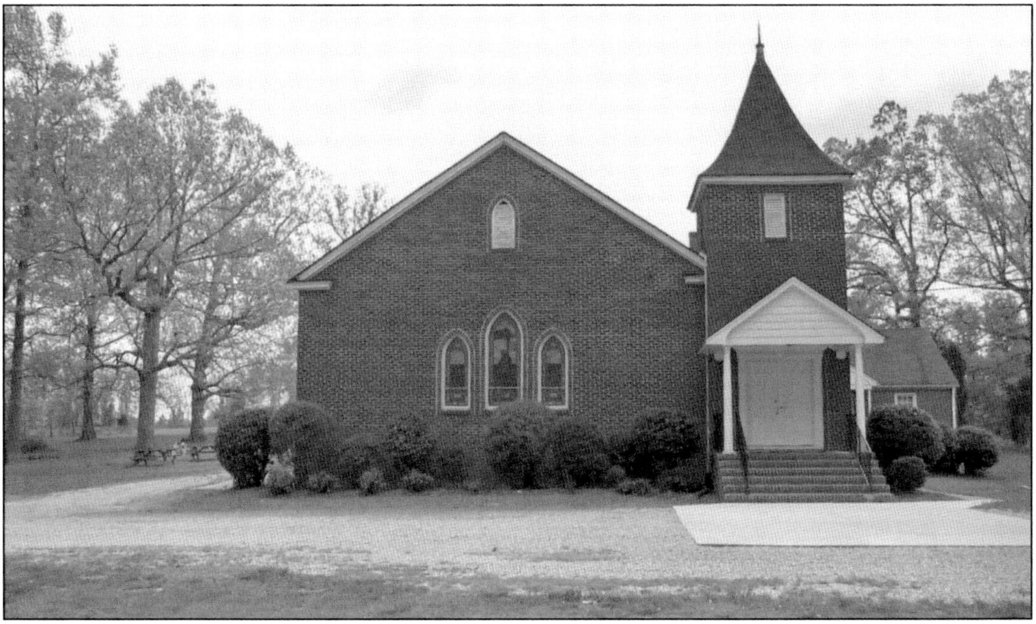

While in Person County today, Lea's Chapel was formed as an Anglican church in 1750 on South Hyco Creek near Leasburg and named for the Lea family. Known as Chapel Church, it was a widely recognized landmark in this frontier region. Francis Asbury, one of the first American Methodist bishops, preached there in 1781, during the Revolutionary War. The church passed to the Methodists after 1784. (CCHA Photograph Archives.)

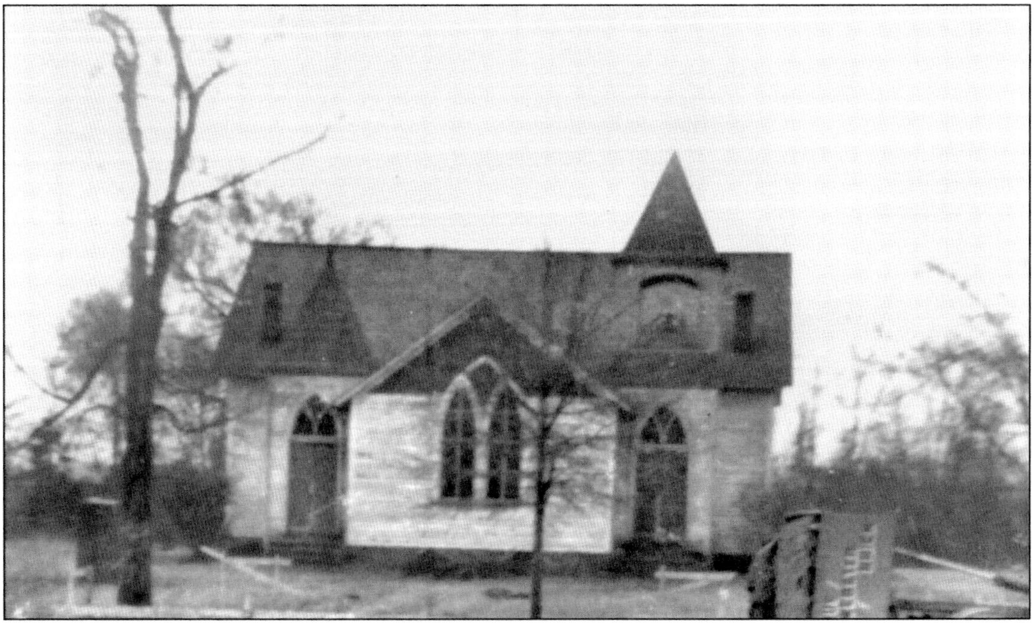

Built in 1857, the Leasburg Methodist Church was the successor to Bethany Church, where the famous Methodist bishop Francis Asbury once preached. The second floor of the building was used by the local Masonic lodge and other community organizations. The Masons disbanded in 1896, and the building was renovated to use all the space for church functions. The church building was demolished in the 1950s. (CCHA Photograph Archives.)

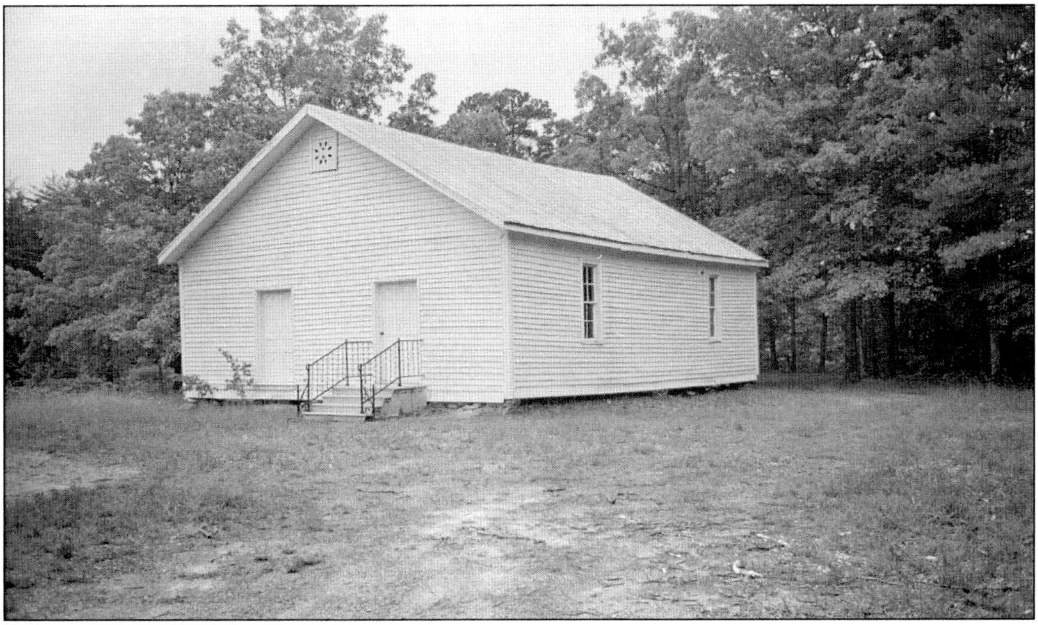

The Country Line Primitive Baptist Church was established in 1792, and the church building above was built during the 19th century. The structure is typical of Primitive Baptist churches of the time, with little ornamentation and separate doors for men and women. This church eventually split into two congregations due to a disagreement over missionary activity. Those favoring missionary work founded the Baptist church in Yanceyville. (NCSHPO.)

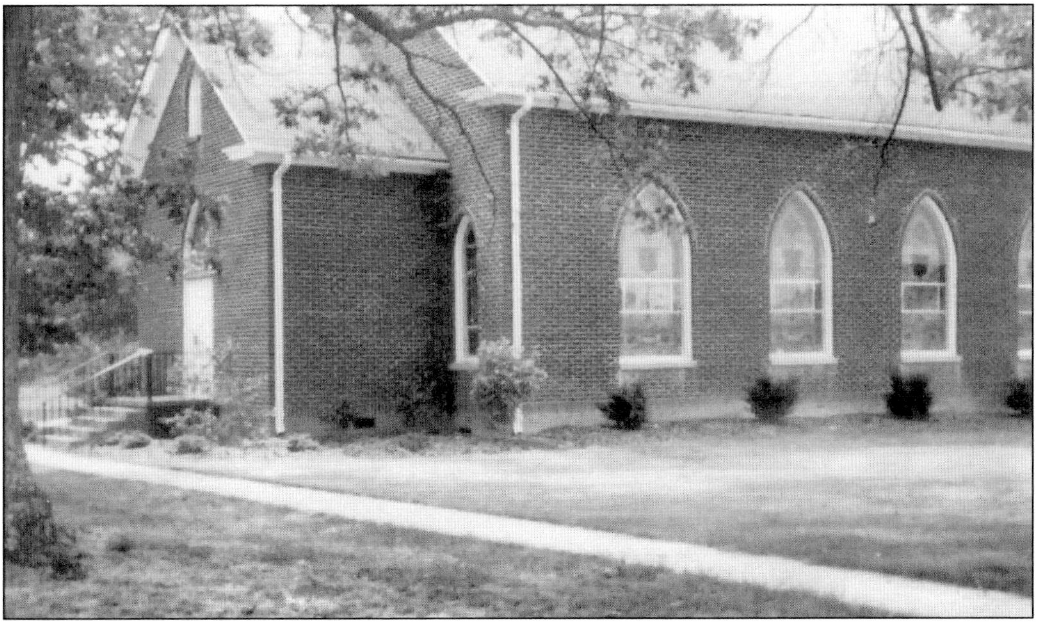

Located in Anderson Township in southern Caswell, the Baynes Baptist Church was established in 1912, and the church building, still in use, was constructed in 1914. The building, which was enlarged and modernized in the 1950s, features beautiful Gothic stained-glass memorial windows. The earliest grave in the cemetery dates from 1923. Church records from 1912 to 1965 are available on microfilm. (Courtesy Nelson and Cindi Straughn.)

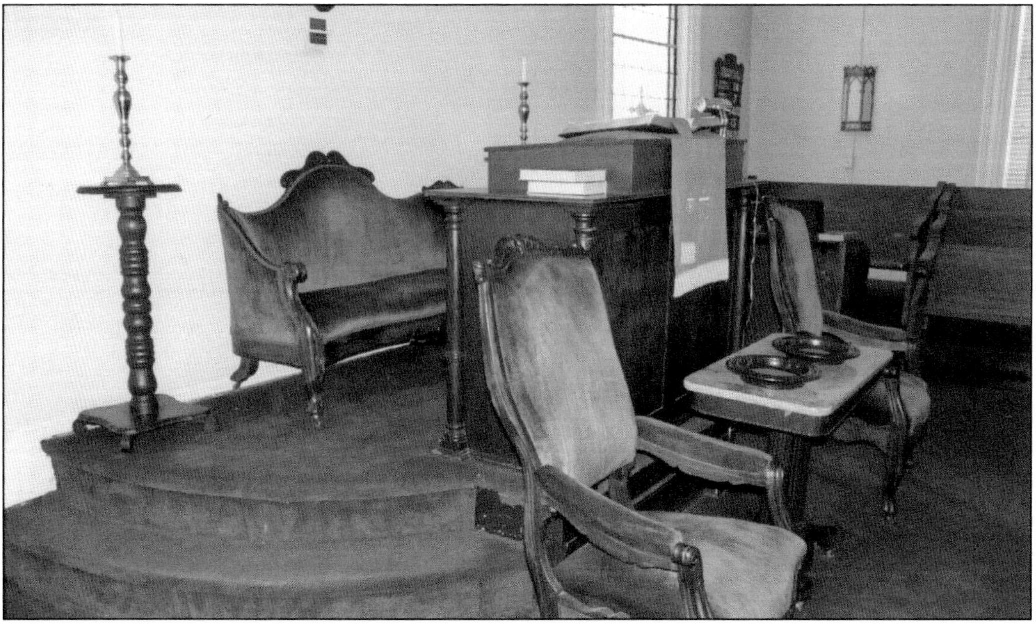

The Presbyterian Church of Milton traces its origins to 1826. This present church building was erected in 1837. Local free black cabinetmaker Thomas Day was a church member, as was his wife, Aquilla Wilson Day. Day made the church's pews, which are in use today. Interestingly, the denomination of the church was determined by a vote of those who paid $4 each to hire the first minister. (Courtesy Houston G. Jones.)

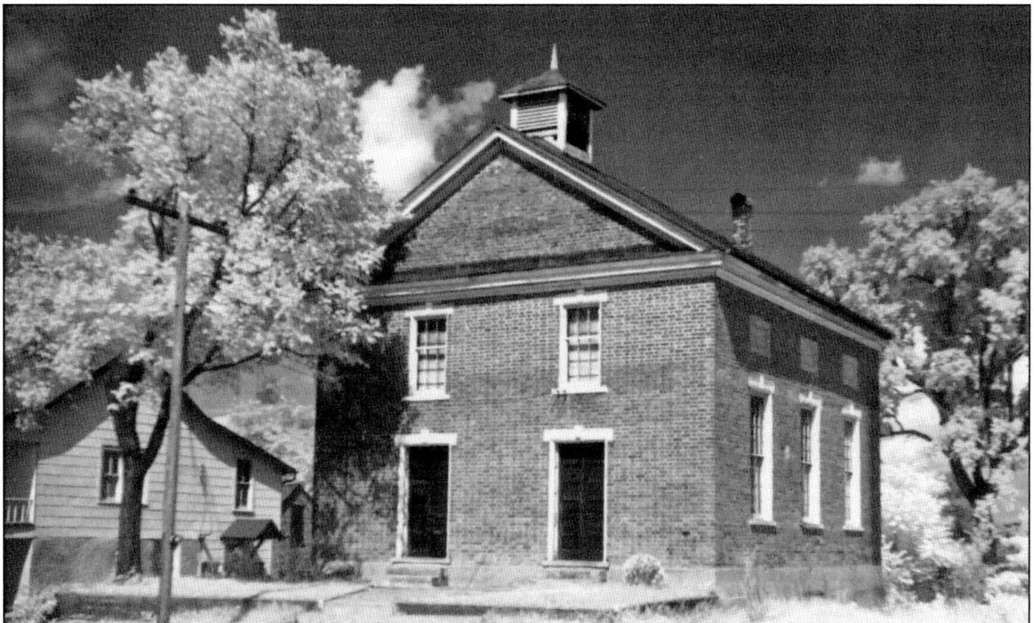

The Milton Baptist Church (also called the Milton Baptist Meeting House) was established in 1828 with Rev. Abner W. Clopton as its first pastor. The handsome little church, which was constructed of locally made brick, remains in use. The original furniture, also still in use, probably was made in the nearby shop of Thomas Day. (Courtesy Jean B. Scott.)

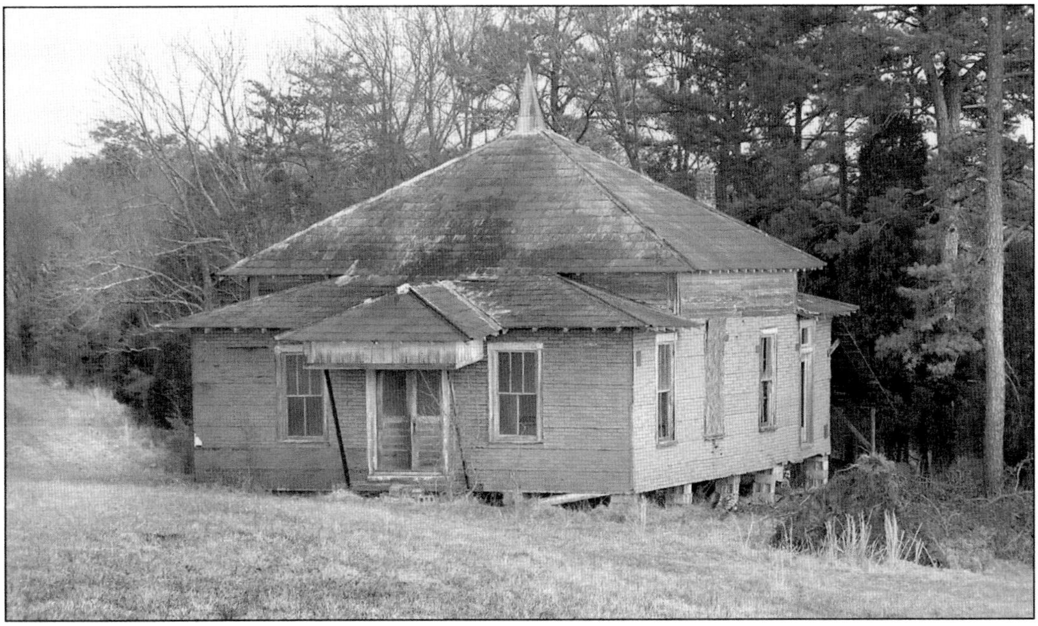

The Beulah Baptist Church was organized in 1834 by Rev. Stephen Pleasant (1779–1852), who served as the first pastor and strongly supported missionary activity. In 1861, Sidney S. Lea donated property for the first church building. The second church building sits abandoned in a pasture; its date of construction is unknown. A third structure now serves the church. (CCHA Photograph Archives.)

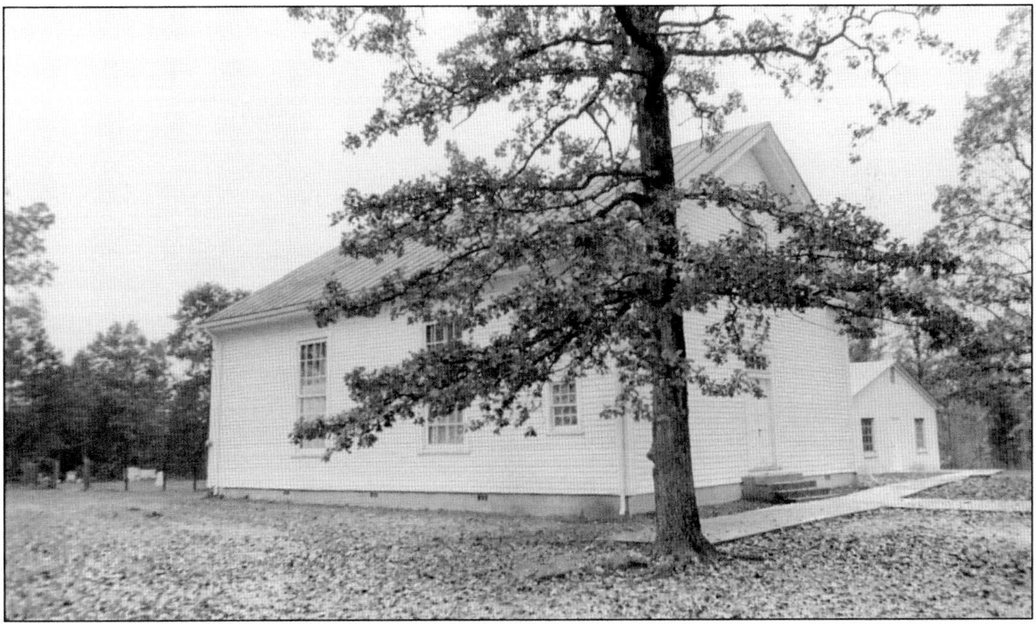

Grier's Presbyterian Church, the oldest church in Caswell County, was organized in 1753 by Rev. Hugh McAden. Originally known as Upper Hyco, it was located about a mile east of the present site in eastern Caswell, where an old cemetery may still be seen. The current location was selected in 1835, and the church still standing was built in 1856. The building is on the National Register. (Courtesy Houston G. Jones.)

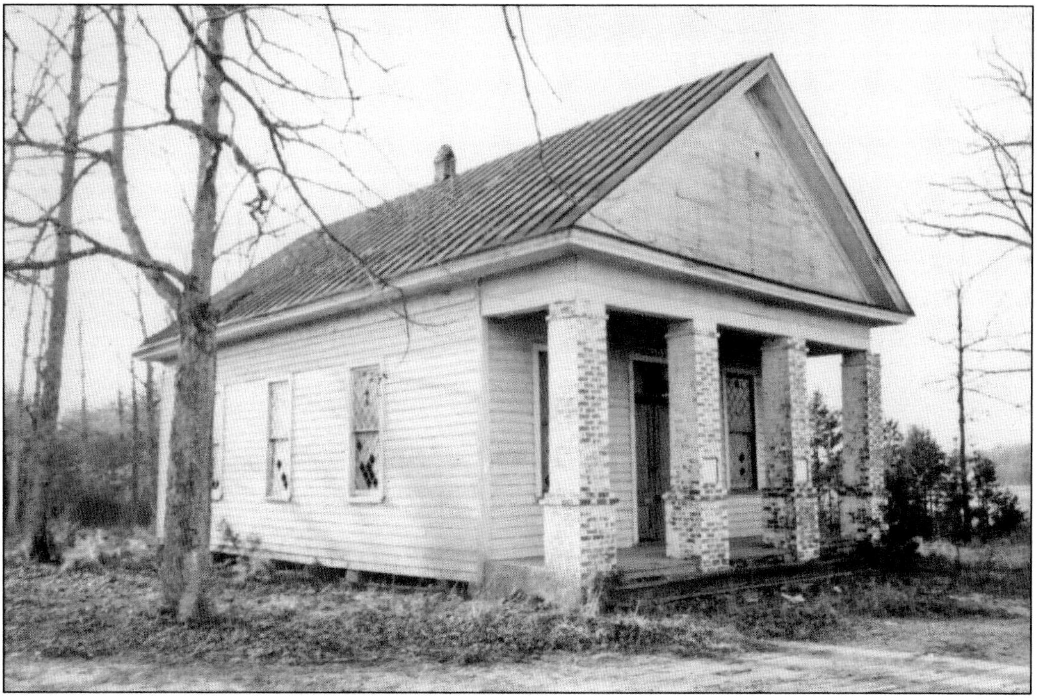

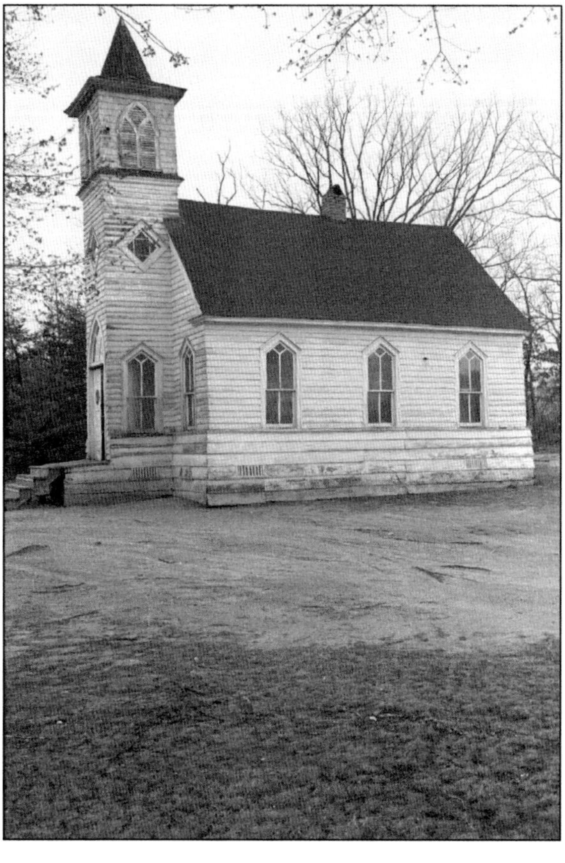

Gilead Presbyterian Church, between Milton and Yanceyville, was formed in 1839. This church building, erected in the early 1900s, was furnished with pews made by famous Milton craftsman Thomas Day. Gilead was dissolved in 1955, the church building sold in 1962, and the Thomas Day pews dispersed, with some being used as benches by the local high school football team. A small cemetery remains. (Courtesy Houston G. Jones.)

In May 1892, a Presbyterian church for blacks was organized near Caswell's Semora community. The church building was erected soon after the congregation was organized. Called Elim Church, it also was known as Palmer's Chapel in honor of the first pastor, Rev. Boswell B. Palmer, who died in 1915. Reverend Palmer had several daughters, all of whom became schoolteachers. The church was active until 1928. (NCSHPO.)

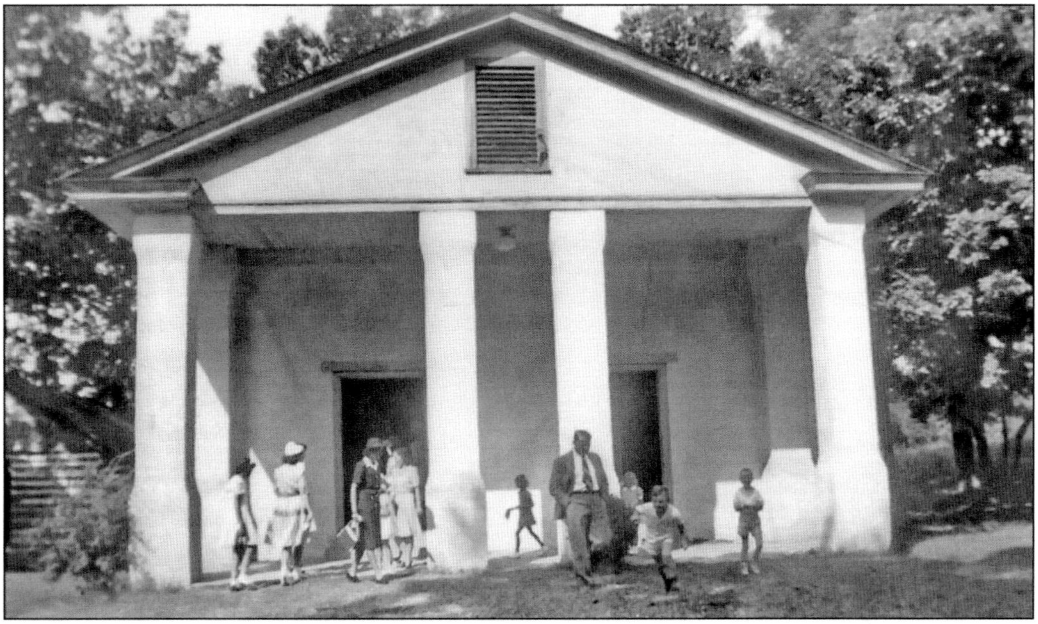

The old Yanceyville Methodist Church building was erected around 1845 beside what today is the Yanceyville United Methodist Church cemetery. Burials in the cemetery date from 1852, but many unmarked native stones could be older. The first Methodist minister stationed in Yanceyville was probably Rev. J. P. Simpson (1856–1857). The old building was used until 1943 and has been demolished. (Courtesy John O. Gunn Estate.)

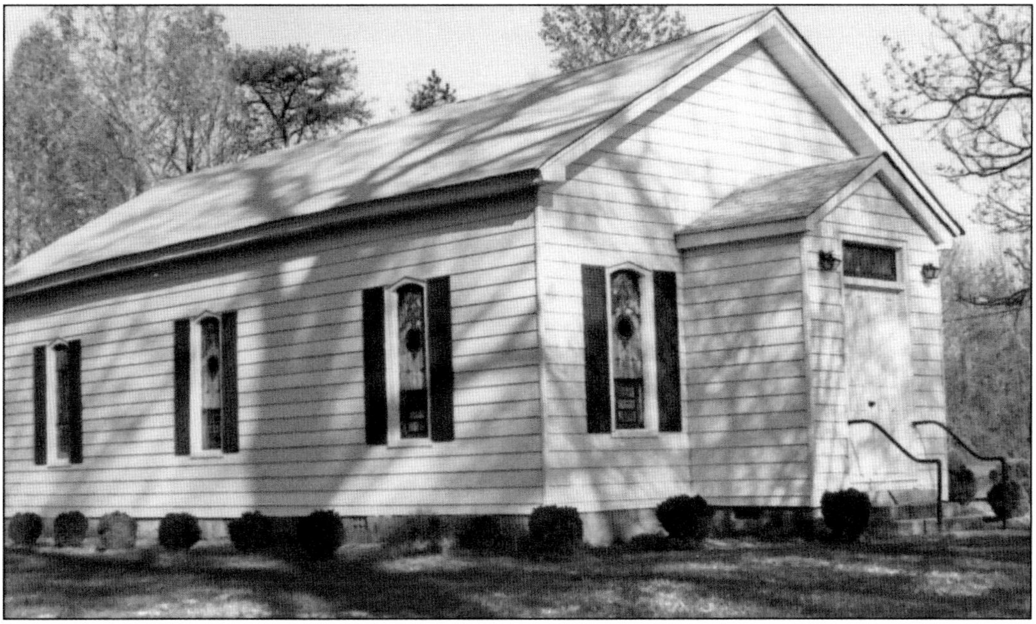

The Locust Hill Methodist Church building was erected in 1886 by members of the church, which was organized a few years earlier. Members and friends contributed the land, trees for lumber, money, and labor. The stained-glass memorial windows found in the church today were contributed by descendants of the charter members. The early church shared a minister with Yanceyville. (Courtesy Houston G. Jones.)

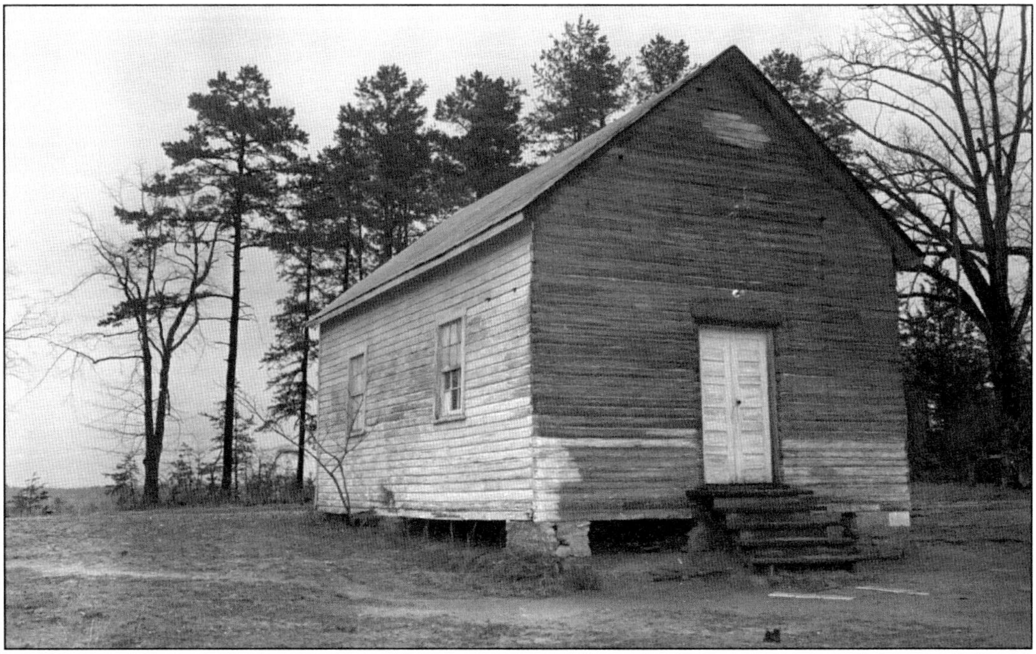

The Oak Level A.M.E. Church in Caswell's Snatchburg community, near Milton, was built in 1919, which is evidenced by a marble cornerstone with name and date. Finding a cornerstone on such a modest structure is unusual. The building was heated with a wood stove, and two large oil lamps provided light. (NCSHPO.)

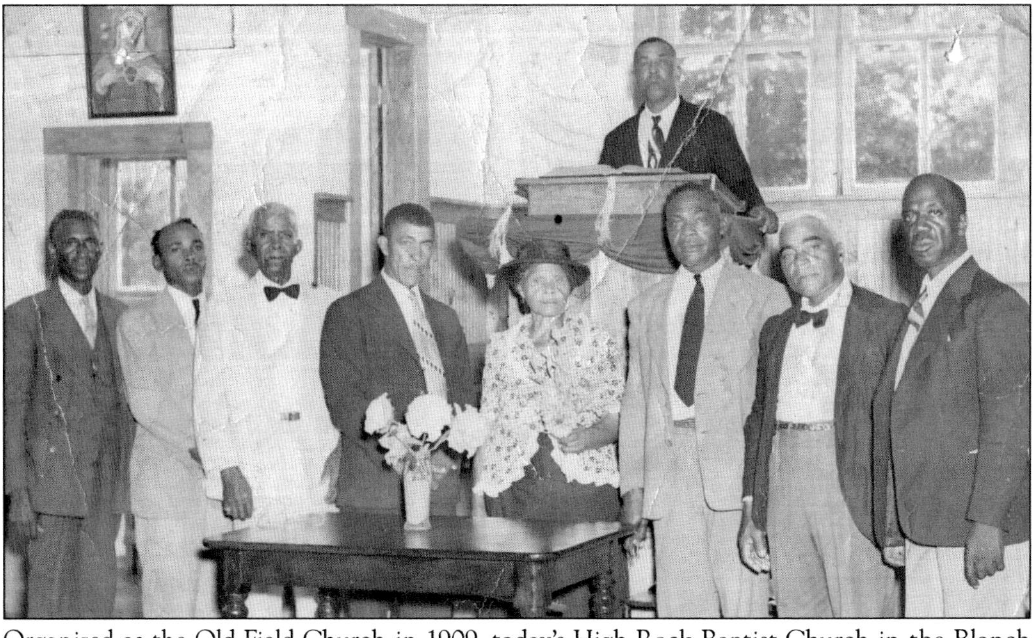

Organized as the Old Field Church in 1909, today's High Rock Baptist Church in the Blanch community has occupied several structures. In 1949, church members gathered after the second church building was completed. From left to right are Ed Long, John L. Lea Sr., Robert Garland, Ernest Garland, Ella Long, John Henry Long, Johnny Poteat, and James Johnson. In the background is Rev. Harvey Gwynn. (Courtesy Monnie Garland Glass.)

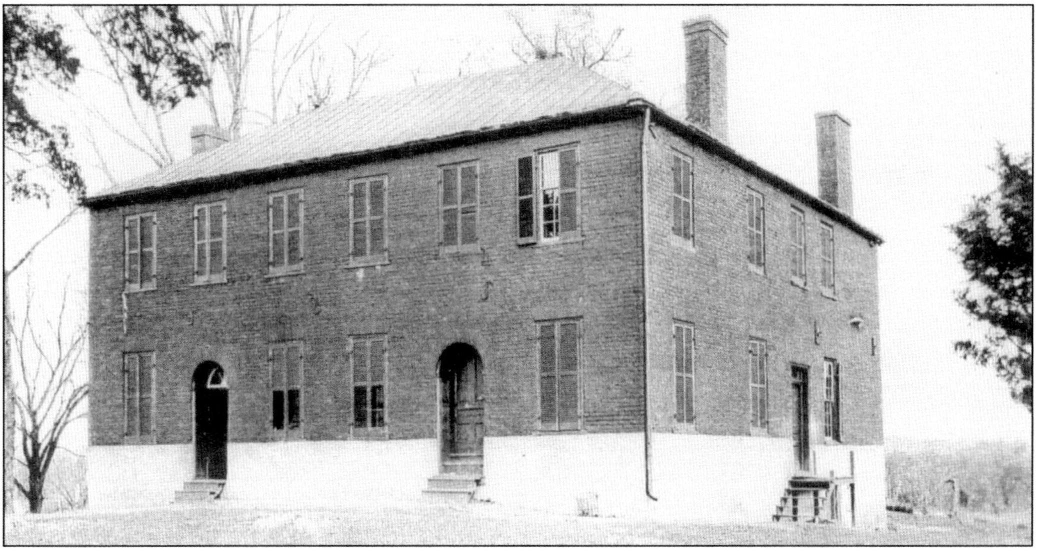

The Milton Female Academy, which began operation in 1820 with Rev. Abner W. Clopton as the first superintendent, was a very successful school. Promotional material in 1854 reported that the academy's buildings were "spacious" and could accommodate 14 to 20 boarders along with the principal's family. The building was dismantled in 1920 and the bricks used to build the Milton public school across the street. (CCHA Photograph Archives.)

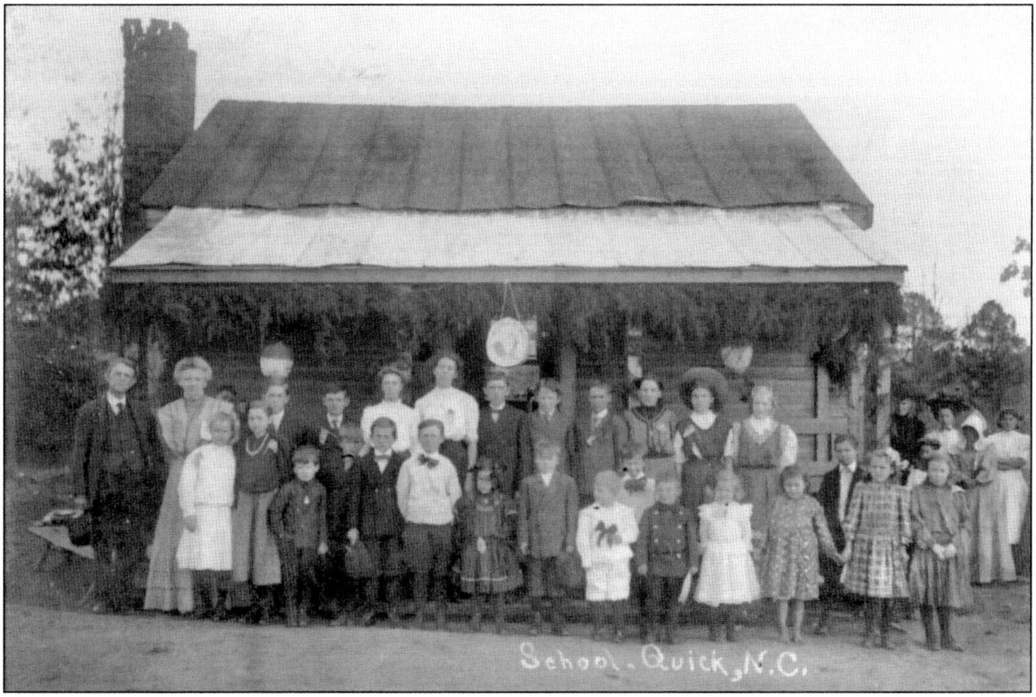

One of the small community schools in use before consolidation was Blackwell's School at Quick in the western part of the county (seen above in 1908). School consolidation was not universally supported, and those who governed the county were criticized harshly for closing these small neighborhood schools. At the far left is Caswell County school superintendent George A. Anderson (1869–1945). (Courtesy James Y. and Nettie Dameron Blackwell.)

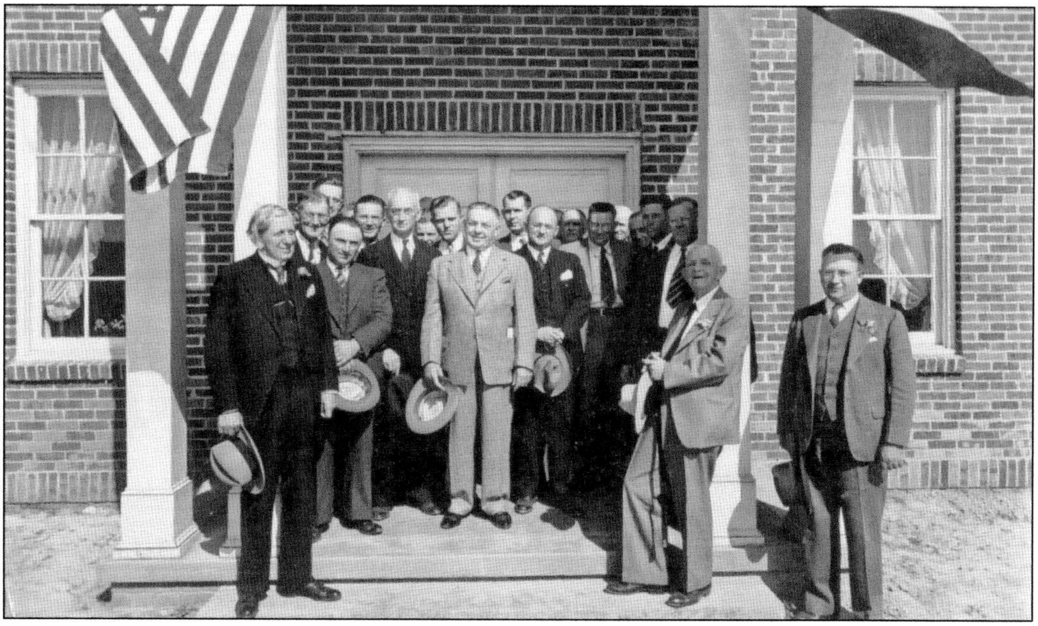

This is the 1940 dedication of the Anderson School building complex in southern Caswell County, which included home economics, agriculture, and a gymnasium. To the left in the foreground is North Carolina governor Clyde R. Hoey (on step). In the center is state superintendent of education Clyde A. Erwin. George A. Anderson, for whom the school was named, is leaning against the column to the right. (Courtesy Gordon Plumblee.)

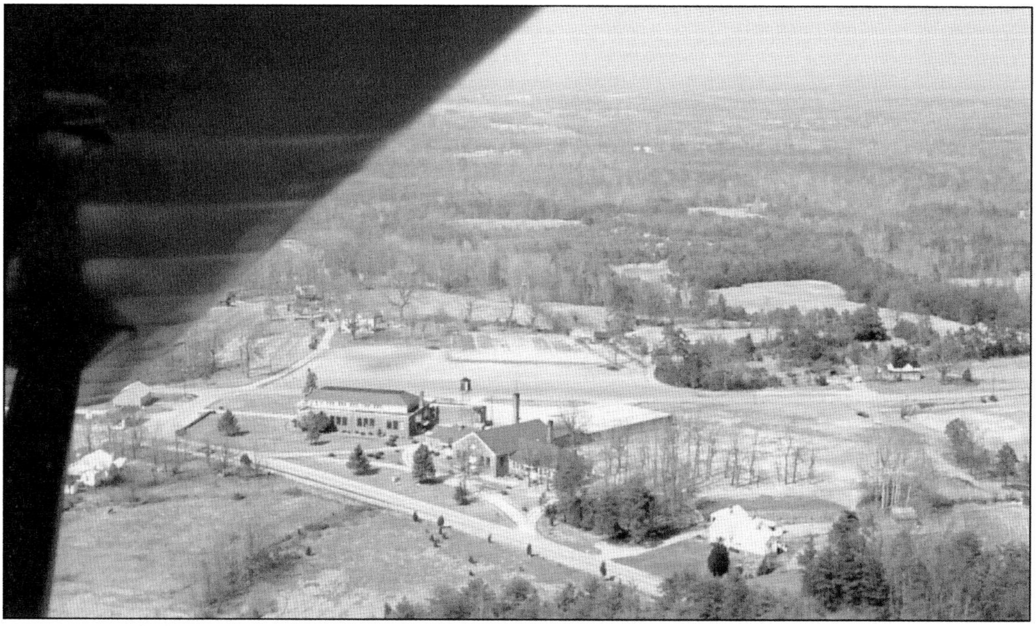

A 1967 aerial photograph of Anderson School in southern Caswell County gives a good view of the campus. The main classroom building to the left was constructed in 1923–1924. To the right of that building is the gymnasium, which is flanked to the left by the home economics building and to the right by the agriculture building, all constructed in 1938–1940 with assistance from the Works Progress Administration. (Courtesy Gordon Plumblee.)

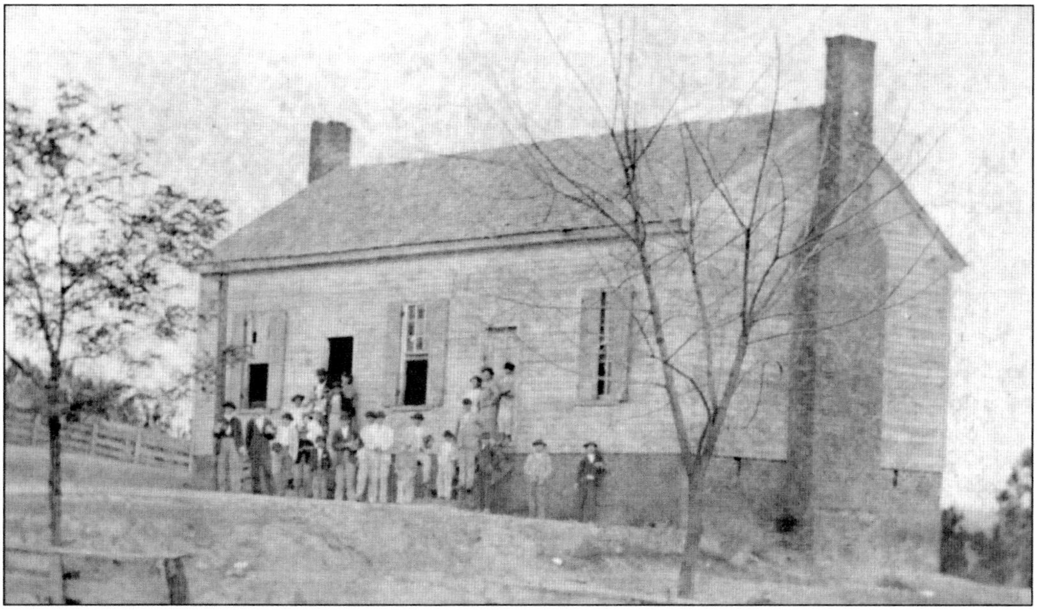

In 1867, James S. Dameron opened a school in northwestern Caswell called the Ruffin Select School. Soon a permanent building was erected of rock, and the school became known as the Rock Academy (successor building shown here). Many Caswell youngsters were educated there, including John Blackwell Cobb (1857–1923), who became a vice president of the American Tobacco Company and a substantial benefactor of the area. (Courtesy James Y. and Nettie Dameron Blackwell.)

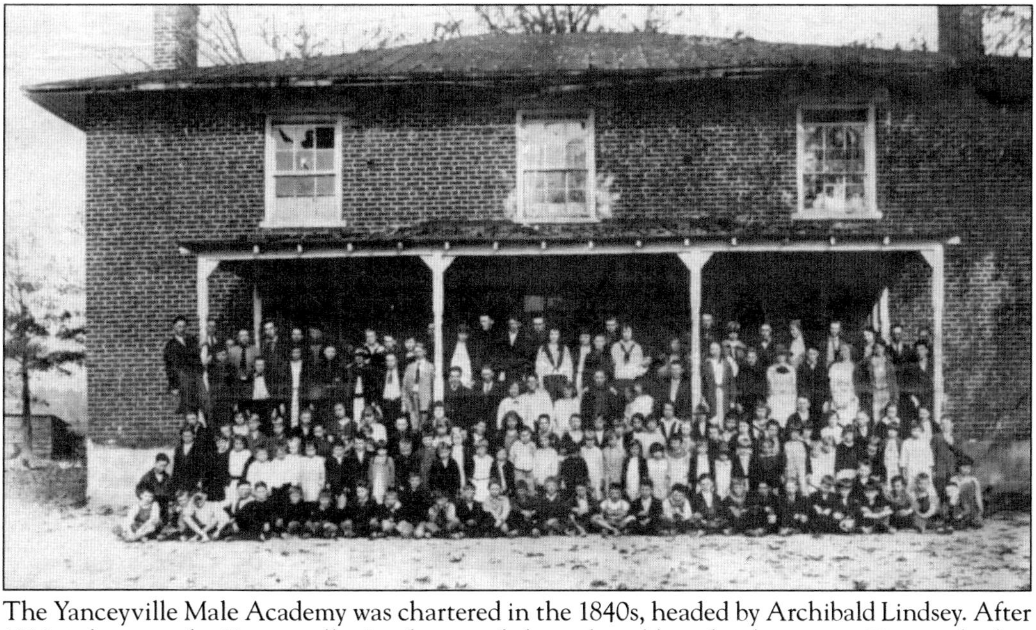

The Yanceyville Male Academy was chartered in the 1840s, headed by Archibald Lindsey. After 1910, it became the Yanceyville Academy and the only public school in town. Here is the last graduating class (1923). The building was used as a teacherage after the new Bartlett Yancey School was built nearby. By 1932, the old academy building was used for overflow students. It was demolished in the 1950s. (CCHA Photograph Archives.)

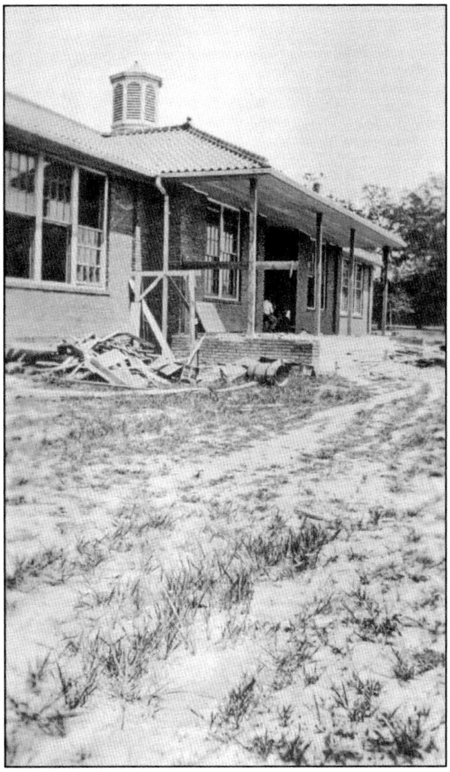

In 1923, the Bartlett Yancey School was built in Yanceyville on land contributed by the family of Bartlett Yancey Jr. Initially there were 11 grades. The design was a central auditorium (with a stage) flanked by classrooms and with two classroom wings at the rear. The wood-floored auditorium doubled as a basketball court. The building was dismantled in the 1950s. (Courtesy Louise Moore Atwater Estate.)

Cobb Memorial School was built in western Caswell County with funds donated by John Blackwell Cobb (1857–1923), a Caswell native who became an executive of the American Tobacco Company. The school, which opened in the early 1920s, no longer operates, and the buildings are in private hands. Three Cobb teachers in 1940 were, from left to right, Virginia Boyd, Hazel Kinlaw, and Lorine Kinlaw. (Courtesy Houston G. Jones.)

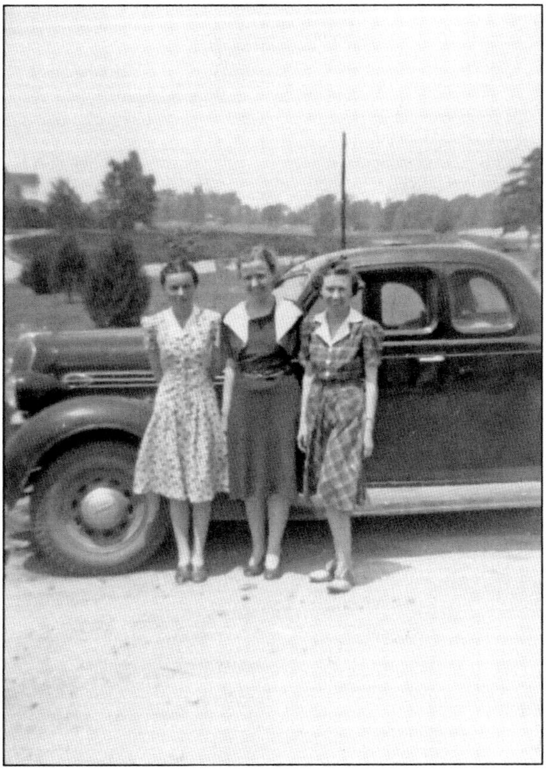

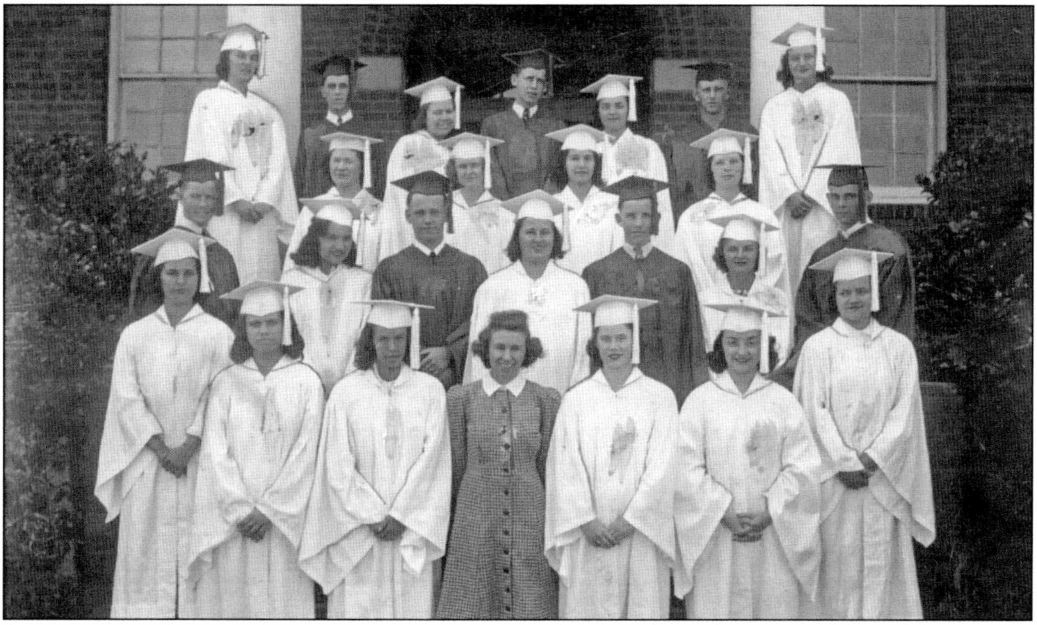

Much beloved by its students, Cobb Memorial High School ceased operation when Caswell County consolidated its high schools in the 1960s. After consolidation, all the county's high school students attended Bartlett Yancey High School in Yanceyville. The 1941 Cobb graduating class is on the front steps of the old Cobb Memorial High School, which burned in 1948 but was quickly replaced. (Courtesy Houston G. Jones.)

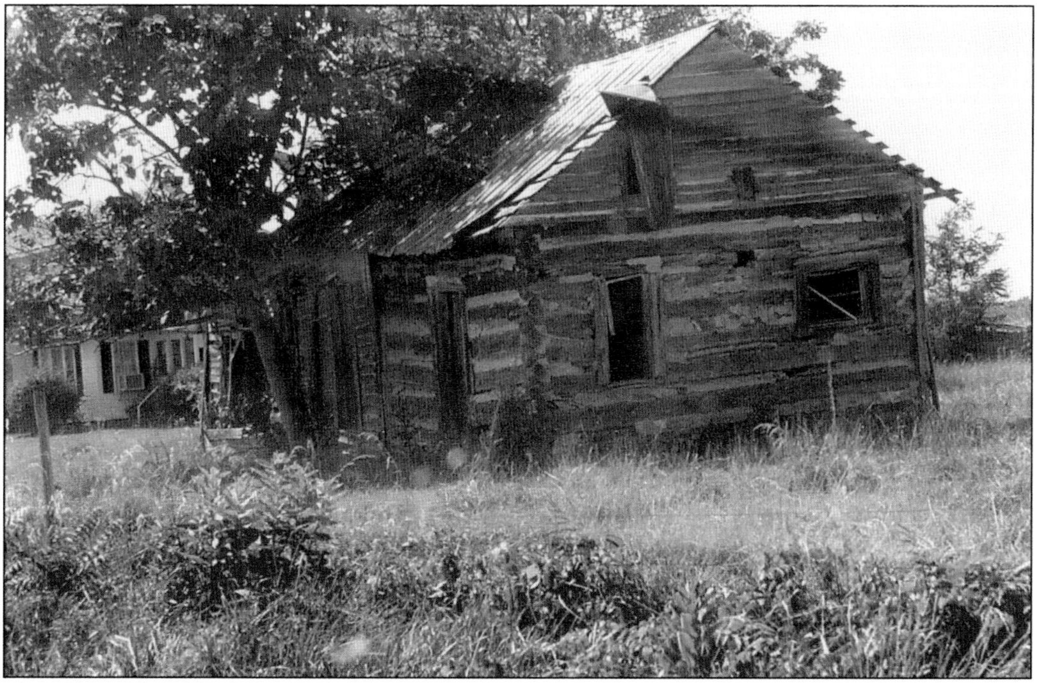

The old log school for black students in the Locust Hill community stood on Highway 158 in western Caswell County near the New Ephesus Church. The school, in operation during the early part of the 20th century, was in ruins for many years and no longer exists. (Courtesy Ada W. James.)

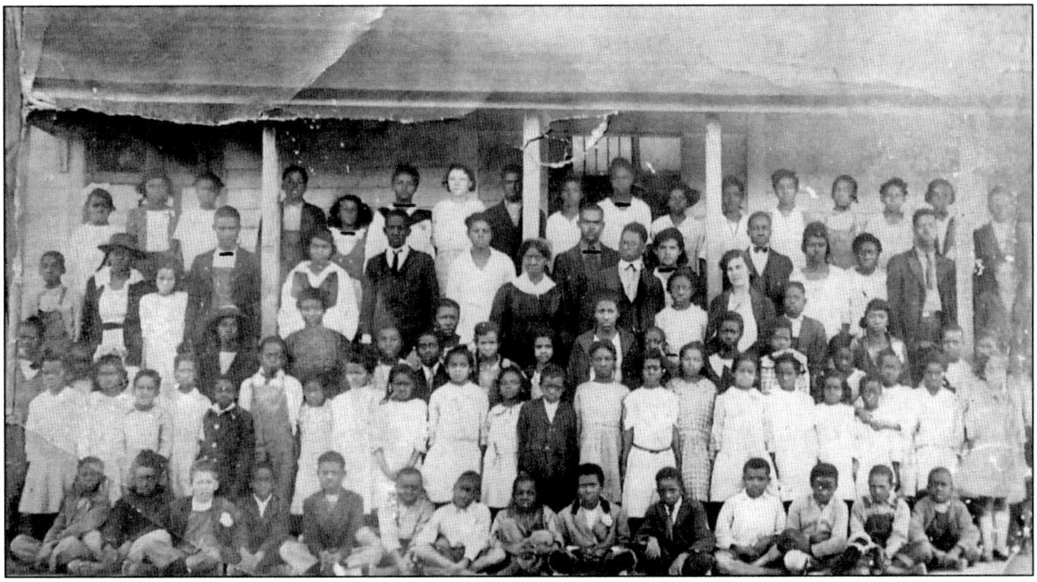

The Yanceyville Colored School was chartered in 1897. The school building was the old Stephens house, purchased in 1906 by local black community leaders. The house stood empty for decades after the murder of owner Senator John Walter Stephens in 1870. Note the large number of students attending school in this four-room house in 1922. (Courtesy Ada W. James.)

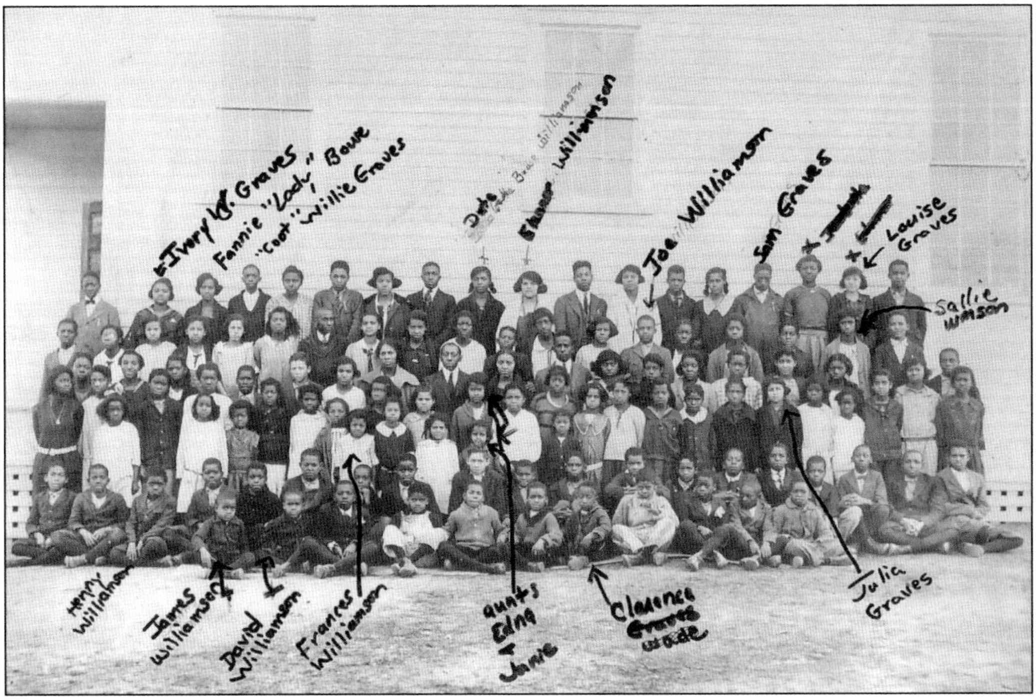

Until 1925, Yanceyville's black students attended school at churches and then in an old house purchased by black community leaders. In 1925, black parents contributed $800 and considerable labor, and a new four-room Rosenwald school was constructed. Philanthropist Julius Rosenwald (president of Sears, Roebuck, and Company) made funds available throughout the South for black schools between the late 1910s and 1932. (Courtesy Ada W. James.)

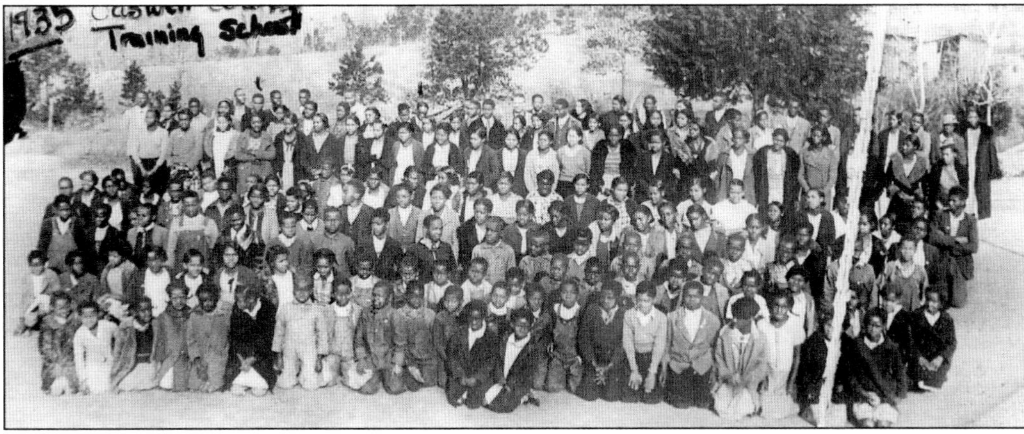

In 1935, with the addition of a high school, the name of the old Yanceyville Colored School (accredited in 1897) was changed to the Caswell County Training School. However, classes continued to be held in the four-room Rosenwald school that was built in 1925. (Courtesy Ada W. James.)

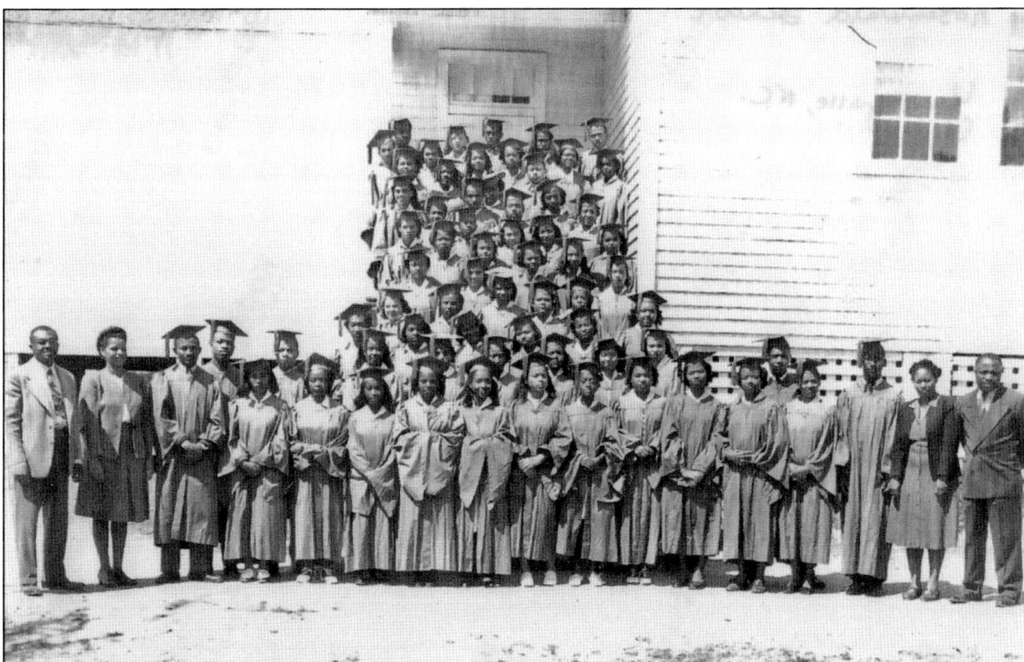

With the 1948 Caswell County Training School graduating class is Principal Nicholas Longworth Dillard (1906–1969) (at far left). He served in that position for 37 years (1932–1969). Dillard was tireless in his efforts to better educational opportunities for Caswell's black children, including work that resulted in a new school building in 1951. Today, a Caswell County middle school is named in his honor. (Courtesy Ada W. James.)

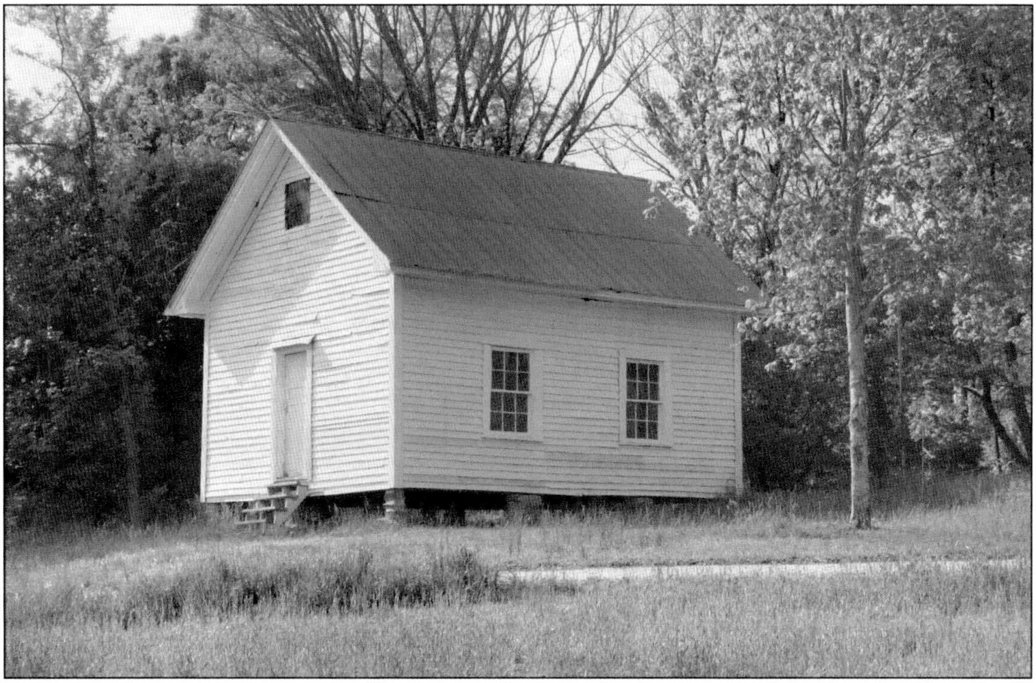

The Poteat one-room schoolhouse was built in 1913 by Albert Lindsey Poteat (1865–1929) on his Caswell County farm using lumber sawn from trees felled on his land. While Poteat had little formal education, he was interested in obtaining better training for his family and neighbors. The school building was moved to the Yanceyville National Historic District and restored by the local Future Farmers of America chapter. (CCHA Photograph Archives.)

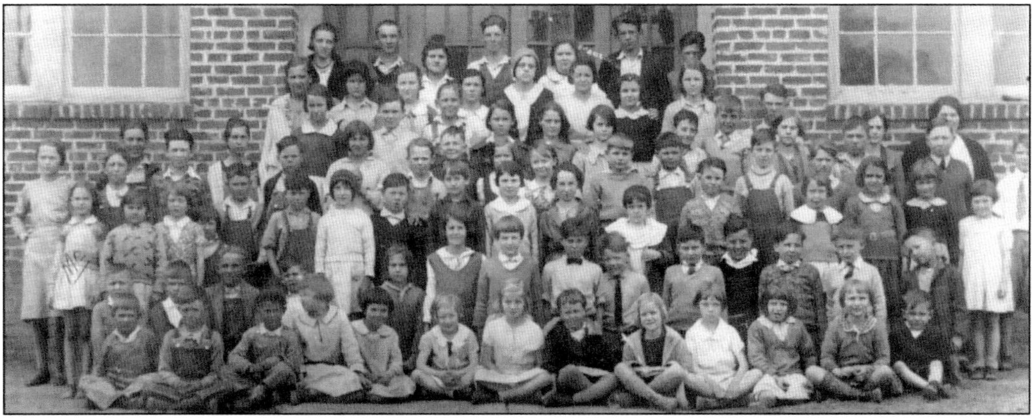

During the early 20th century, many small schools remained scattered throughout the county, some still of log construction. However, by 1924, Cobb, Milton, and Semora were offering instruction in consolidated schools from the first grade through high school. The 1932 Milton Elementary School student body poses here with the school in the background. Purportedly, this building was constructed with bricks from the Milton Female Academy. (Courtesy Lois Angle Love.)

Three

Business and Farming

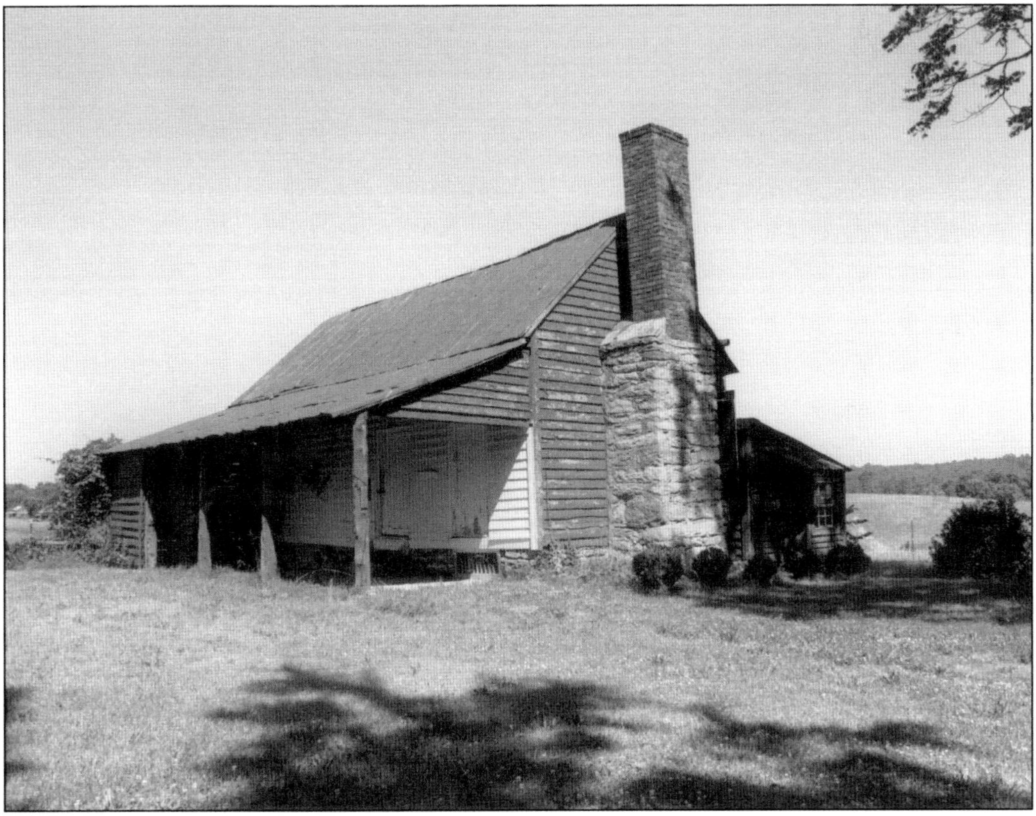

Brown's Store, built around 1780 in Locust Hill, is one of the oldest commercial structures in Caswell County. It was built by or for the Brown family and operated by Jethro Brown (1766–1828) as a country store, stagecoach stop, and post office. The building remains intact today, including its original Federal trim, brick chimney, full fieldstone basement, and some original hardware. The store is on the National Register of Historic Places. (Courtesy Susan Lassiter.)

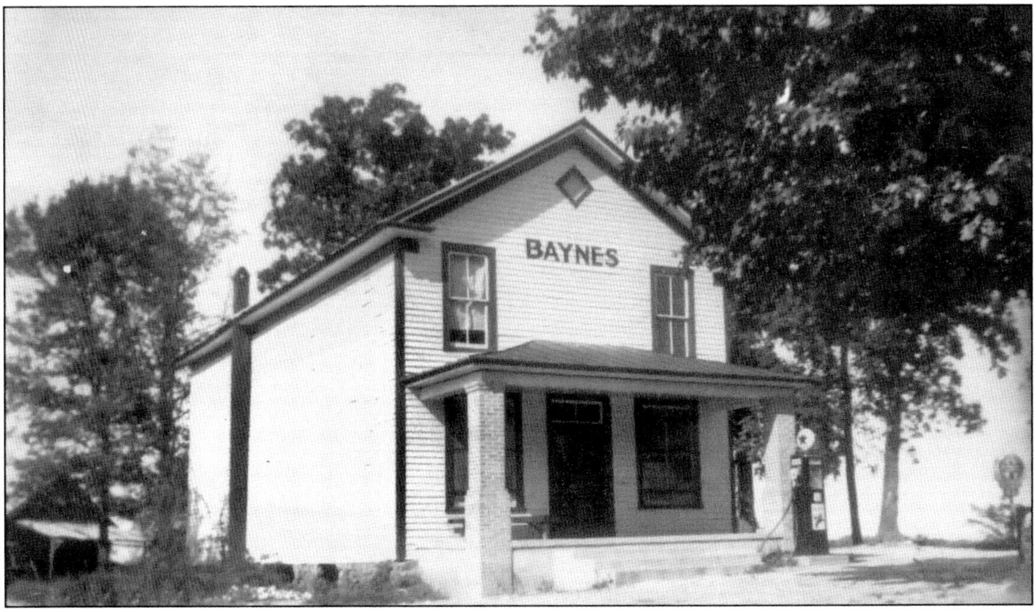

Erected in 1907 and still in business today, Baynes Store in Anderson Township initially was owned and operated by James Rainey Baynes (1855–1923) and his brother-in-law Leonidas Franklin Harrelson (1858–1939). It was a typical Southern country store: sawdust on the floor; barrels of flour and beans; coveralls and boots on the shelves; and a pot-bellied stove as a social gathering point. Caskets also were sold. (Courtesy Nelson and Cindi Straughn.)

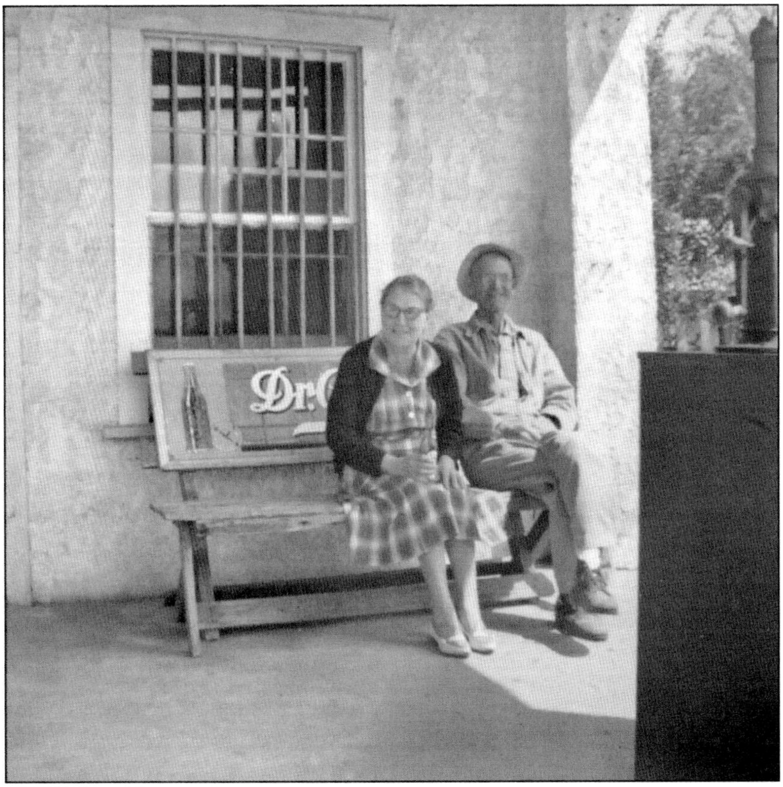

Storeowner Robert Ashley Briggs (1891–1967) and wife Mary Henry Oakes Briggs (1898–1973) are taking a rest break at their store in Leasburg during the 1950s. A hand-pumped kerosene tank is to the right. The old store, once a local landmark, stands today derelict and abandoned. At one time, the small town of Leasburg had six general stores, with several operated by the Briggs family. (Courtesy Mildred Wade Henderson.)

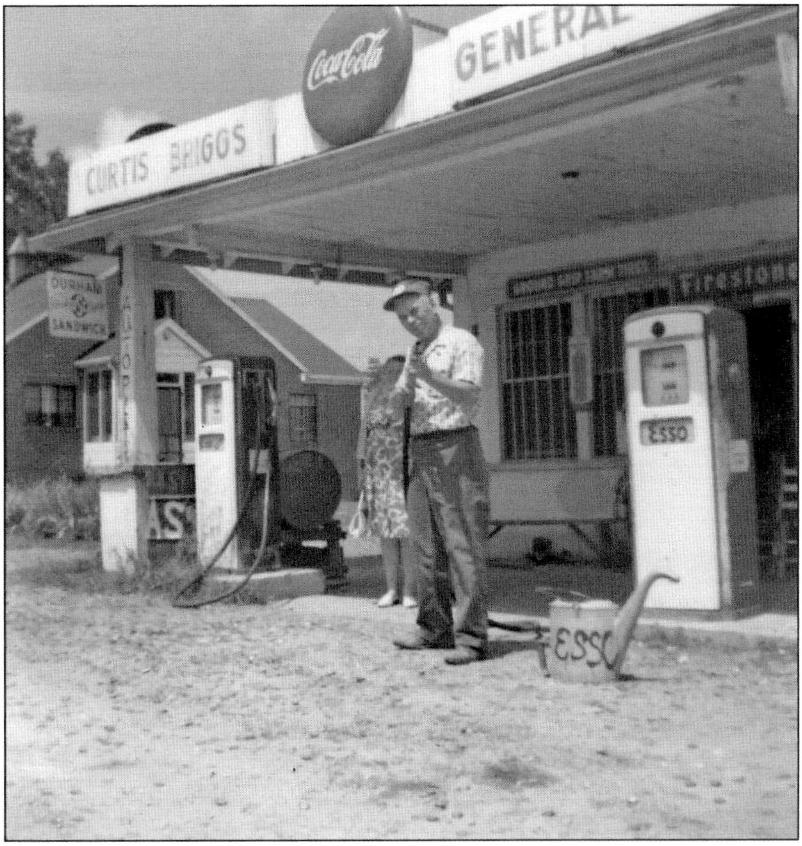

Clyde Curtis Briggs (1917–1981) owned and operated Briggs General Merchandise in Leasburg, directly across from the old Leasburg Post Office. In a playful mood, Briggs is aiming the gasoline nozzle at the photographer. Curtis carried on the Briggs family mercantile tradition in Leasburg. His business was just up the road from the store of Ashley Briggs, his father. (Courtesy Mildred Wade Henderson.)

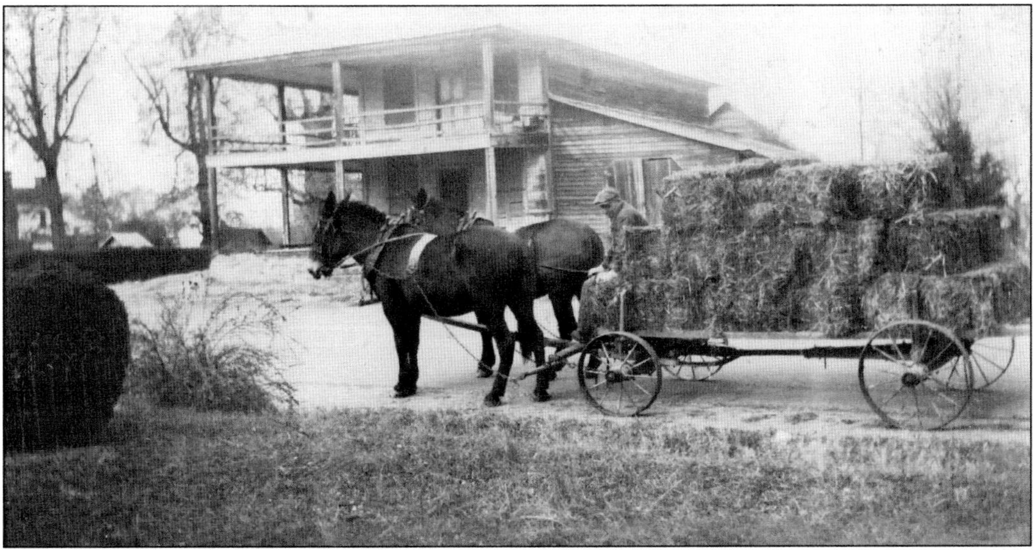

The unpaved road and the mode of transporting goods date this scene at around the turn of the 20th century, possibly earlier. The building across the way is the Leasburg store of Samuel Pinkney Newman (1860–1934). "Pink" Newman also was a tobacconist who worked in the tobacco trade in Danville, Virginia, during the week but returned to his home in Leasburg for the weekends. (Courtesy Mildred Wade Henderson.)

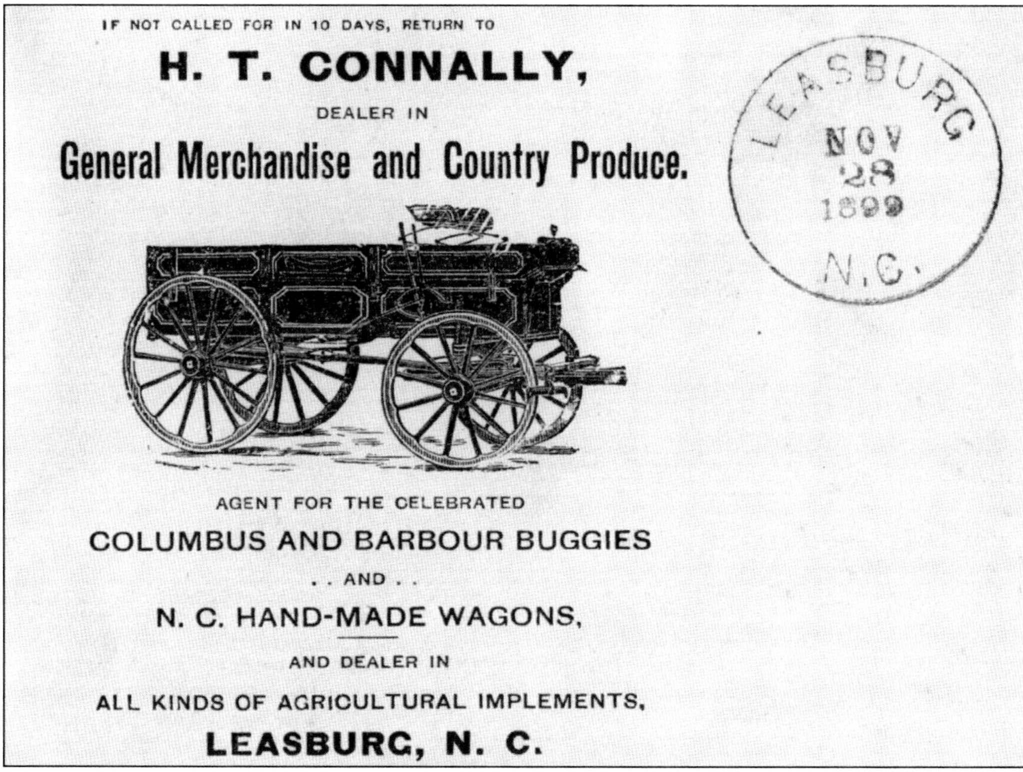

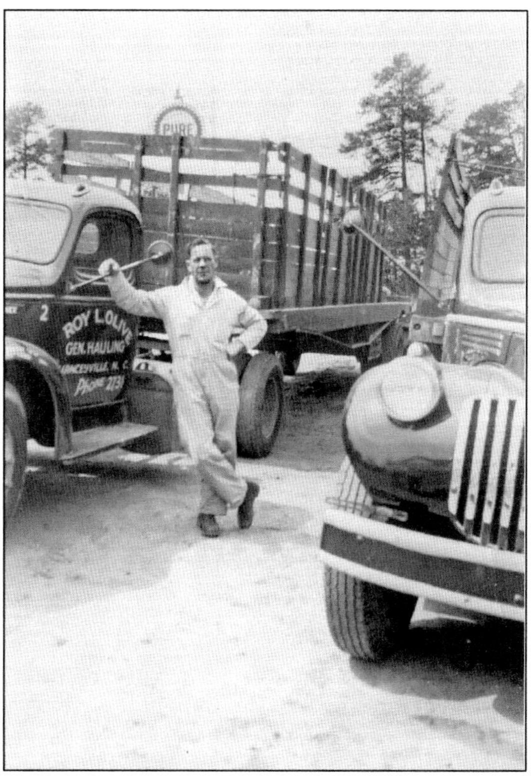

Henry Thomas Connally (1849–1914) owned and operated a successful general store in Leasburg. The business earlier was called Pulliam's Store, having been operated by Berryman Green Pulliam (1801–1877), who became Connally's father-in-law. The building was dismantled in the early 1960s, and much of the interior was donated to the Greensboro (North Carolina) History Museum, where it was on display for many years. (Courtesy Chris Holaday.)

From the beginning, Caswell County's focus was on agriculture. However, a few ventured into non-agricultural businesses. One was Roy Lee Olive (1918–1989). George Gunn Henderson (1915–2002) is standing beside one of Olive's trucks in the 1940s, probably at the Pure gasoline station in Hightowers. (Courtesy Mildred Wade Henderson.)

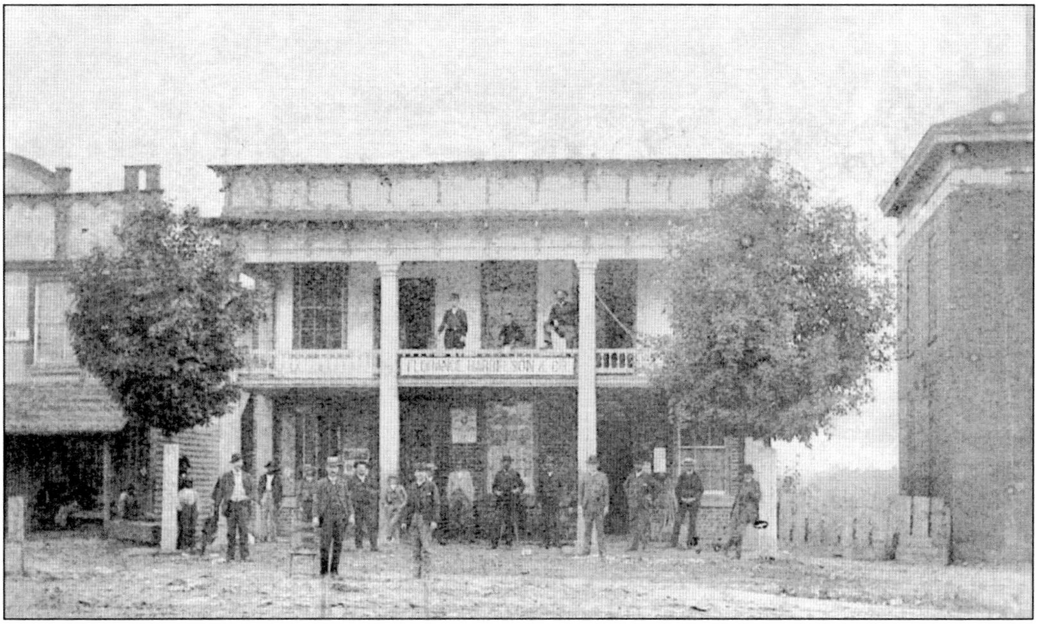

In the 1880s, Florance, Harrelson, and Co. was a thriving concern on the Yanceyville Square. Walter N. Harrelson (1859–1933) is beside the chair, with Thomas Jefferson Florance (1858–1926) to his left. The trees were wrapped to prevent horses from eating the bark. To the left (partially behind the tree) is a saloon. The building on the right is believed to be the Masonic lodge. Many of these buildings burned around 1890. (CCHA Photograph Archives.)

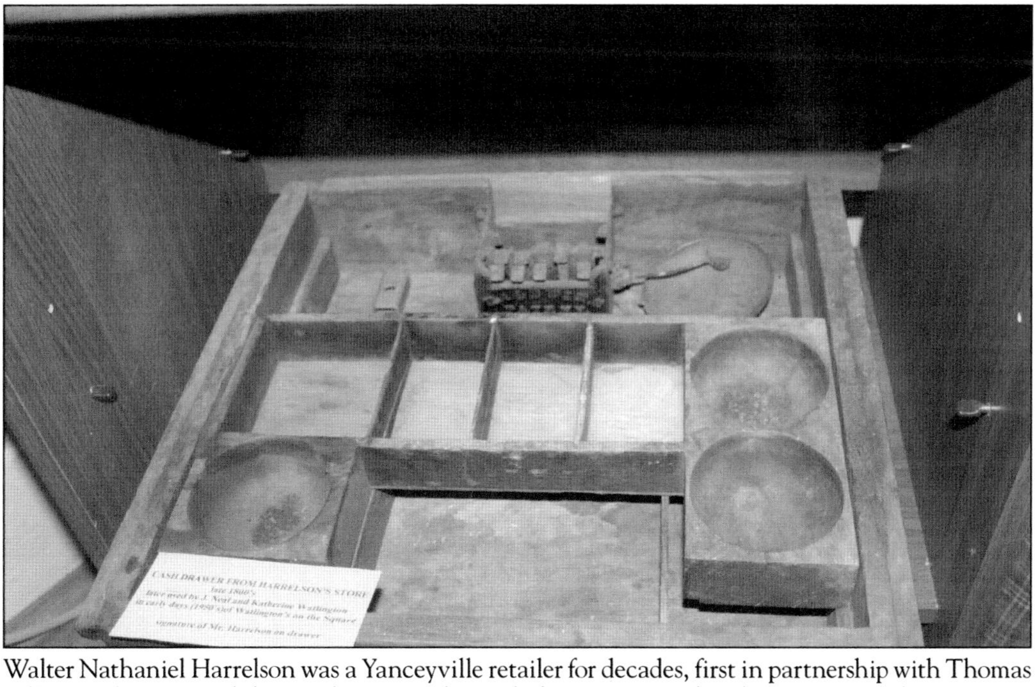

Walter Nathaniel Harrelson was a Yanceyville retailer for decades, first in partnership with Thomas Jefferson Florance and then on his own. This cash drawer was used at the W. N. Harrelson store on the Yanceyville Square and is on display at the Richmond-Miles History Museum in Yanceyville. It dates from the late 1800s. (CCHA Photograph Archives.)

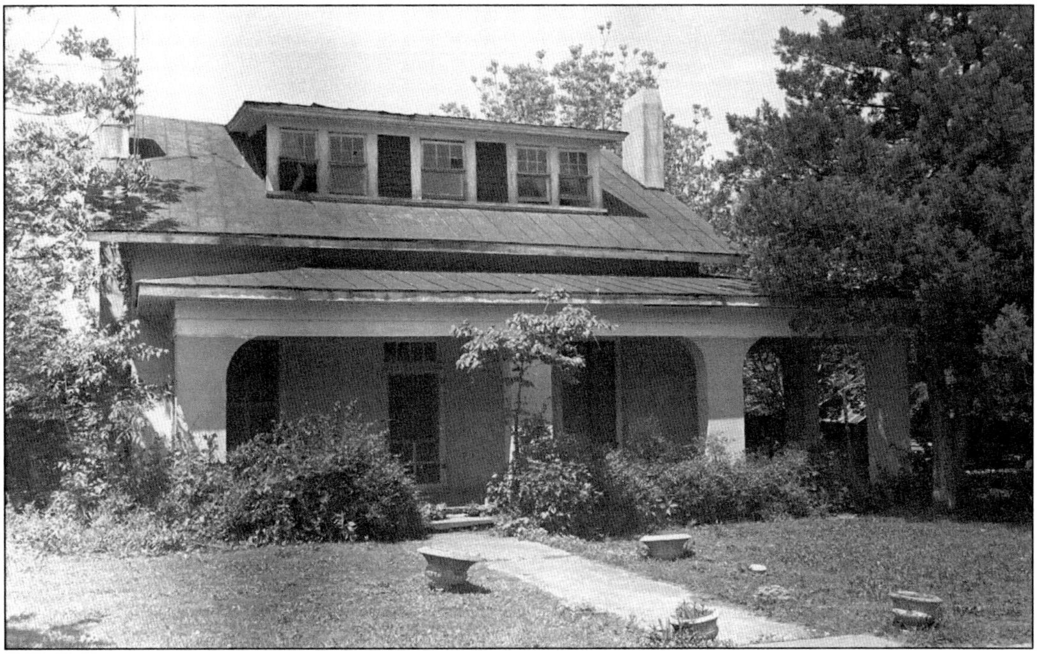

The house, built around 1850 on West Main Street in Yanceyville but no longer standing, purportedly was the first office of the Bank of Yanceyville, chartered 1852. J. J. Lawson, a Bank of Yanceyville teller, once lived there. Legend has it that when the house was owned by the Fitch family, they were so proud of their indoor toilet that it was placed in the kitchen. (NCSHPO.)

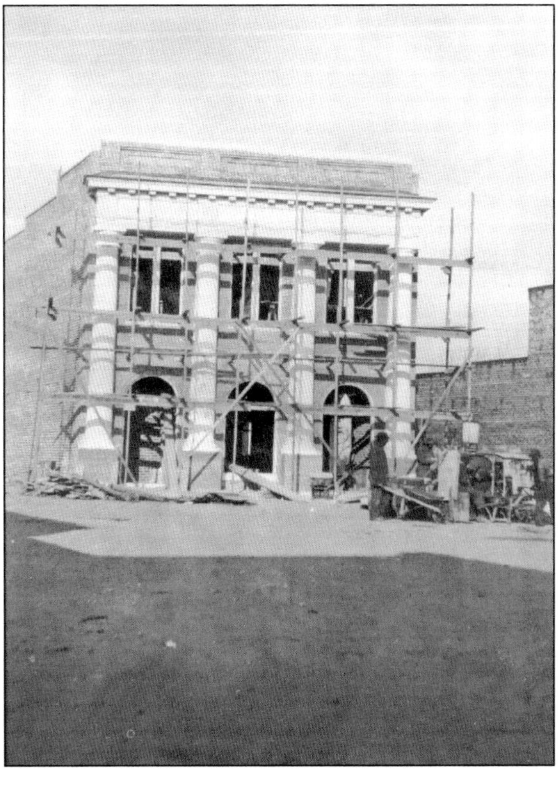

The Bank of Yanceyville began business in 1852, during the boom era in Caswell County. By the start of the Civil War, it was one of the best-capitalized banks in North Carolina and made substantial loans to the State of North Carolina to help finance the war. In 1922, construction began on a new bank building. (Courtesy Louise Moore Atwater Estate.)

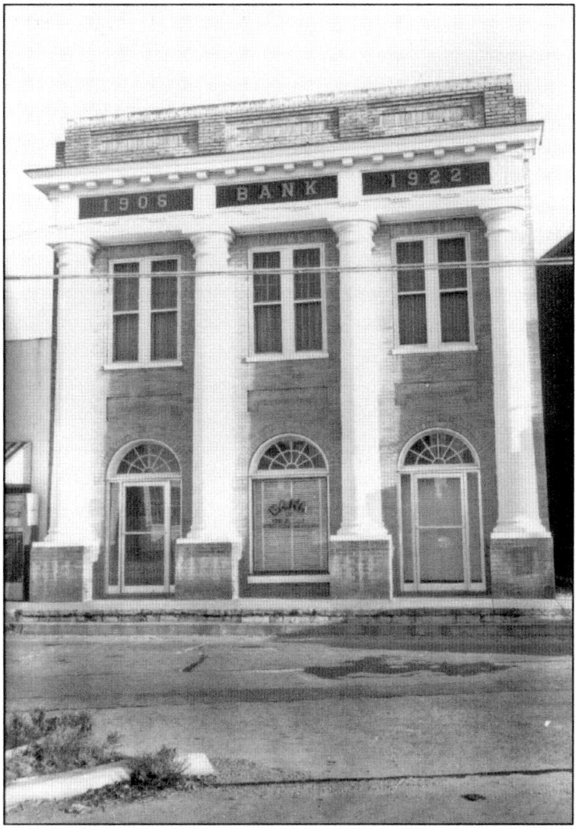

Wealthy Caswell County planter and businessman Thomas Donoho Johnston (1800–1883) founded the Bank of Yanceyville in 1852. The initial authorized capital was $200,000, and the bank issued its own notes, which circulated as currency. The original bank failed as a result of the Civil War and surrendered its charter in 1866. The Bank of Yanceyville that occupied this building dates from 1906. (CCHA Photograph Archives.)

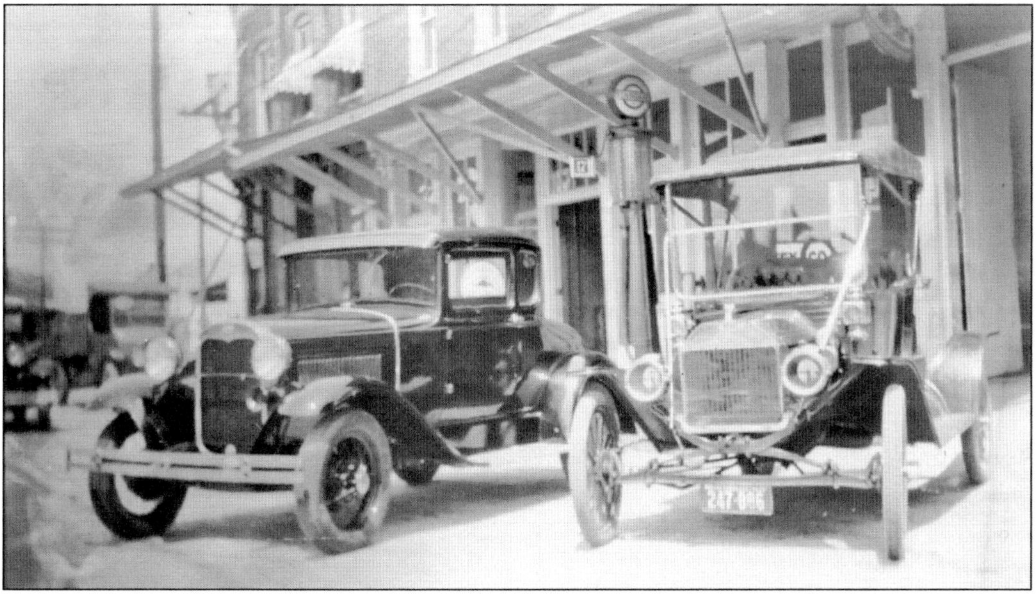

In 1927, the first Ford Model A in Caswell County was displayed in front of Crowell Auto Co. in Yanceyville. The older vehicle is a Model T, which had been phased out. The dealership eventually would become Caswell Motor Co., owned by John Oliver Gunn (1892–1992). (Courtesy John O. Gunn Estate.)

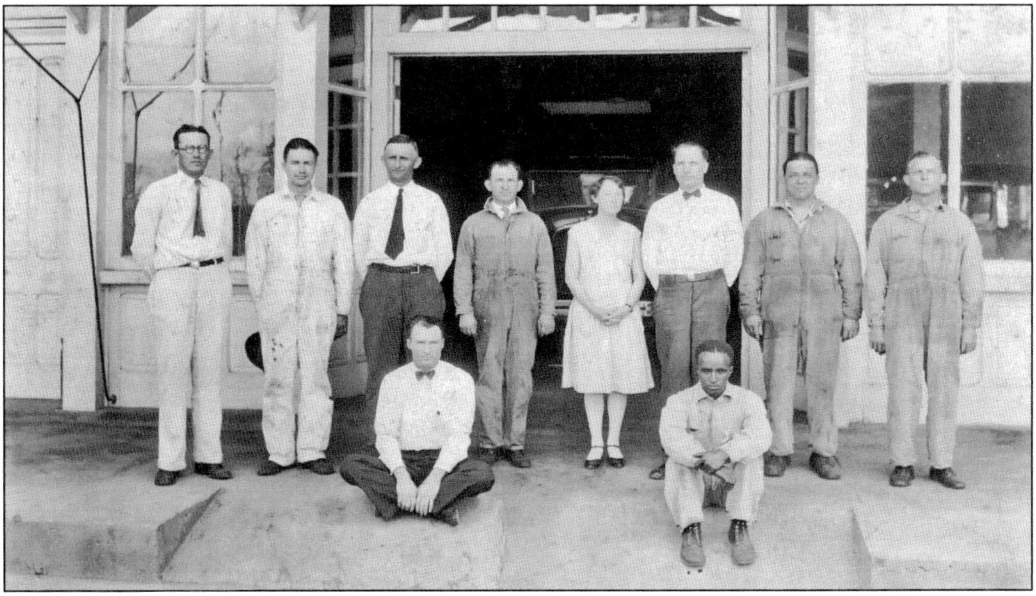

In 1927, employees of Crowell Auto Co. in Yanceyville gathered in front of the dealership. They are, from left to right, (seated) John Oliver Gunn (white shirt) and Lynn Bowe (born 1905); (standing) Earmine Lee Poteat (1898–1979), Otis A. Powell (1900–1966), Thomas Hiram Hodges (1888–1972), Woody Lillard (born *c.* 1893), Pattie Griffin Gunn (1895–1956), Hubert Hodnett Page (1897–1974), Harry Bradner (1898–1980), and Loyd Johnson (born *c.* 1883). (Courtesy John O. Gunn Estate.)

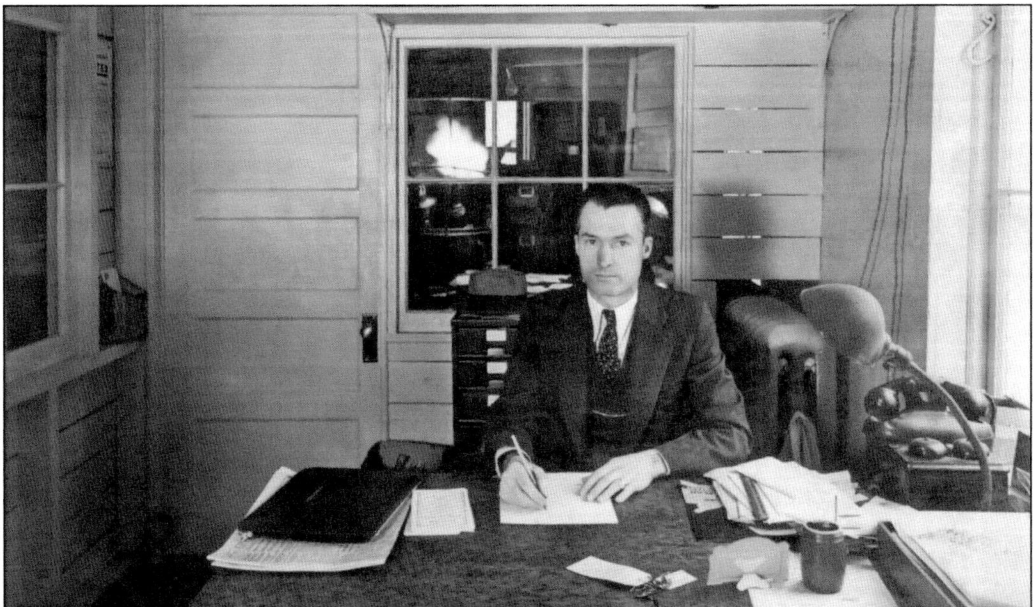

John Oliver Gunn was the manager of Crowell Auto Co. in Yanceyville. The dealership was an authorized outlet for Ford automobiles and Fordson tractors. Gunn eventually purchased the dealership and renamed it Caswell Motor Co. The business flourished, and Gunn became a leader in the community. The photograph was taken in 1927. (Courtesy John O. Gunn Estate.)

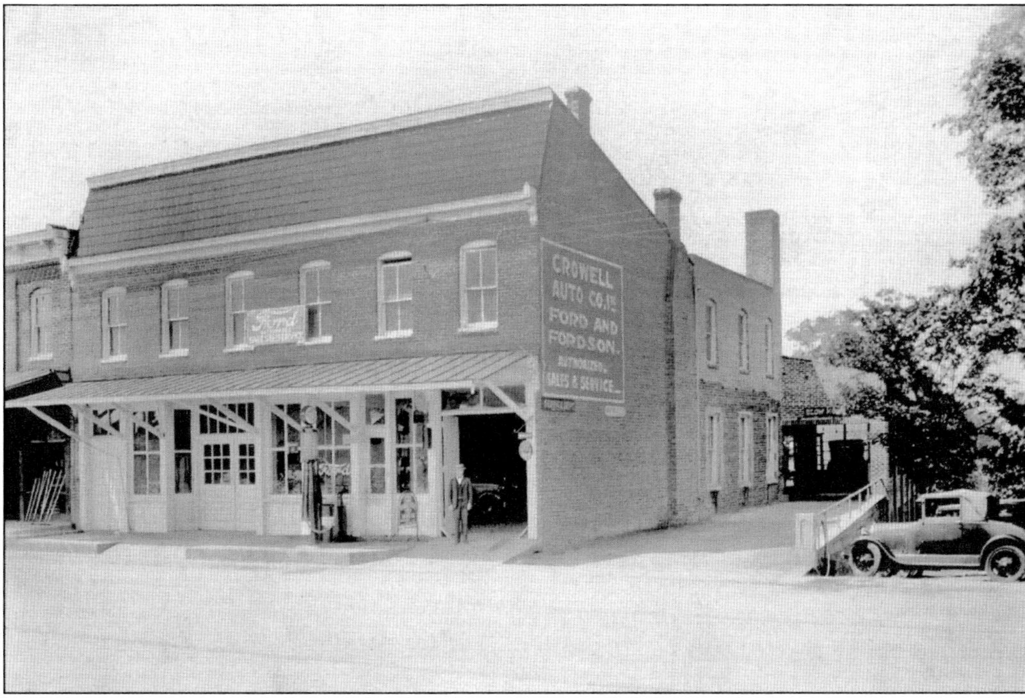

Crowell Auto Co. was established around 1917 as the authorized Ford and Fordson dealer in Yanceyville. The 1927 building, which began life in 1897, had a rear section added to provide a garage and service area. The driveway to the addition covered an old well that had been on the square for decades. (Courtesy John O. Gunn Estate.)

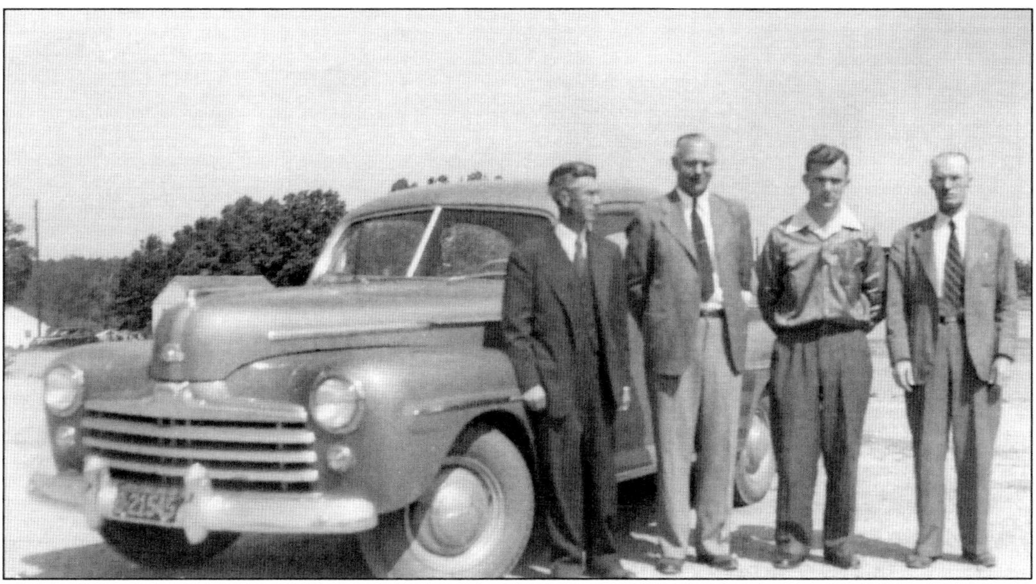

Standing beside what is believed to be a driver education car provided by Caswell Motor Co. to the Yanceyville high school are, from left to right, Norman Stroupe Upchurch (teacher), Sheffield H. Abel (principal), Billy Hunt (student), and John Oliver Gunn (owner of Caswell Motor Co.). The image dates from the 1940s. (Courtesy John O. Gunn Estate.)

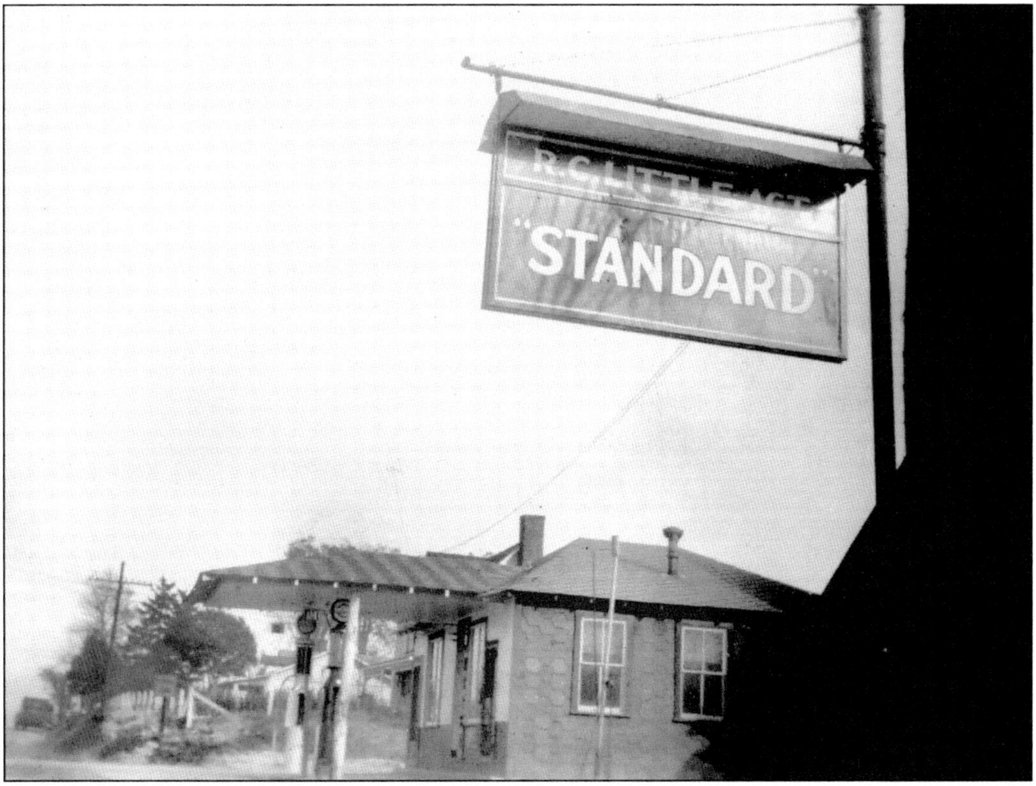

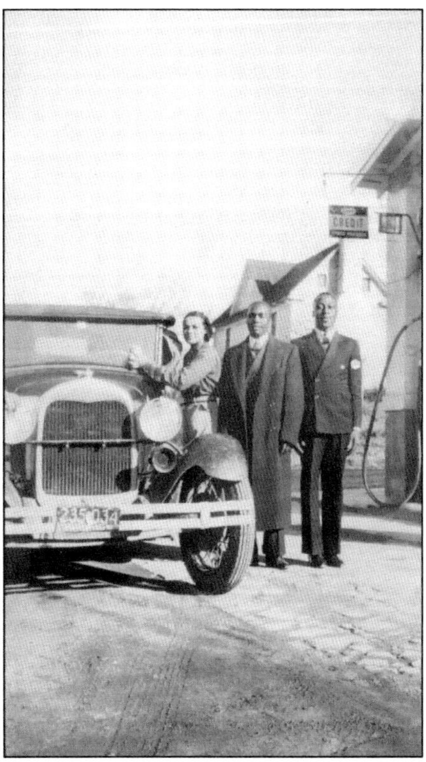

Martha Louise Lea Little (1904–1983) and her husband, Roy Charles Little (*c.* 1893–1938), owned Little Service Station in Yanceyville, one of the early successful local black businesses. It began operation in the 1920s as a Standard agency, purchasing gasoline from Standard Oil of New Jersey. When the photograph above was taken, the building was fairly new. Note the gravity-fed gasoline pumps. In the left photograph, Martha Little is servicing a customer's car around 1928, after the brand had become Esso. The father of Martha Louise Lea Little, Thomas Sidney Lea (1873–1963), provided financial support for local black educational efforts, including participating in the purchase of a building in 1906 that was used as the first black school in Yanceyville. In the background of both images is the home of Yanceyville dry goods merchant Julius Spencer Watlington (1895–1972). (Both courtesy Helen Little.)

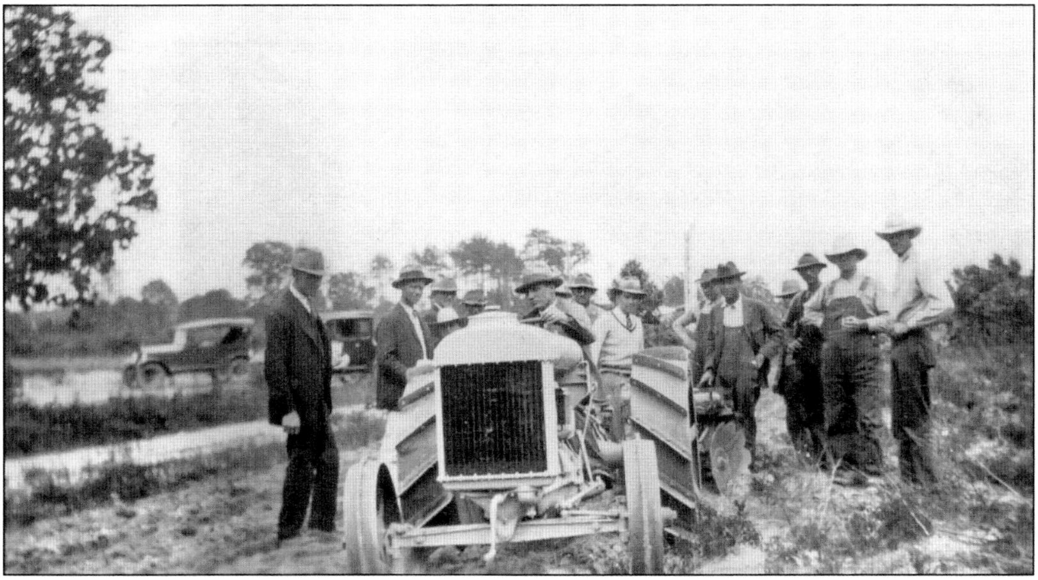

Caswell County farmers are participating in a 1920s Fordson tractor demonstration being held by Crowell Auto Co., the authorized Fordson dealer in Yanceyville. While few of the participants are identified, the man in the large hat second from right probably is Edgar Archibald Allison (1879–1955). The tractor is a Fordson Model F, which was in production from 1917 to 1928. (Courtesy John O. Gunn Estate.)

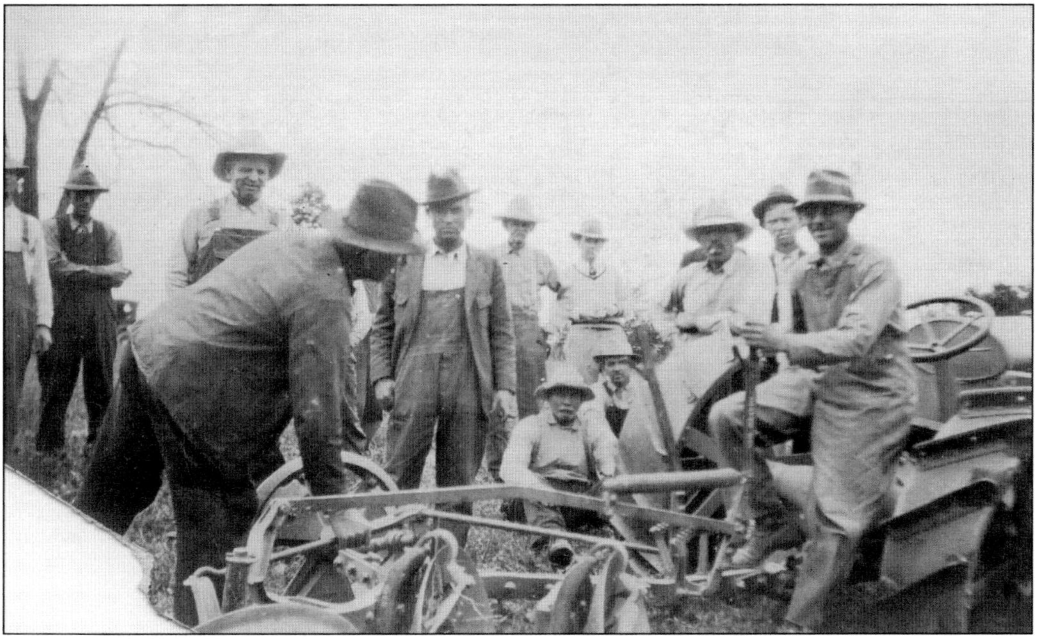

At the same 1920s Fordson tractor demonstration seen above, local farmers are inspecting the implement hitch mechanism at the rear of the tractor. This probably was wise, because the Fordson Model F tractor had a habit of rearing up on its back wheels and turning over. One farm magazine recommended that Ford paint a message on each Fordson: "Prepare to Meet Thy God." (Courtesy John O. Gunn Estate.)

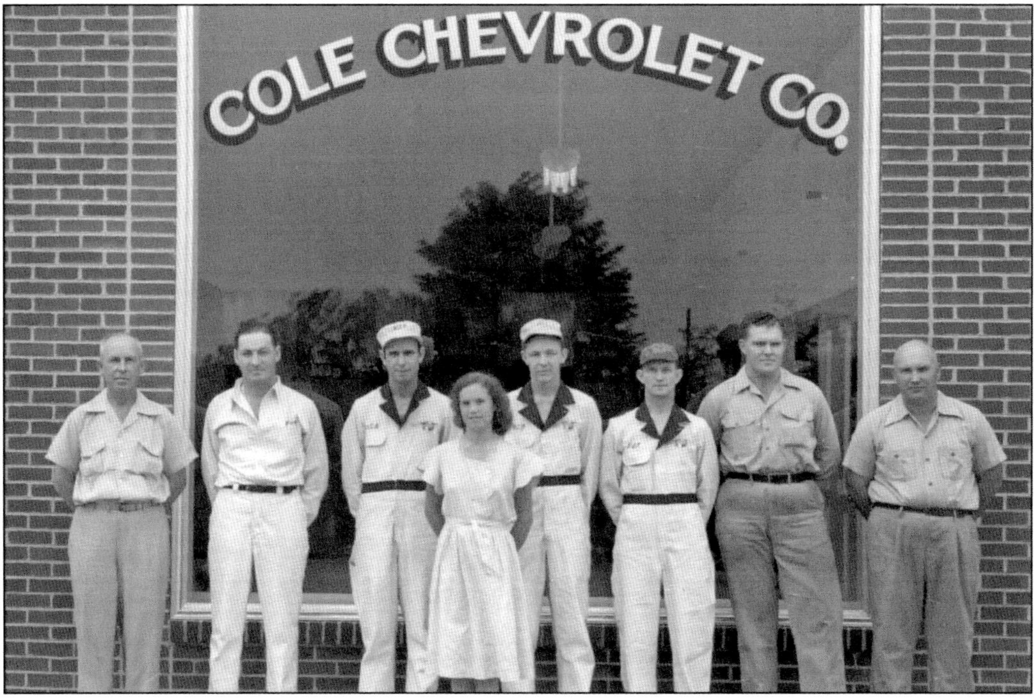

In 1928, Clyde Caviness Cole (1903–1969) opened a Chevrolet dealership in Yanceyville, having secured the first Chevrolet franchise granted in Caswell County. In 1947, Cole built a new dealership. The employees gathered in front of the new building are, from left to right, Clyde Cole, Irving Reagan, Wallace Burke, Billy Oakley, Steve Poteat, Billy Aldridge, Jim Aldridge, and Bessie Shaw (in front). (Courtesy Jerry L. Cole.)

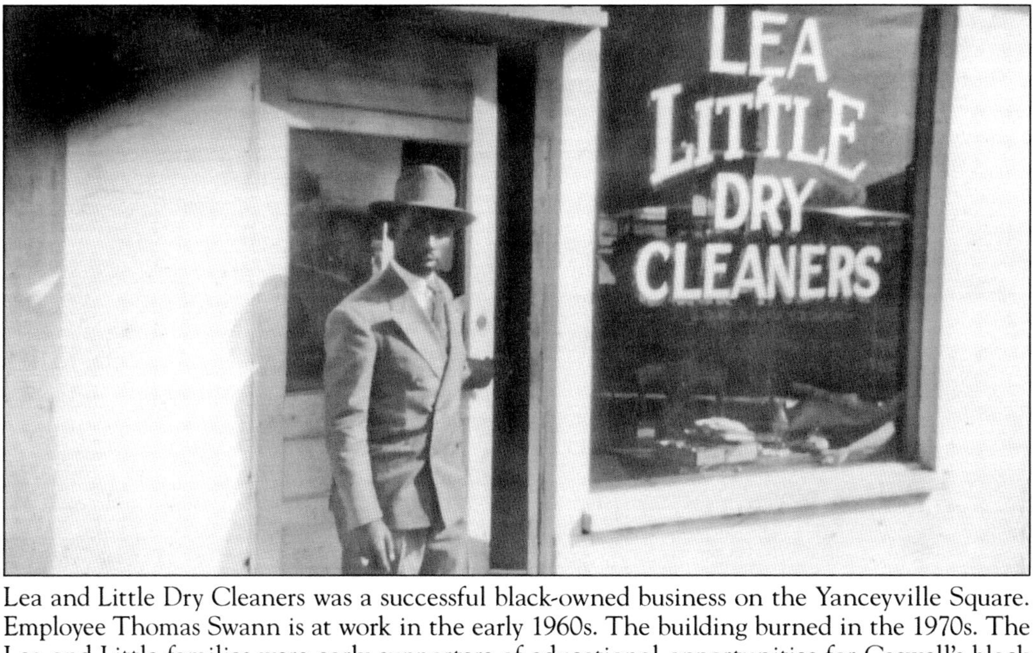

Lea and Little Dry Cleaners was a successful black-owned business on the Yanceyville Square. Employee Thomas Swann is at work in the early 1960s. The building burned in the 1970s. The Lea and Little families were early supporters of educational opportunities for Caswell's black children, both with their time and money. (Courtesy Helen Little.)

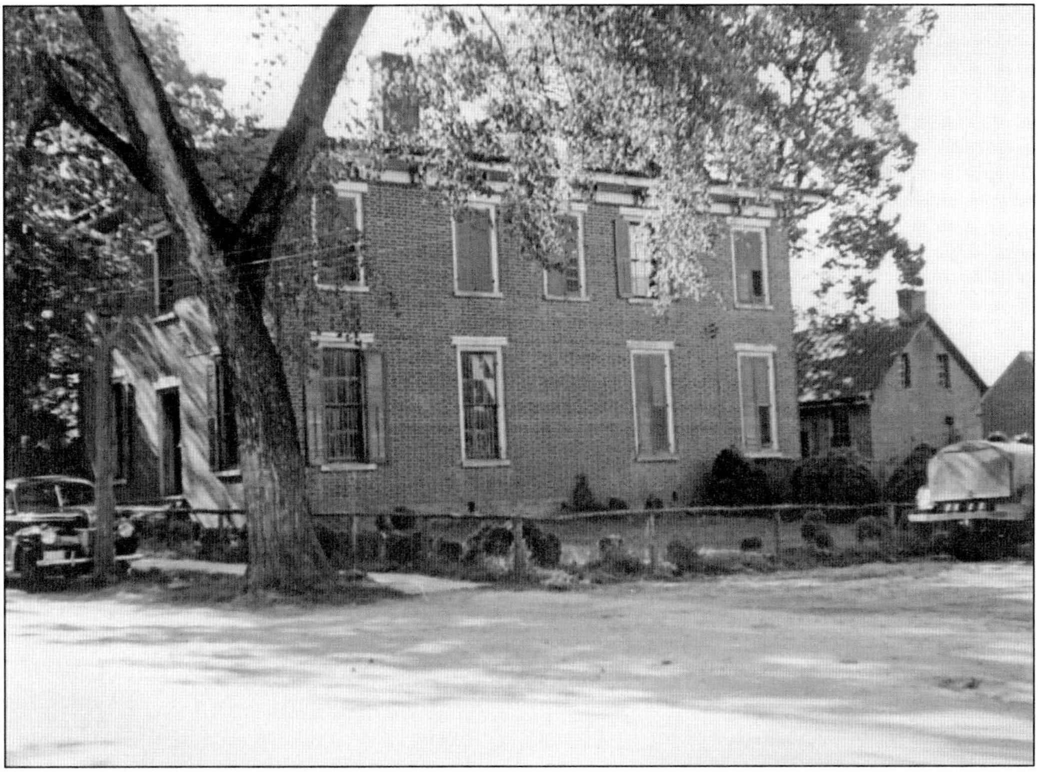

Milton was the home of Caswell County's first bank, with a branch of the State Bank of North Carolina established there in 1818. The building in this photograph was erected in 1859 to house the Milton branch of a successor institution with a similar name, the Bank of North Carolina. The structure, now a private residence, is on the National Register of Historic Places. (Courtesy Jean Bradsher Scott.)

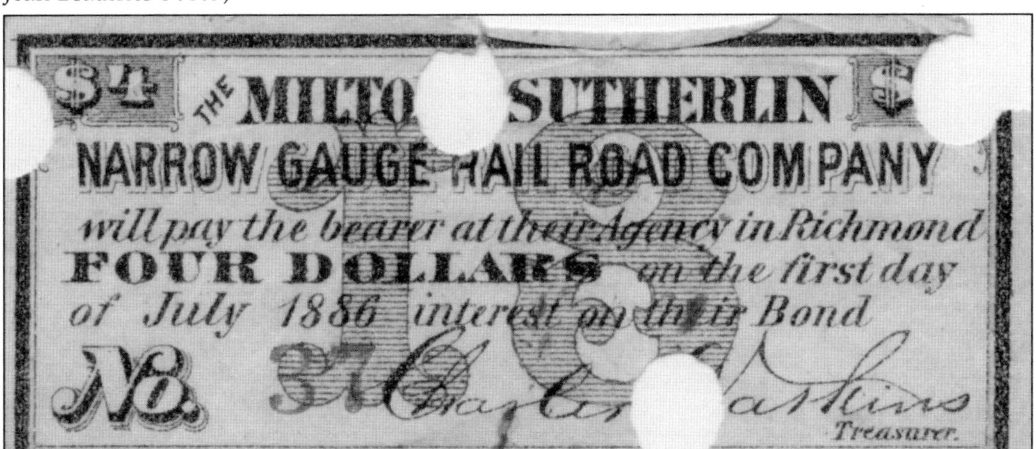

Caswell County suffered economically because it lacked adequate transportation infrastructure to attract industry. Several attempts were made at railroads. All eventually failed. One, the Milton and Sutherlin Narrow Gauge Railroad, became operational in 1877 but was out of business by 1895. It ran 7 miles from Milton to Sutherlin, Virginia, which was on the Richmond and Danville Railroad. Bonds were issued to finance the railroad's construction. (Courtesy Jean Bradsher Scott.)

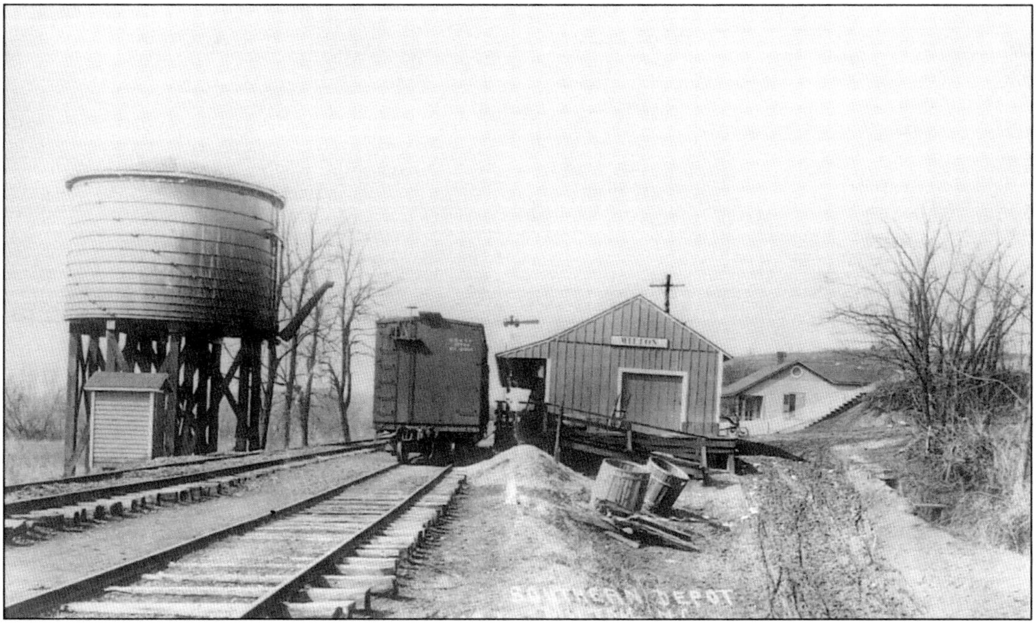

The Milton railroad station was built around 1900. In the early days, steam-powered locomotives of the Southern Railway provided freight and passenger service. Note the large water tower across the tracks, often used by local boys for unauthorized swimming. The house to the right was occupied by the railway section foreman, whose job was to keep the tracks in good repair. (CCHA Photograph Archives.)

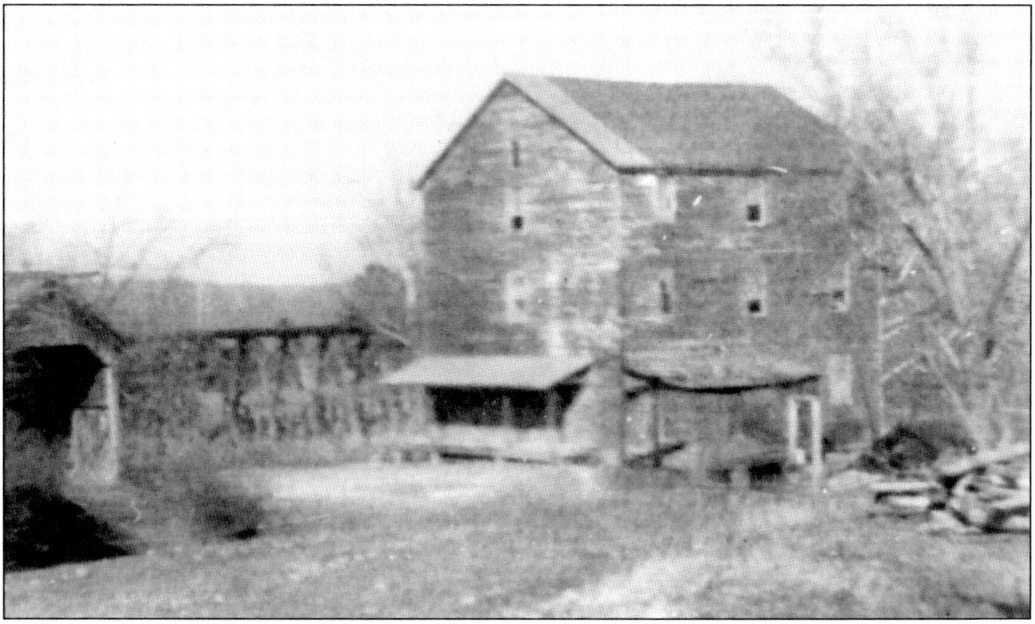

For decades, Caswell's millers converted grain to flour and meal by grinding it between rotating stones. This technology was replaced by the roller mill, which crushed the grain between rollers. The old Milton roller mill stood on Country Line Creek. Beside it was the high trestle bridge over the stream. The open-ended building to the left was used to store coal for sale. (Courtesy Jean Bradsher Scott.)

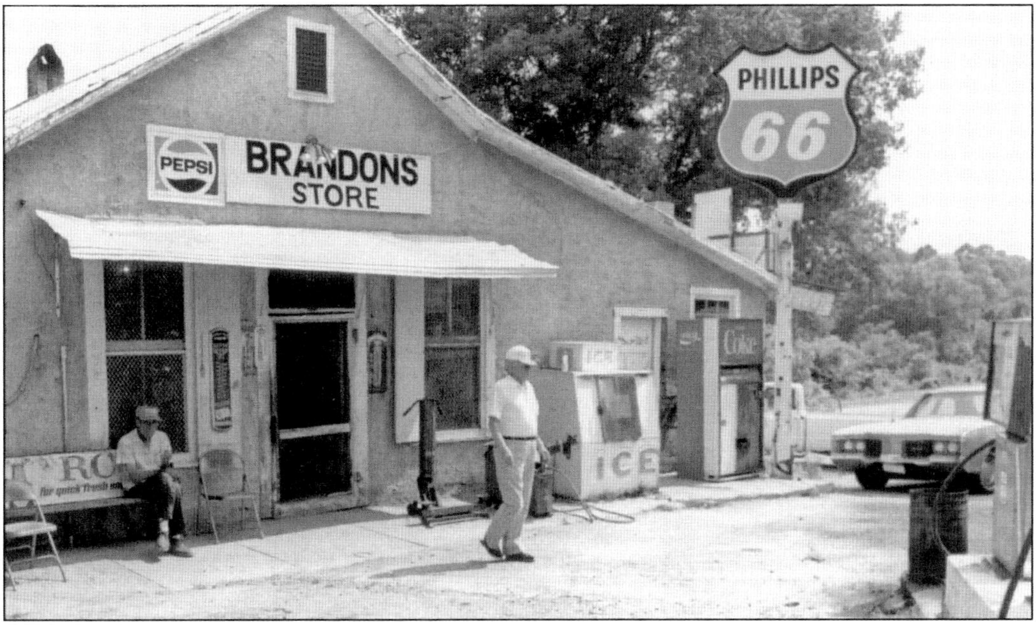

The traditional country store gave way to service stations, often in the same building. This store in Blanch was opened before 1926 by Charles S. Walters (1884–1961), who built the structure in stages and operated it until he died. It occupied a prime location across from the Blanch railroad station and once housed the Blanch Post Office. Henry R. Brandon (1937–1988) was the last operator. (CCHA Photograph Archives.)

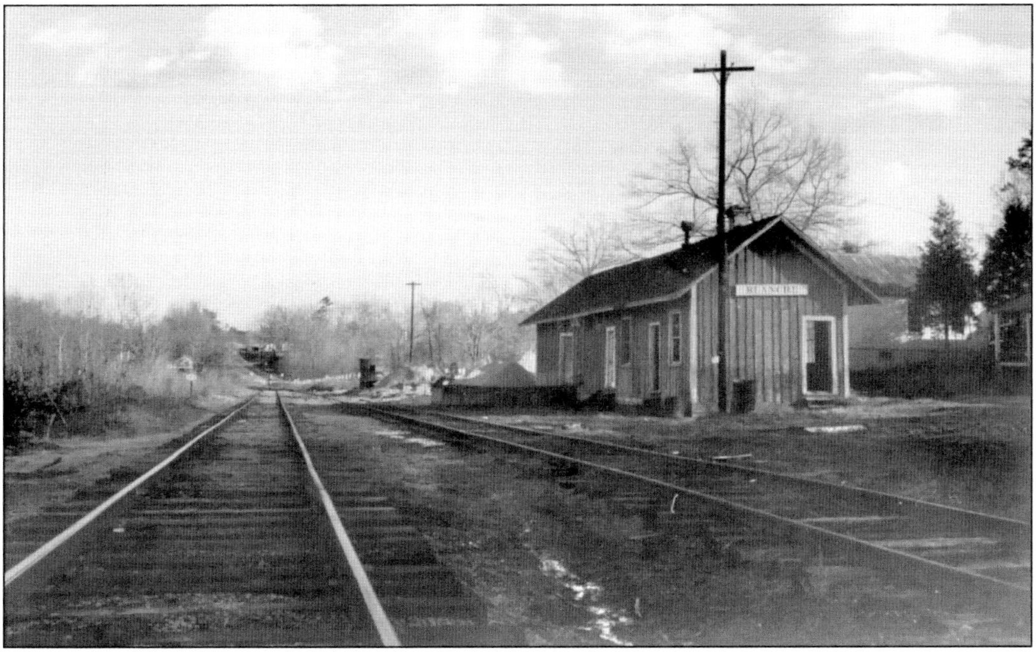

The Blanche (Blanch) railroad station was built around 1900. It is very similar in design to the Milton railroad station and probably was constructed at the same time. The two communities, only a few miles apart, were served by the same railroad. The Blanche station, a one-story gabled board-and-batten building, was demolished in the 1970s. (NCSHPO.)

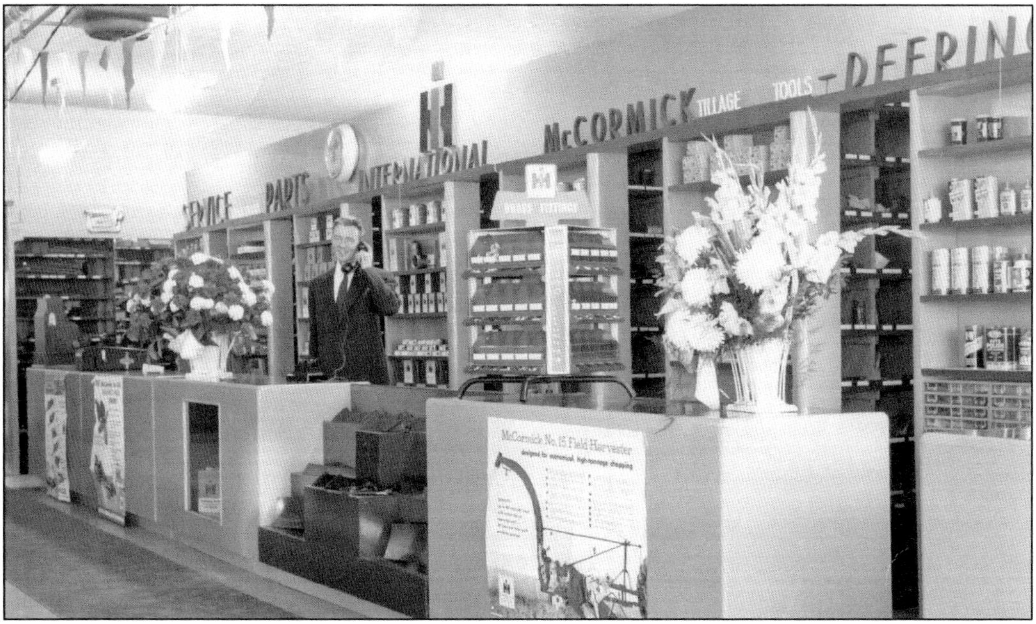

Caswell Hardware and Implement Company in Yanceyville was the authorized dealer for Pontiac, International Harvester, Farmall, McCormick, and Deering. It also offered a wide range of hardware and household goods. Seen here at the front desk in the 1950s is Richmond Stanfield Frederick (1918–1983). Now closed, the old building remains on what was Greensboro Street. (Courtesy Richmond S. Frederick Jr.)

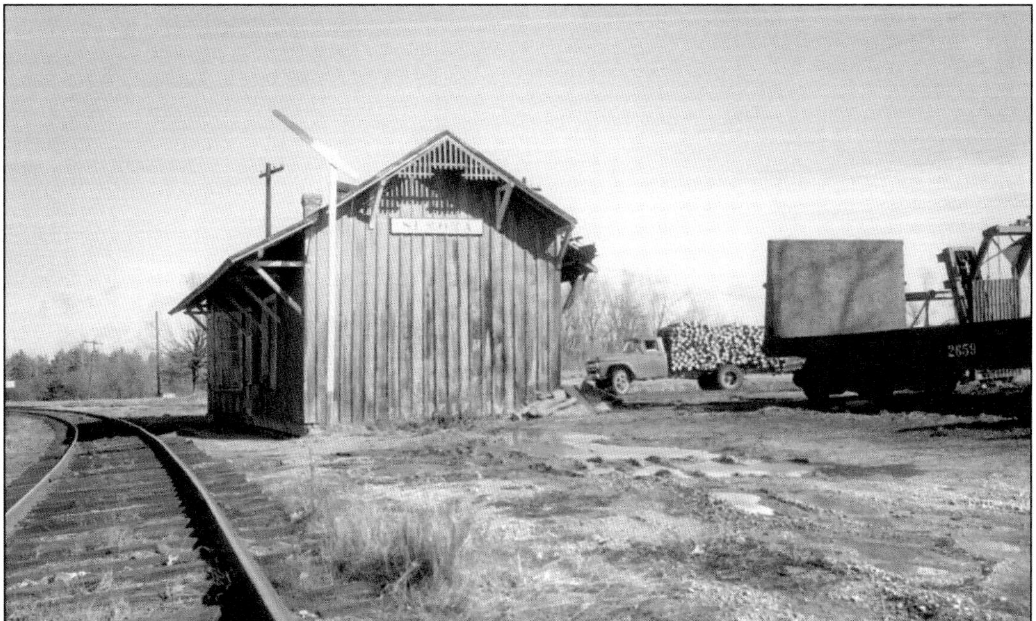

The Norfolk, Franklin, and Danville Railroad once ran through the Semora community in Caswell's northeast corner. Caswell never had a railway that served the main portions of the county. No railroad track ever ran to Yanceyville. This lack of transportation infrastructure is one reason little industry developed in the area. (NCSHPO.)

William Long (1801–1876) owned substantial acreage in Caswell County and built this mill in the mid-1800s. Located on Country Line Creek, it operated until 1941, using waterpower to turn grinding stones that made flour and meal. The millstone now is on display at the Caswell County Courthouse. Long also built a water-powered sawmill, and he used lumber from it in 1856 to construct Cherry Hill, his imposing home. (NCSHPO.)

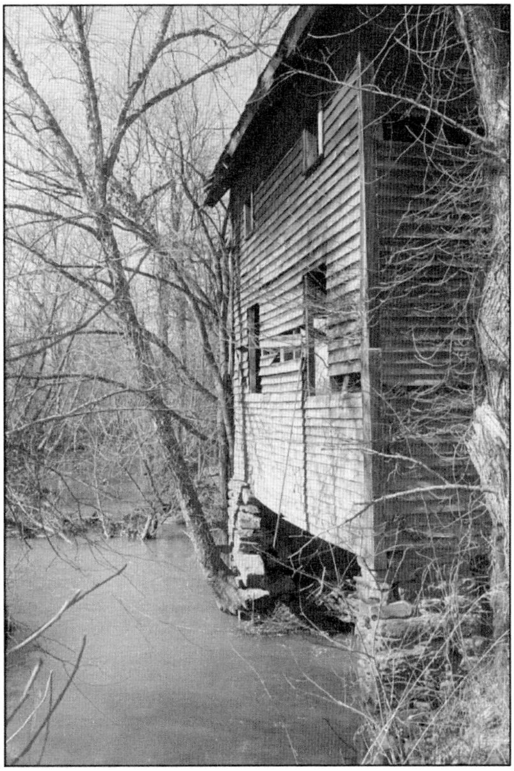

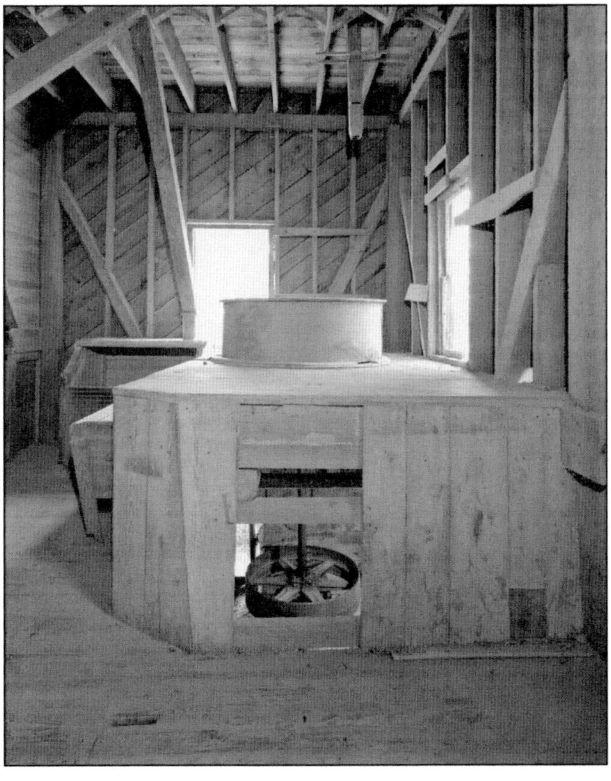

Womack's Mill was located on Country Line Creek southwest of Yanceyville. The water-powered grain mill was built around 1909 but was not the first mill to stand on the site. This photograph shows the encased gristmill stone with the driving pulley beneath. The milldam dates from 1826. Womack's Mill was dismantled in 1980, and the site is now covered by Farmer Lake. (Courtesy Library of Congress.)

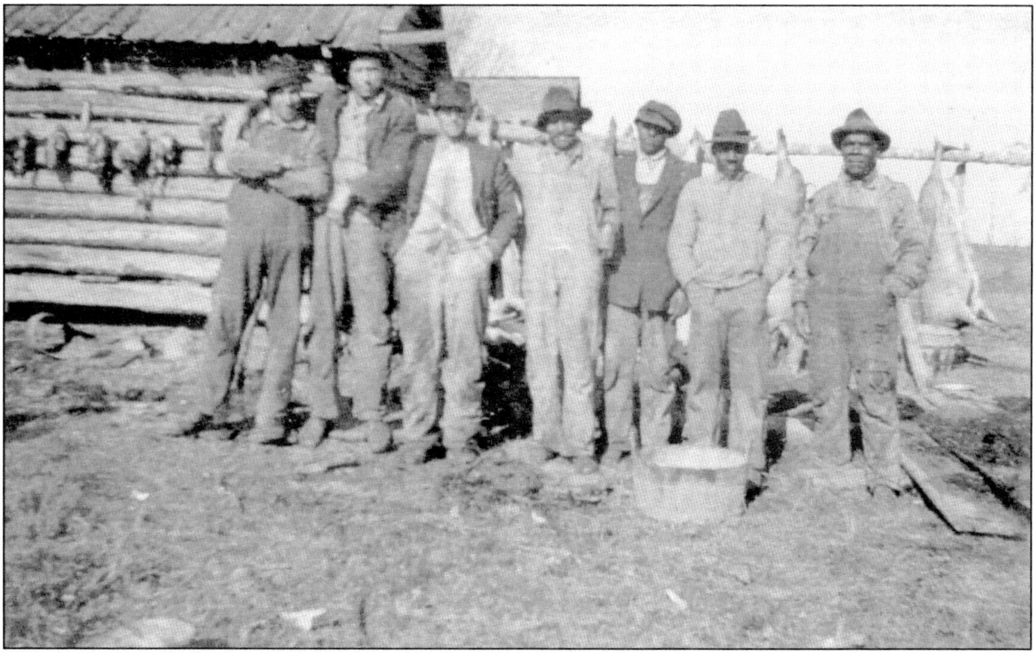

This group of Caswell County men is conducting the annual fall hog killing. The recently slaughtered hogs are hanging in the background to drain their blood. The next step before the carcasses are butchered is to remove the bristles. This could be done by singeing or by placing the carcass in hot water. (Courtesy John O. Gunn Estate.)

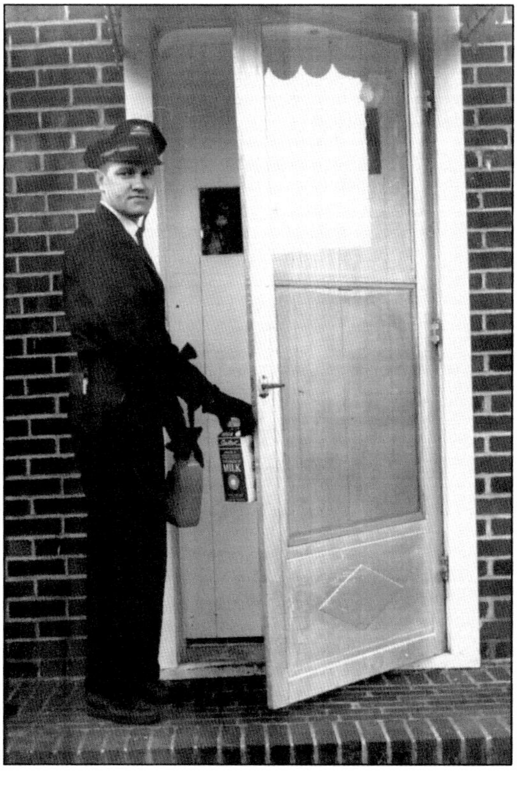

Willard Bodenhammer Dabbs (1923–1972) was better known as Pete. In the 1950s, milk and other dairy products were delivered to one's home, and Pete was a popular milkman. He was tragically killed in 1972 when his Sealtest milk truck ran off the road west of Yanceyville and overturned. Pete was a marine in World War II. (CCHA Photograph Archives.)

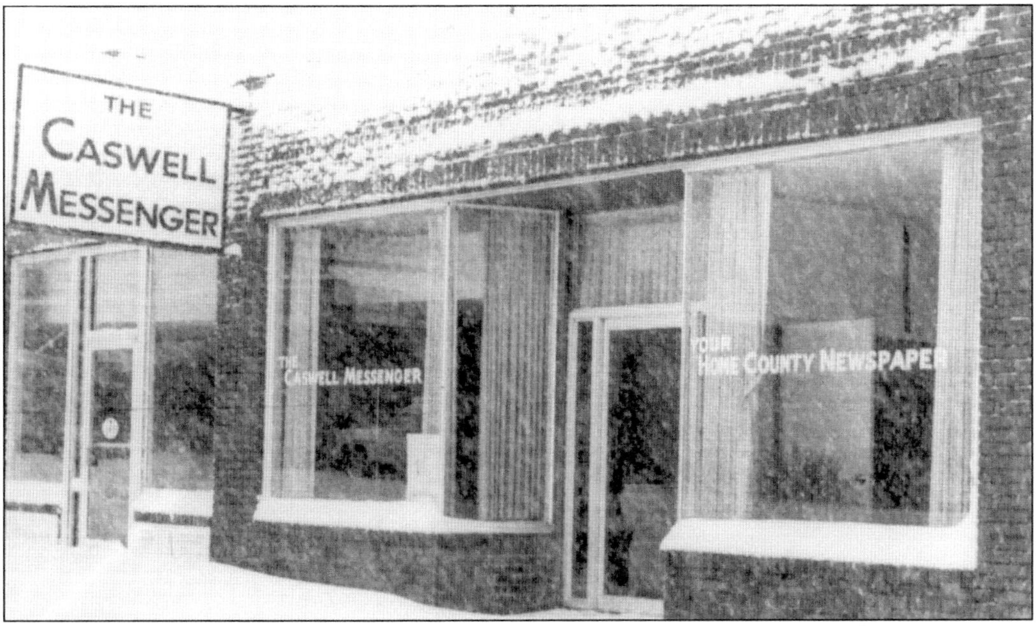

The Caswell Messenger weekly newspaper was established in Yanceyville in 1926 under the editorship of Cecil Jones. A contest was held to select a name, and the winners were Miss Lenora Hill and Miss Elizabeth Chandler. The first issue appeared on February 25, 1926, and the newspaper continues to be published today, with the old hot-type Linotype machine giving way to the computer. (CCHA Photograph Archives.)

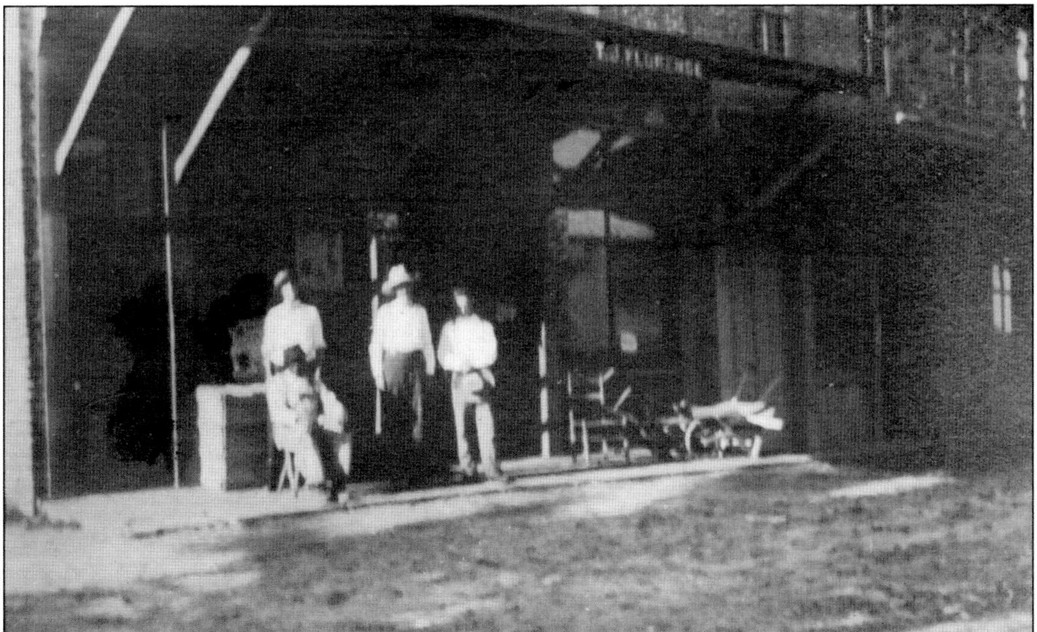

Thomas Jefferson Florance had been a partner with Walter Nathaniel Harrelson in a Yanceyville general store that burned around 1890. After the fire, the T. J. Florance building was erected near the same site on the north side of the Yanceyville Square. From this location, the Florance family operated a store for decades. (CCHA Photograph Archives.)

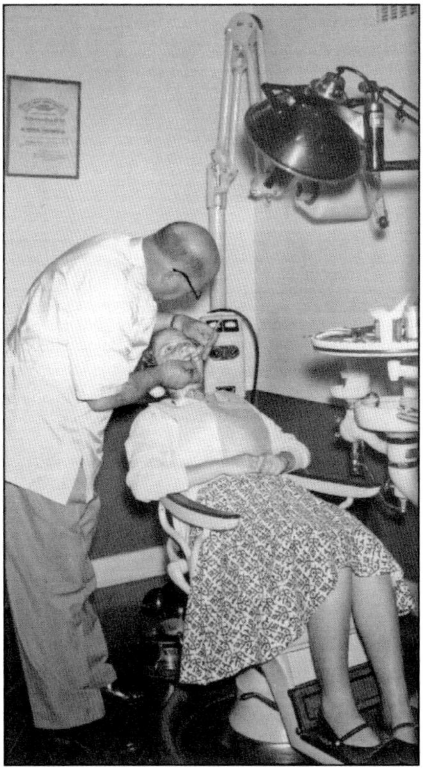

Dr. Ludolphus Graham Page, D.D.S., (1902–1970) conducted a large dental practice from his West Yanceyville office. He provided care to the famous Fultz Quads when the four black sisters had been refused treatment elsewhere. Dr. Page also provided custom-fitted mouth guards for the local high school football team at no charge. (Courtesy Dr. Graham Allison Page.)

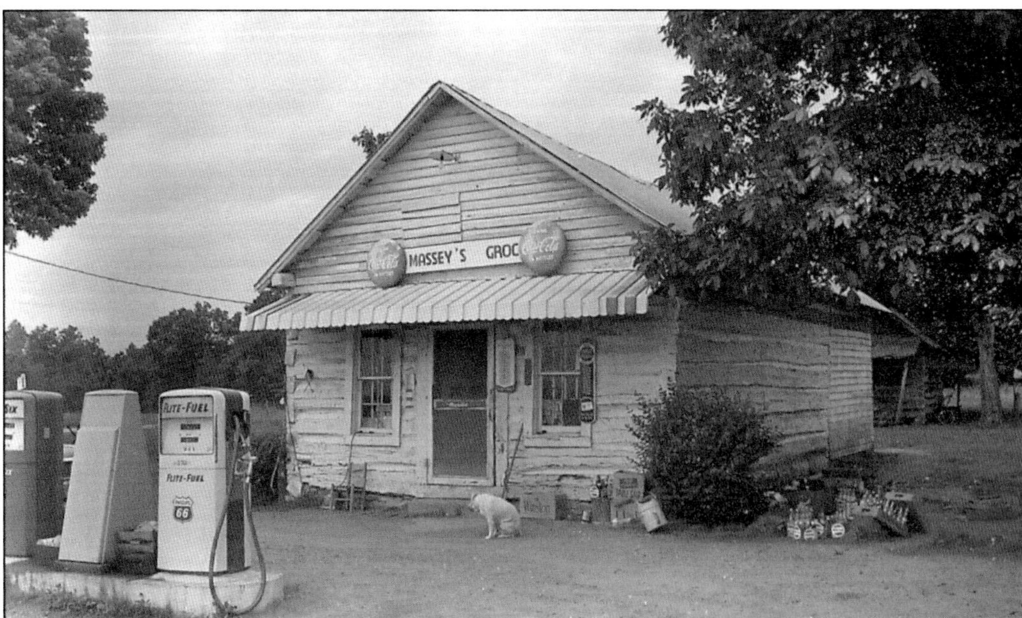

Massey's Grocery Store, a log building of half-dovetail design, was erected around 1890 by Graham Massey and his neighbors. This Stoney Creek Township business was in operation for over a century and is a good example of a rustic country store built with native materials. The rear section was an addition. (NCSHPO.)

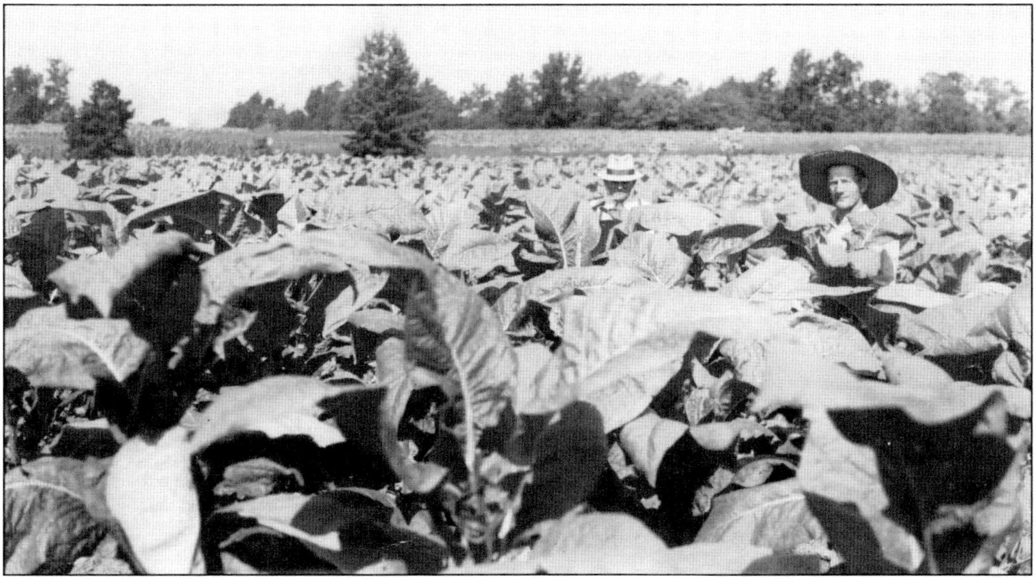

Tobacco has been both a blessing and a curse for Caswell County for over 200 years. Other than the land itself and the people who occupy it, no single tangible element better defines Caswell County than tobacco. All who lived here were affected directly or indirectly by the health of the tobacco economy. (Courtesy Tim Ross.)

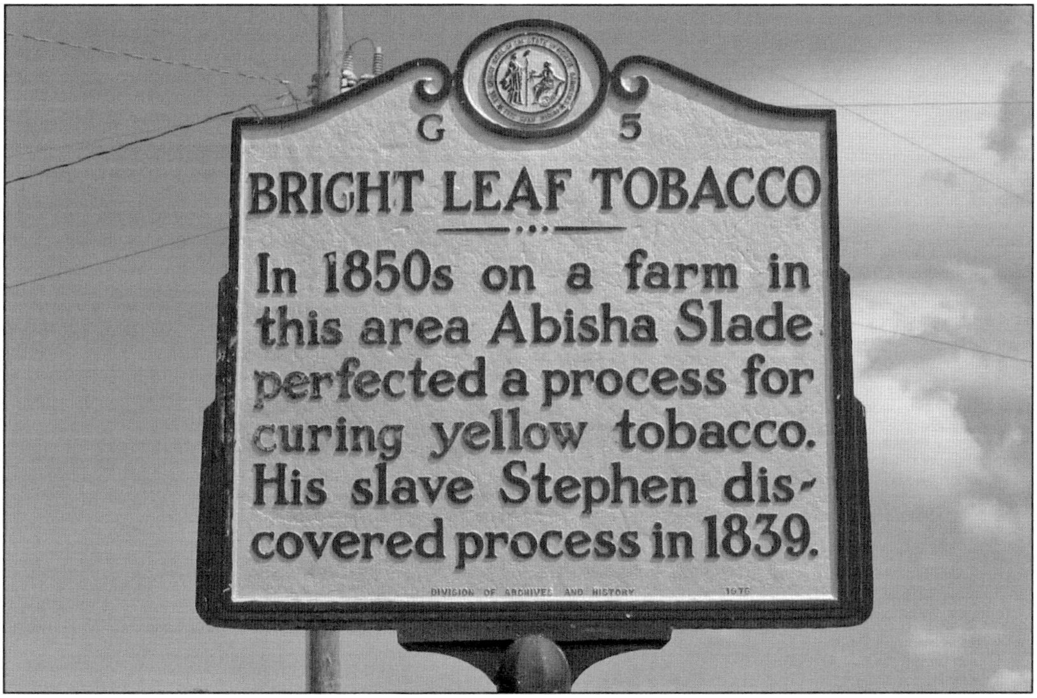

Discovery of the bright-leaf tobacco curing process by slave Stephen made his owner, Abisha Slade (1799–1869), famous and wealthy. The event also greatly contributed to the economic boom era in Caswell County. Stephen was the farm's blacksmith and borrowed charcoal to feed a dwindling tobacco barn fire. The unusual heat generated by the charcoal turned the leaves golden, and they sold at a premium. (CCHA Photograph Archives.)

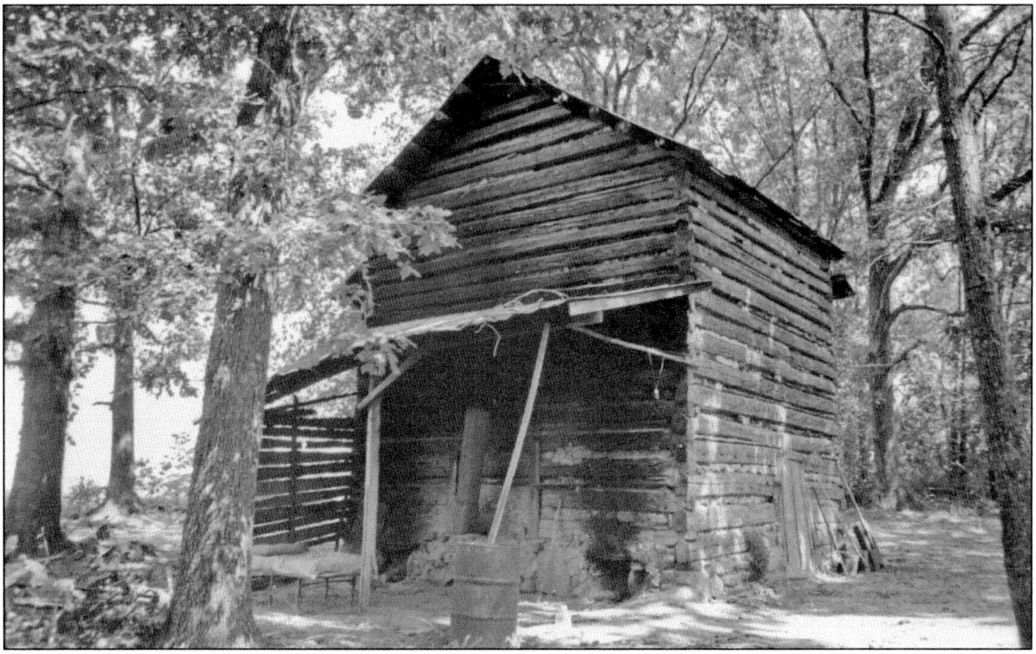

This old chinked-log tobacco barn stood on the Paul H. Jones (1896–1952) farm in Locust Hill Township. Tobacco was cured inside the barn using wood-burning flues. Note the cot employed by the farmer because the fire had to be tended continuously. Also at hand is water in a barrel to be used in case the barn ignited. (Courtesy Houston G. Jones.)

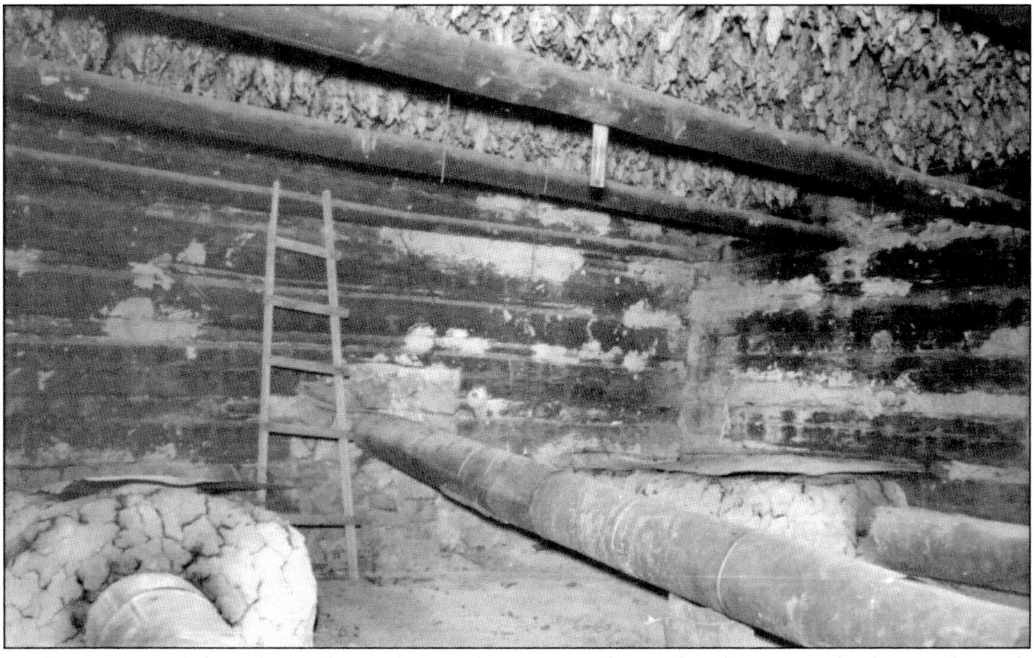

In the interior of the tobacco barn shown above, the tobacco has been attached to sticks with twine and hung in the barn for curing. The barn has flues that run from externally fed fireboxes, thereby heat-curing the tobacco without exposing it to smoke. The temperature is slowly raised over the course of the curing, which generally took several days. (Courtesy Houston G. Jones.)

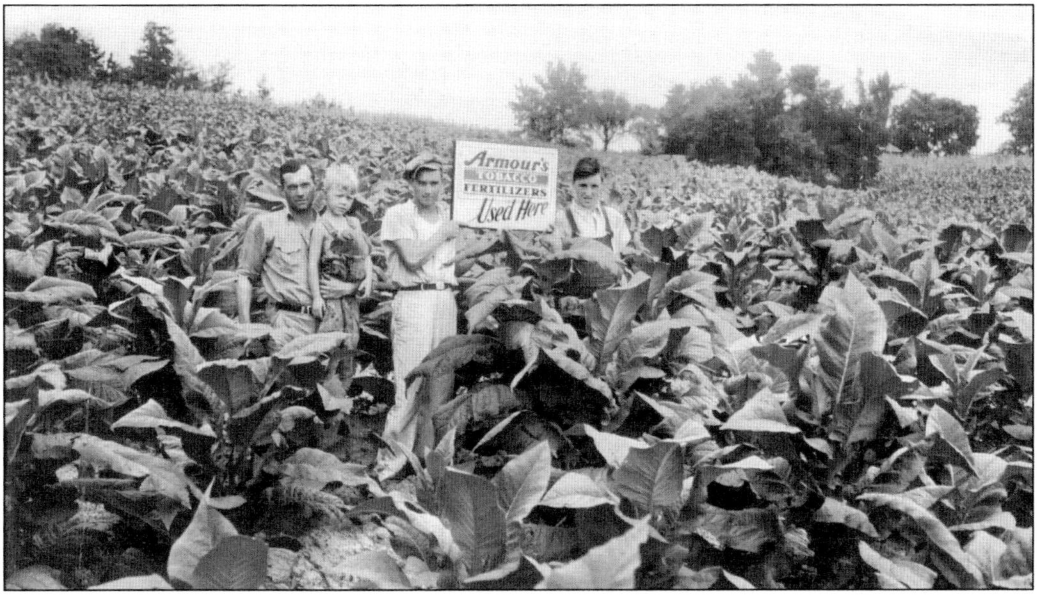

The male members of the Moorefield family in the early 1930s let all know that Armour's fertilizer is used on their tobacco. From left to right are Arthur William Moorefield (1893–1976), Frank James Moorefield, Arthur William Moorefield Jr. (1917–1975), and Jesse James Moorefield (1920–1973). The farm, just south of Yanceyville, once belonged to Sallie Womack Wiggins (1864–1929), a granddaughter of Bartlett Yancey Jr. (Courtesy Frank J. and Mozelle White Moorefield.)

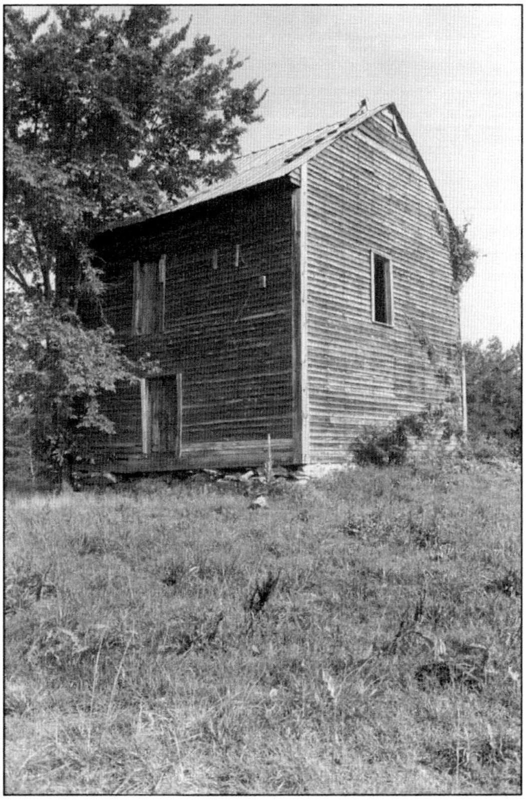
South of Yanceyville stood Johnston's Tobacco Factory (erected around 1870), one of many such enterprises that flourished in Caswell County and the region generally before the tobacco trust drove out the smaller competitors. Most, including Johnston's, manufactured plug chewing tobacco. The tobacco often was flavored. Johnston used licorice, and the interior walls of the old building were blackened with the substance. (NCSHPO.)

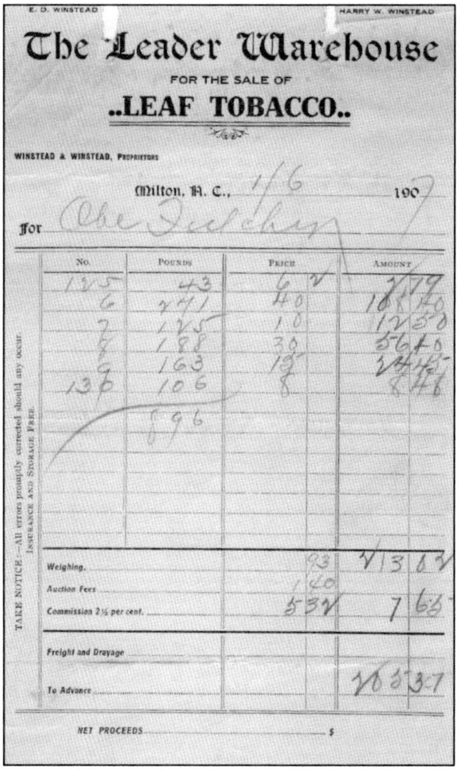
E. D. WINSTEAD HARRY W. WINSTEAD

The Leader Warehouse

FOR THE SALE OF

..LEAF TOBACCO..

WINSTEAD & WINSTEAD, PROPRIETORS

Milton, N. C., 1/6 1907

For Obe Fulcher

No.	Pounds	Price	Amount
125	43	6	2 79
6	271	40	108 40
7	125	10	12 50
8	188	30	56 40
9	163	15	24 45
130	106	8	8 48
	896		

Weighing. 93 | 13 62

Auction Fees 1 40

Commission 2½ per cent. 5 32 | 7 65

Freight and Drayage

To Advance 205 37

NET PROCEEDS $

TAKE NOTICE:—All errors promptly corrected should any occur. INSURANCE AND STORAGE FREE.

At one time, Caswell County was home to a number of tobacco warehouses. Milton was incorporated in 1796 as a center for inspecting and warehousing tobacco and flour. This 1907 tobacco warehouse receipt was issued to local tobacco farmer Obediah Fulcher (1847–1928) by the Leader Warehouse in Milton. (Courtesy Mildred Wade Henderson.)

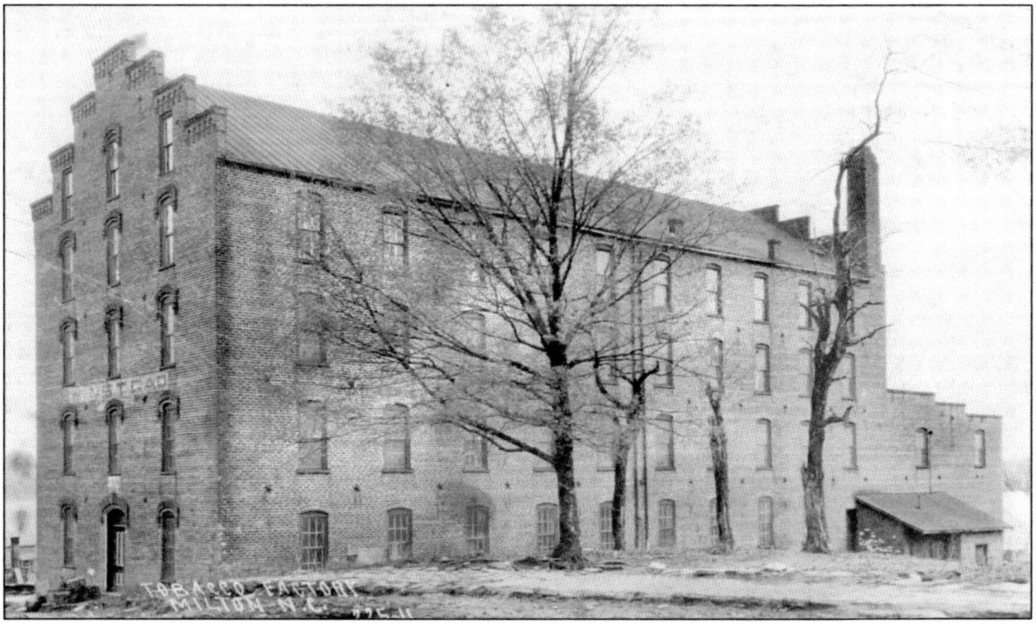

Edward D. Winstead (1852–1925) owned the Winstead Tobacco Factory in Milton. The size of the five-story building gives some indication of the town's economic robustness. Winstead also owned a roller mill and a cotton gin, all in Milton. Sanborn's 1893 Fire Insurance Map shows this structure and notes, "No Watchman, Heat Steam, Work Rms 1st and 2nd, Storage 3rd and 4th." By 1908, the building was vacant. (Courtesy Jack Williams.)

Four

Caswell's Buildings

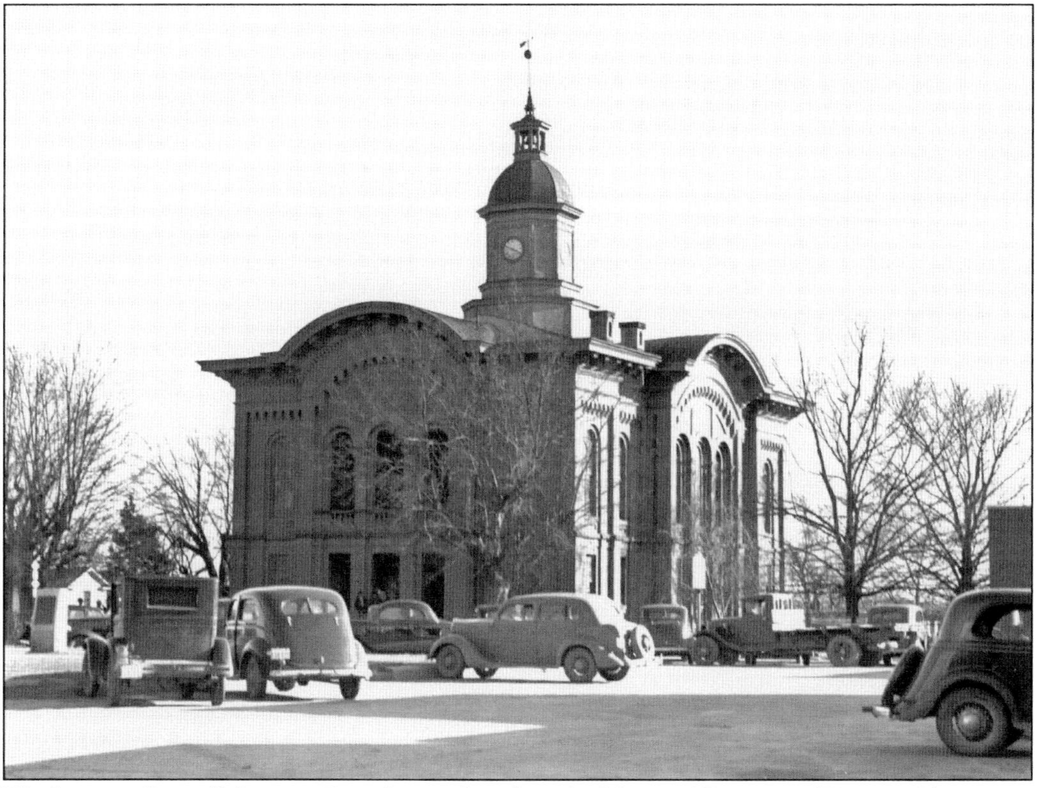

The historic Caswell County Courthouse, listed on the National Register of Historic Places, was the heart of Caswell's government for over a century. The building, designed by award-winning architect William Percival, was completed in 1861, just as the Civil War began. The cost was $28,000. The old building has seen proud times, troublesome times, and tragic times. It has endured occupation, murder, and fire. This image was captured in 1938. (North Carolina Collection.)

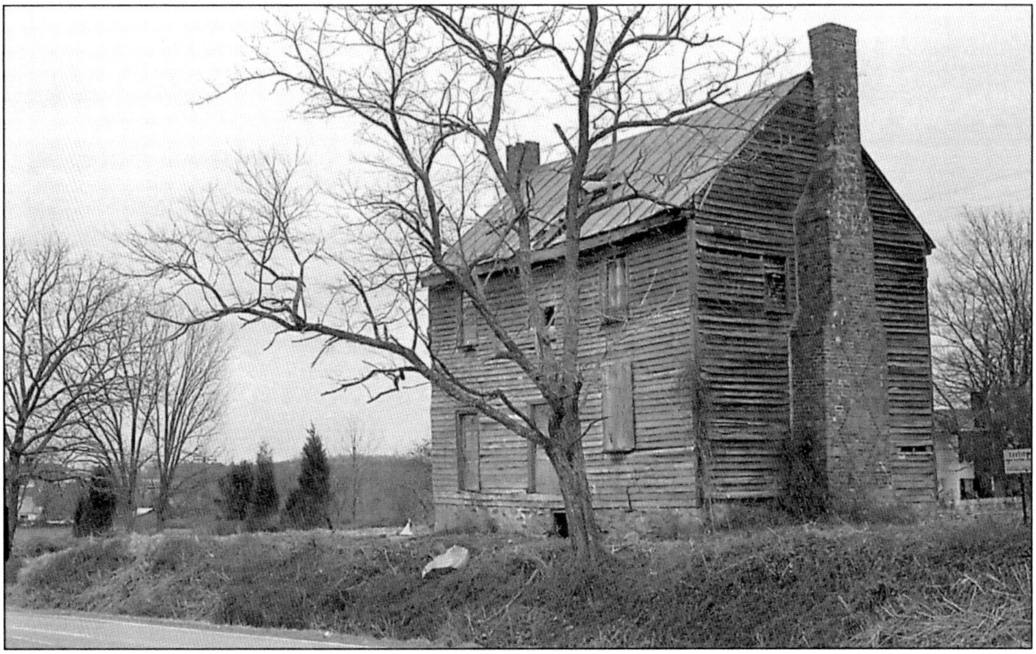

The old two-story Leasburg Tavern was built around 1809, which was evidenced by an unusual terra-cotta plaque in one of the chimneys with the inscription "P. T. 1809." The tavern was a stop on the stagecoach line that ran south to Hillsborough and north to Milton. The building was dismantled in the 1970s, when the highway was widened. (NCSHPO.)

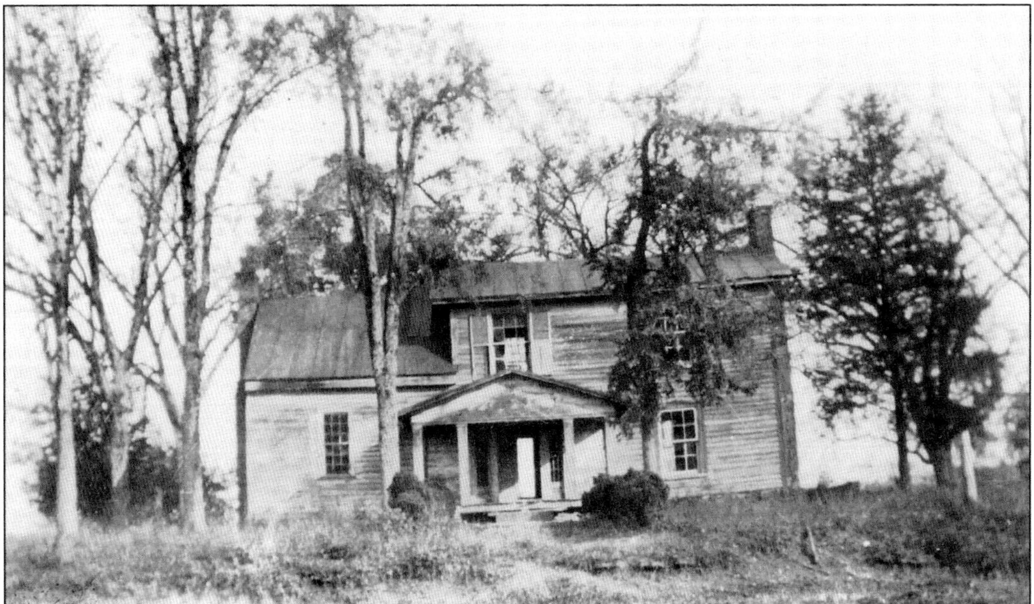

The Stanfield House in Leasburg was built around 1830 by Benjamin Franklin Stanfield (1802–1862). Subsequent owners were William Henry Wade and Rom Stanford Rittenbury (1894–1956). After the death of her husband in 1956, the structure came to be known as the Mary Rittenbury house. Mary Stanfield Rittenbury (1901–1979) was an artist and served as Leasburg's postmaster. (Courtesy Mildred Wade Henderson.)

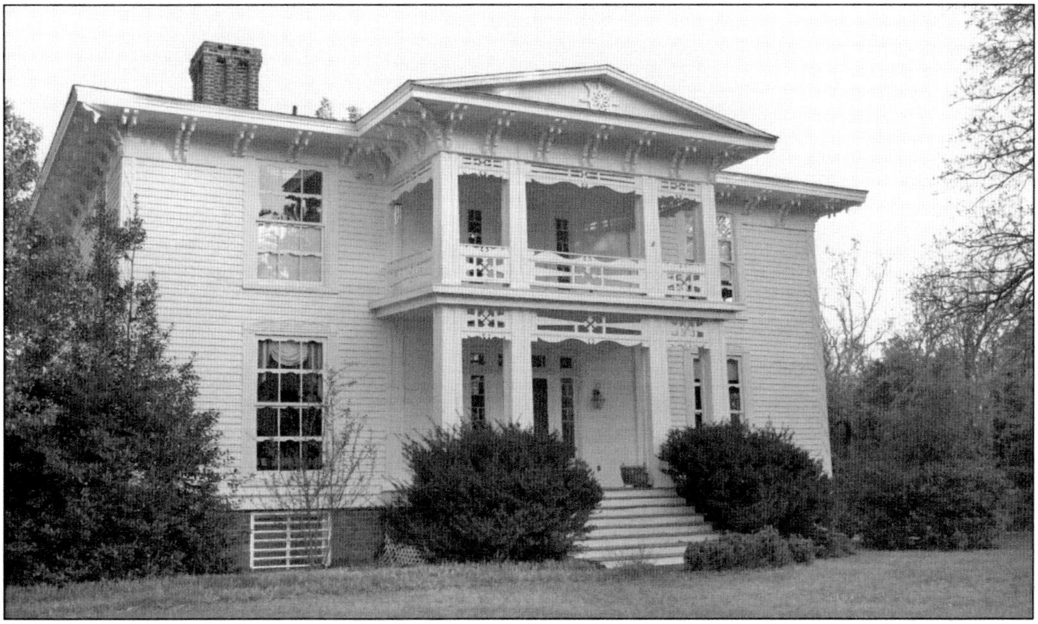

On the National Register of Historic Places, the Garland-Buford House just north of Leasburg was built around 1860 by wealthy Milton physician Dr. John Tabb Garland (c. 1795–1874), who may have never lived there. Garland owned and lived in Longwood, a Milton house also on the National Register. The family continued to live at Longwood until 1954, when the last child of Dr. John Tabb Garland died. (CCHA Photograph Archives.)

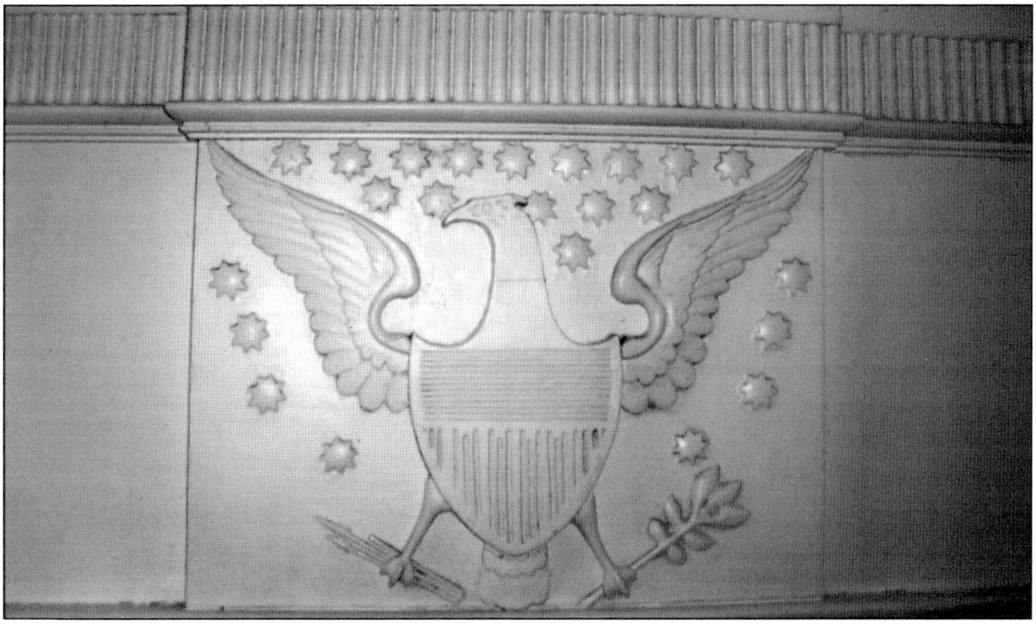

The Dr. Jacob A. Thompson house in Leasburg was built around 1814 by the Lea family. The parlor had a Federal mantel decorated with the Great Seal of the United States that displayed 23 stars. Maine, the 23rd state, attained statehood in 1820, which helps date the mantel. Since being removed from the house in the late 1950s, the mantel's location has been a local mystery. (Courtesy Karen Wade Avants.)

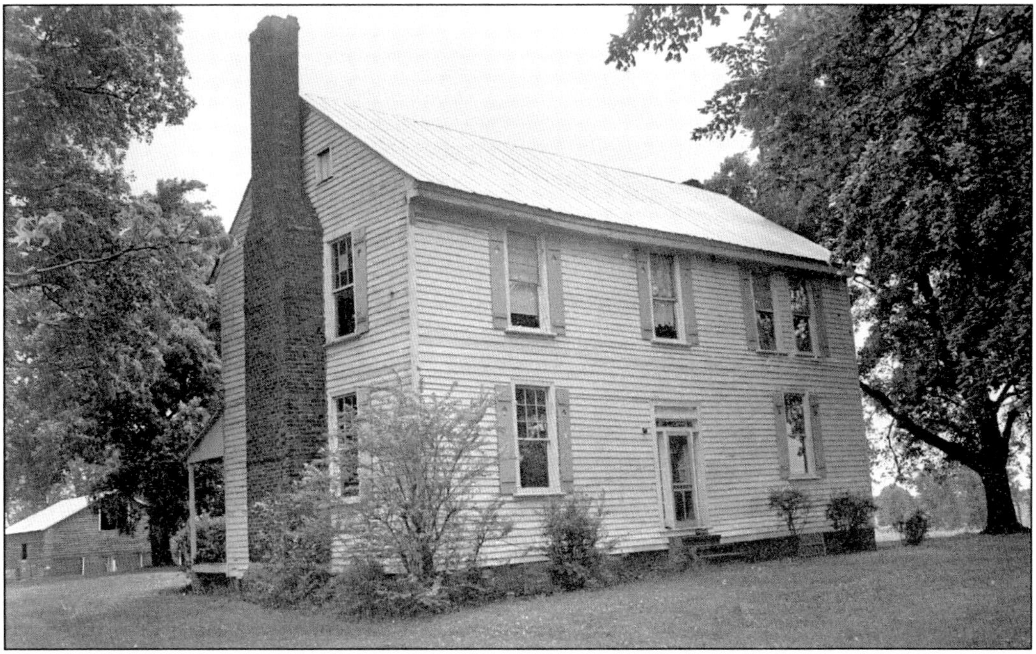

The Kerr House was built around 1853 by James Kerr (1788–1848), wealthy storeowner, planter, slave owner, teacher, member of the North Carolina House of Commons, and state senator. Kerr also was a major in the North Carolina Militia. He donated the land for Kerr's Chapel Missionary Baptist Church in southern Caswell County. (NCSHPO.)

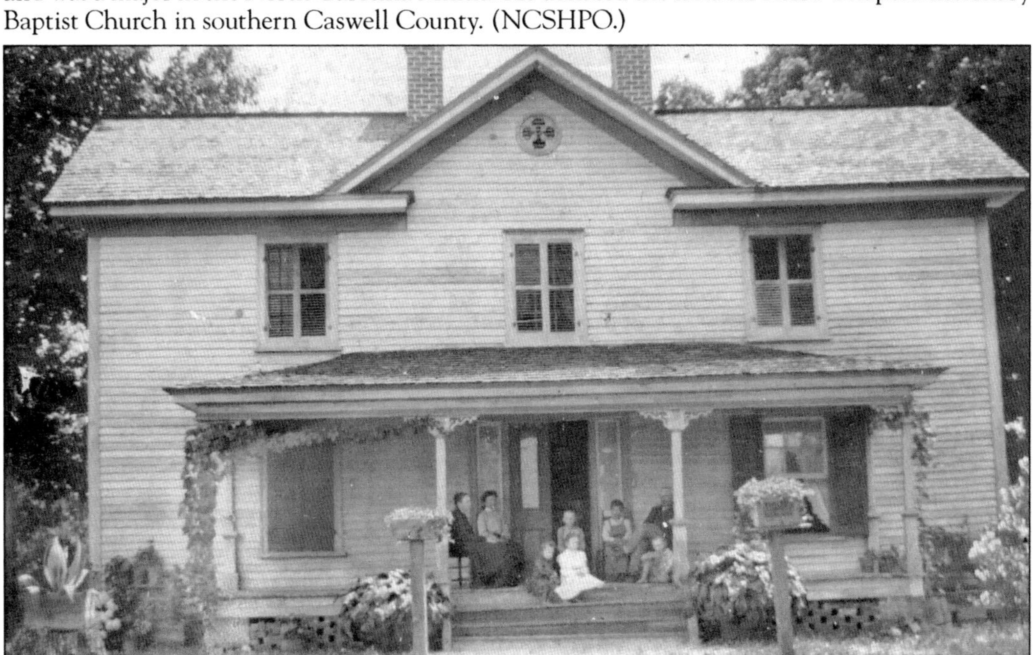

The Baynes House in Anderson Township was built in the 1890s by James Rainey Baynes (1855–1923) and his wife, Laura Louella Harrelson Baynes (1860–1940). James Rainey Baynes was one of the original owners of Baynes Store, which stood near his house and was a community landmark. The area eventually became known as Baynes. (Courtesy Nelson and Cindi Straughn.)

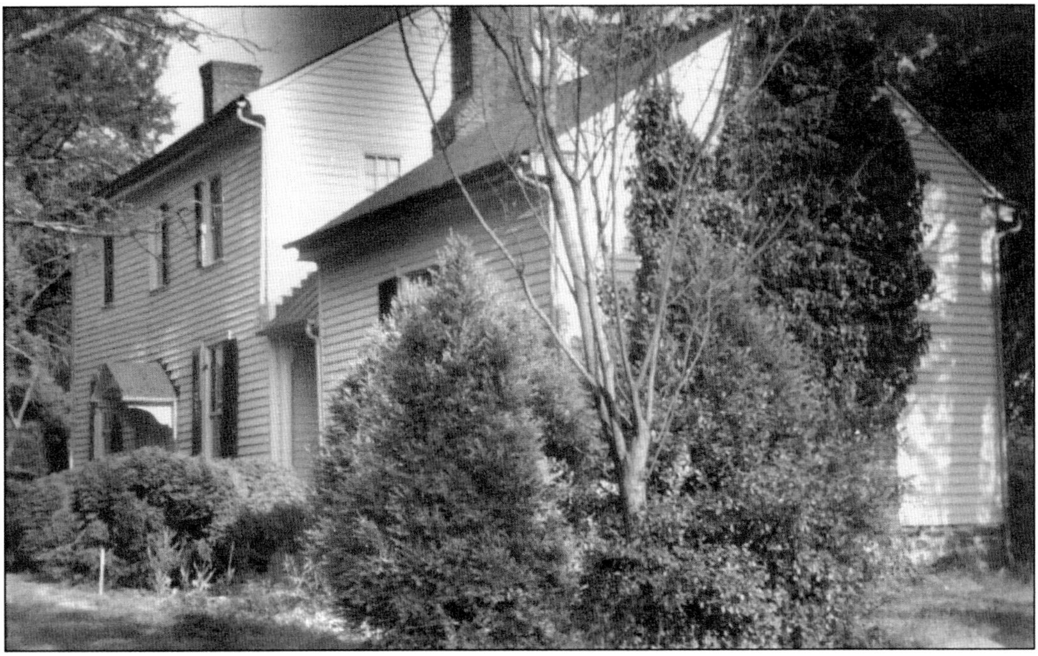

On the National Register of Historic Places, Rose Hill was built around 1800 by Jethro Brown (1766–1828). In 1816, he gave the house to his son Sen. Bedford Brown (1795–1870) as a wedding gift, along with 1,000 acres of land and 100 slaves. The new bride planted hundreds of rose bushes, thus the name. (Courtesy Houston G. Jones.)

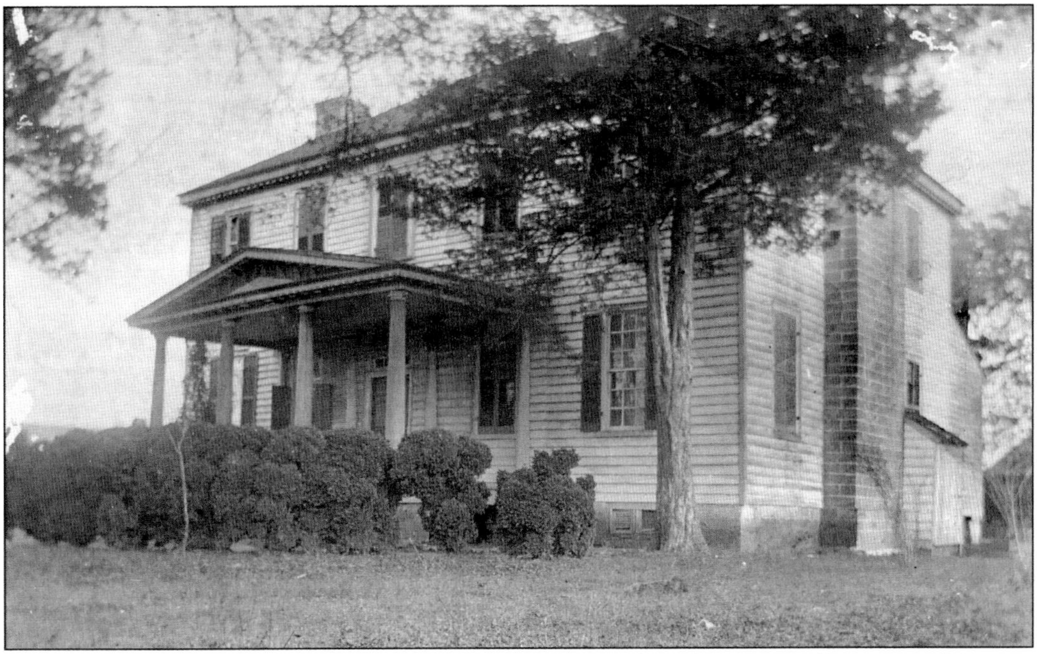

The Brown-Graves-Yarbrough house, built around 1780 and on the National Register of Historic Places, is so called because it was built by the family of Jethro Brown, was the home of lawyer and state legislator Calvin Graves (1804–1877), and eventually was owned by Charles Joel Yarbrough (1850–1919). The law office of Calvin Graves stands separately in the front yard. (NCSHPO.)

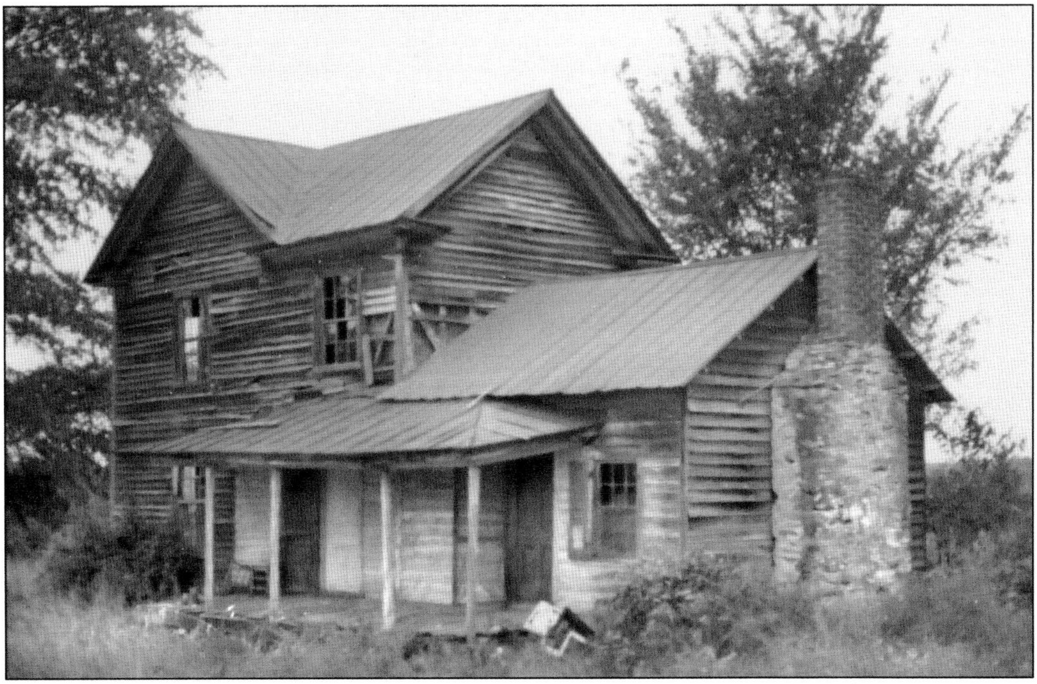

Around 1875, Caswell County farmer Thaddeus Cornelius Jones (1849–1919) built the nearest section of this house (originally made of logs and later weather-boarded) in the Locust Hill community. Jones, twice married, produced a large family of 13 children. Thaddeus and his brother Robert struggled after the Civil War to pay debts secured by a mortgage on the family farm. They were successful and divided the property between them. (Courtesy Houston G. Jones.)

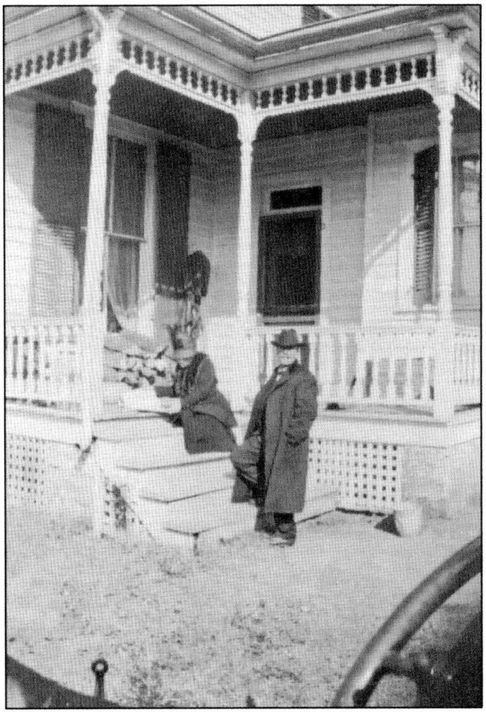

Built around 1815 by nationally known statesman Bartlett Yancey Jr., this house was inherited by his grandson Thomas Pancoast Womack (1861–1916), seen here with his wife, Mattie Hatchett Womack (1873–1954), probably in the 1910s. Mattie Womack donated the Yanceyville land upon which the Bartlett Yancey School was built. Thomas and Mattie are buried in the Yancey family cemetery beside the house. The building is on the National Register. (Courtesy John O. Gunn Estate.)

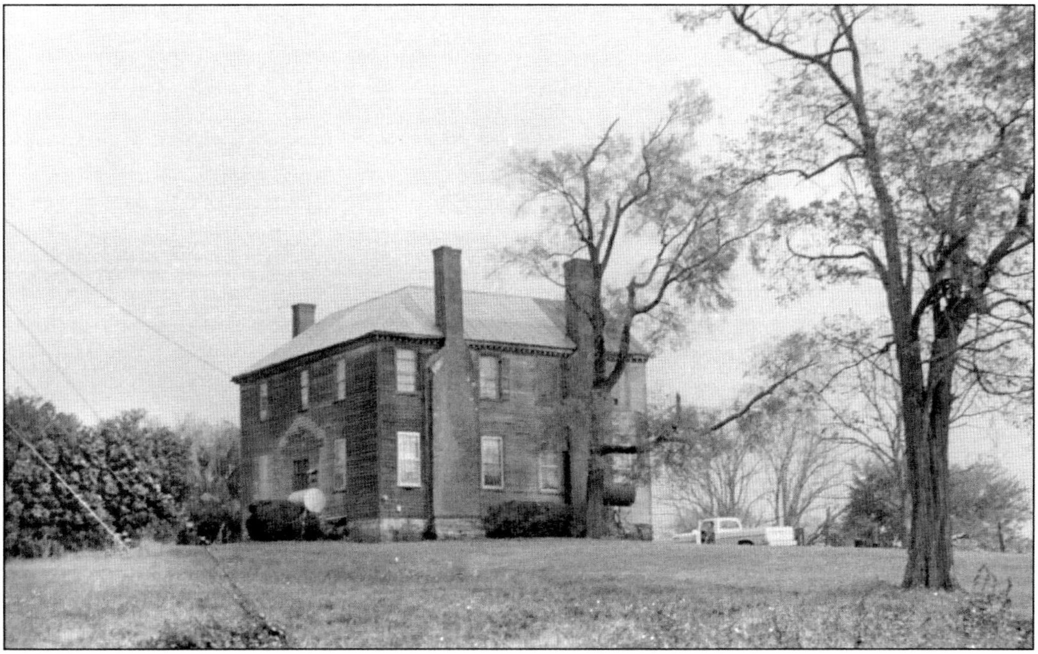

The large wood-framed Irvine House was built around 1790 and stood in the Red House community of northeast Caswell County. A stagecoach route ran nearby. In 2001, the house was dismantled and most of the structure moved to Virginia. The heart-pine parlor flooring was used to restore a Milton house. A small Irvine family cemetery is on the grounds. (Courtesy Houston G. Jones.)

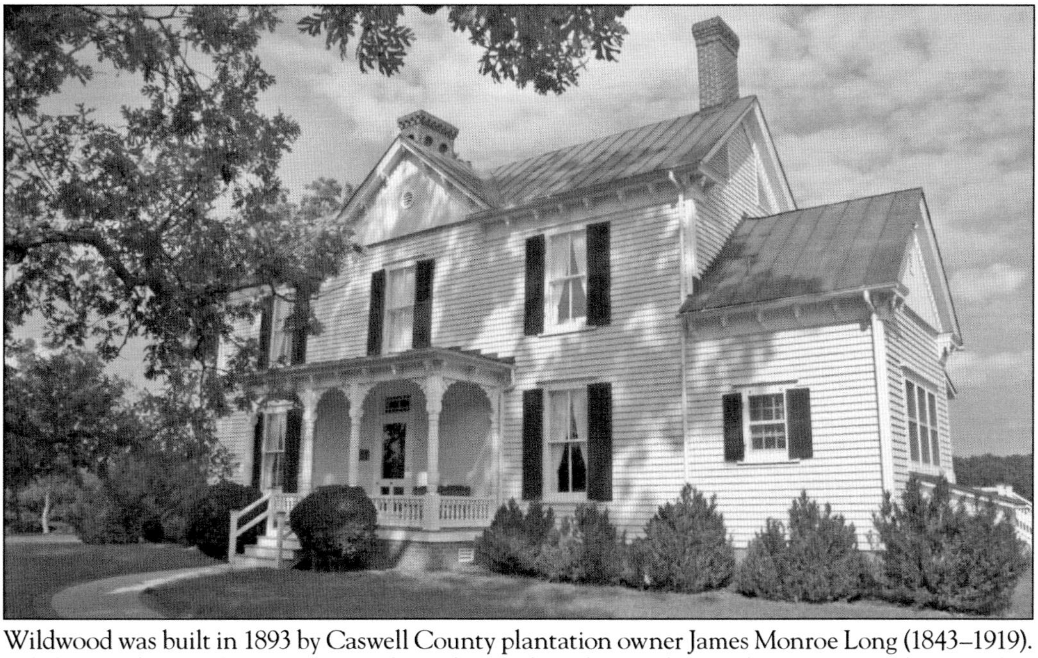

Wildwood was built in 1893 by Caswell County plantation owner James Monroe Long (1843–1919). While a student at the University of North Carolina during the Civil War, Long volunteered to serve in the Confederate army. Many years later, he was awarded a bachelor of arts degree. Long is buried at Red House Presbyterian Church, where a large obelisk marks his grave. Wildwood is on the National Register of Historic Places. (CCHA Photograph Archives.)

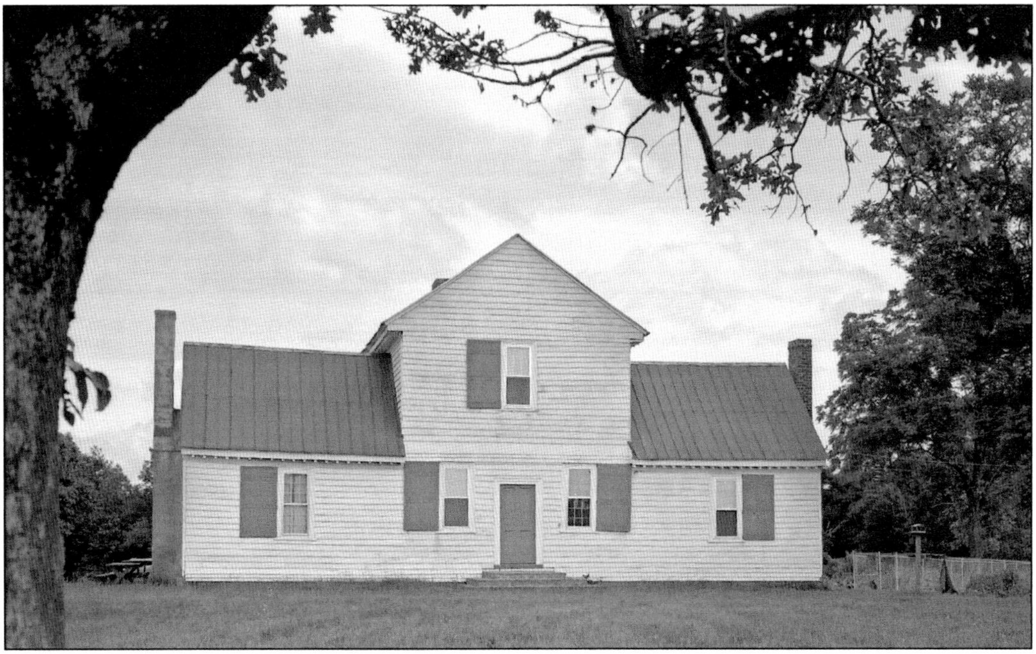

The Azariah Graves House, built during the 1700s for this member of the influential and wealthy Graves family of Yanceyville, is on the National Register of Historic Places. Azariah Graves (1776–1837) was a lawyer, planter, businessman, teacher, and North Carolina state senator. He should not be confused with Gen. Azariah Graves, also covered herein. On the house grounds is a Graves family cemetery. (NCSHPO.)

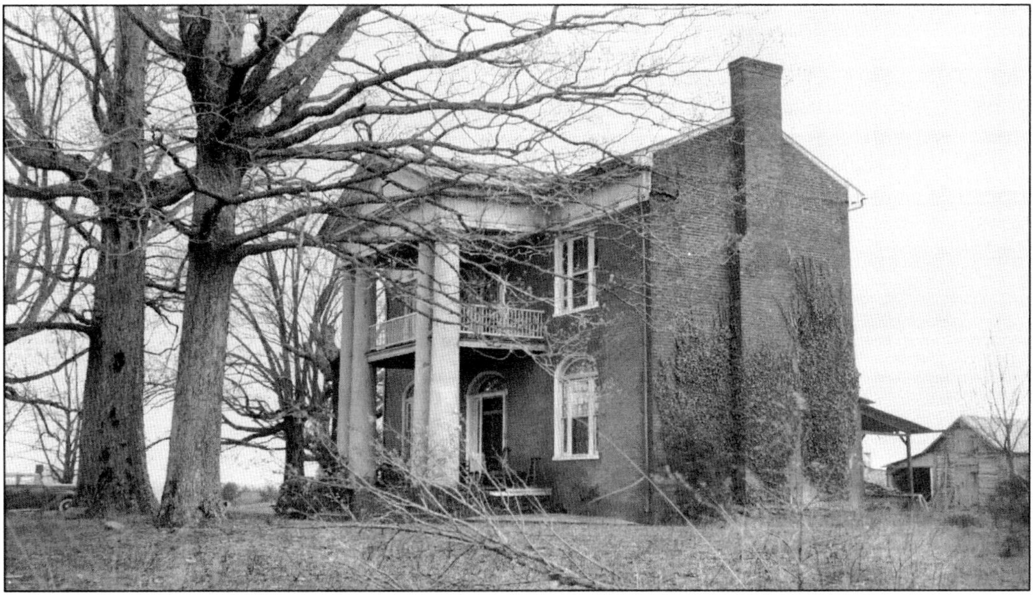

Dongola was built in 1833 by wealthy tobacco plantation owner Jeremiah Graves. The Graves family moved to the area in the 1750s and owned most of the land that became the town of Yanceyville. When the photograph was taken in 1940, only two people were living in the large house: bachelor Robert Sterling Graves (1870–1962) and his twice-widowed sister, Sallie Willie Graves (1880–1960). (Courtesy Library of Congress.)

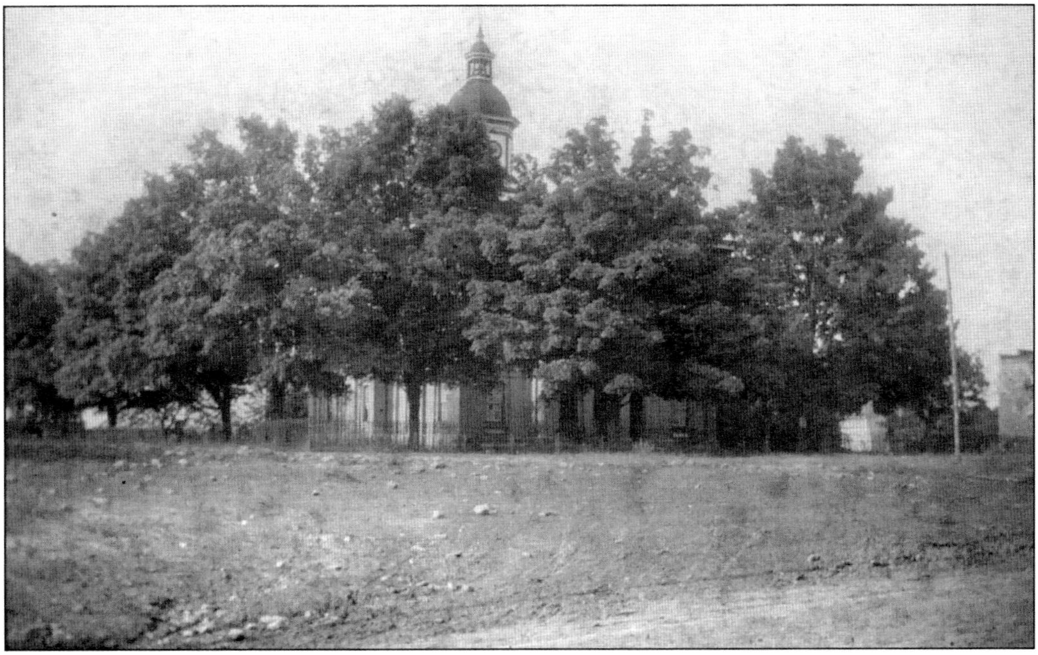

In the early 1900s, the public square in Yanceyville had not been formed into a raised rectangle. It was not until 1921 that the streets of Yanceyville were paved and the public square elevated and enclosed with concrete walls. That year also saw erection on the square of the Confederate memorial monument. The Caswell County Courthouse is in the background. (Courtesy Tim Ross.)

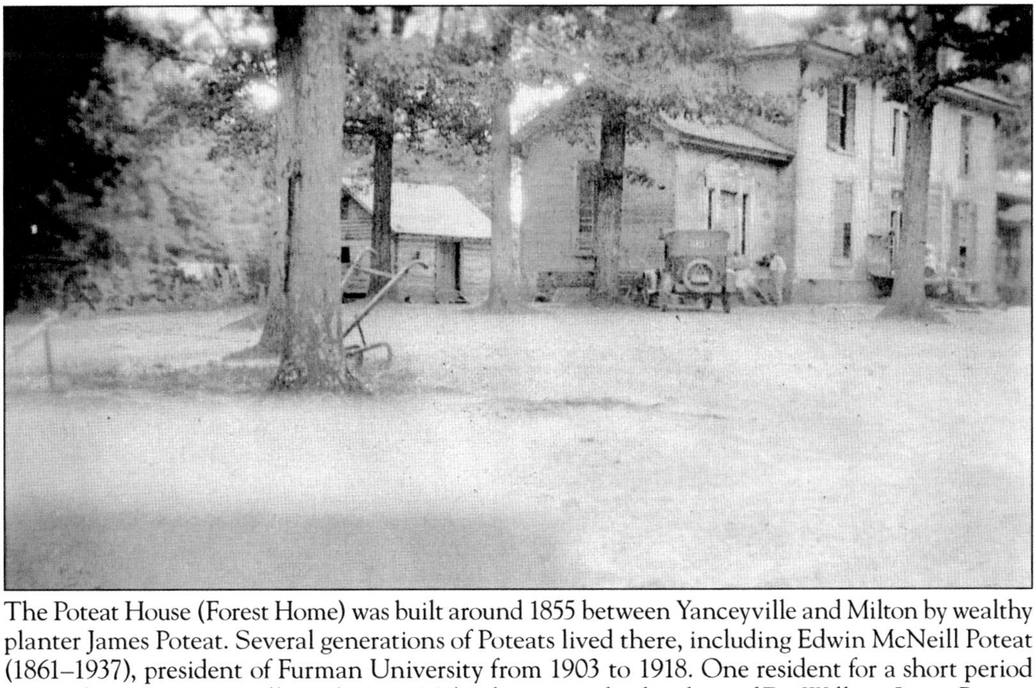

The Poteat House (Forest Home) was built around 1855 between Yanceyville and Milton by wealthy planter James Poteat. Several generations of Poteats lived there, including Edwin McNeill Poteat (1861–1937), president of Furman University from 1903 to 1918. One resident for a short period was author Laurence Stallings (1894–1968), who married a daughter of Dr. William Louis Poteat, longtime president of Wake Forest College (now University). Forest Home is on the National Register. (NCSHPO.)

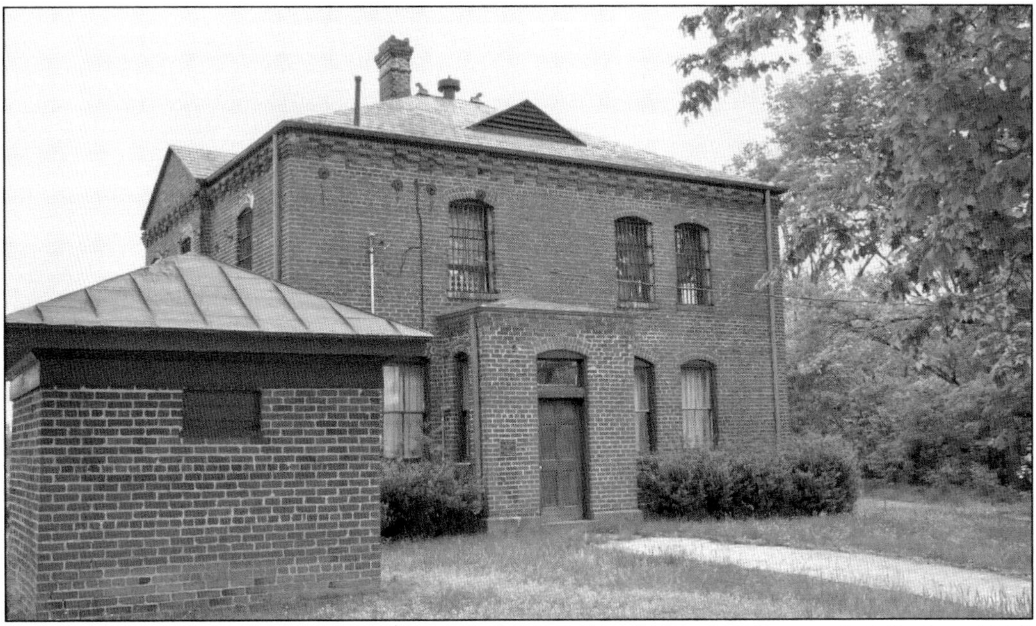

One of the most interesting buildings in the county is the old Caswell County Jail. Built in 1906, the jail housed the county's prisoners until the 1970s, when a new facility was constructed. The CCHA leases the building, and the structure has been restored to near its condition when still in use. Today the old jail remains a popular stop on tours of the Yanceyville Historic District. (CCHA Photograph Archives.)

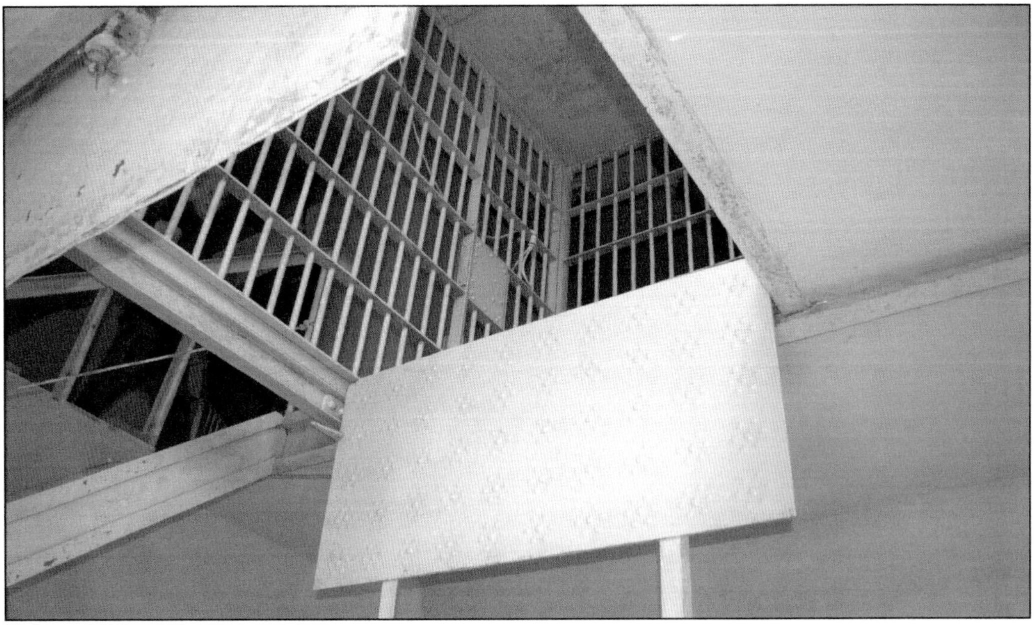

A fully operational metal gallows is in the old Caswell County Jail cell block. It consists of a separate cell with a hangman's noose and a trapdoor released by a lever that would have been controlled by the executioner. This disturbing piece of machinery was never used for the intended purpose. While the jail was under construction, North Carolina law was changed to outlaw hanging cells. (CCHA Photograph Archives.)

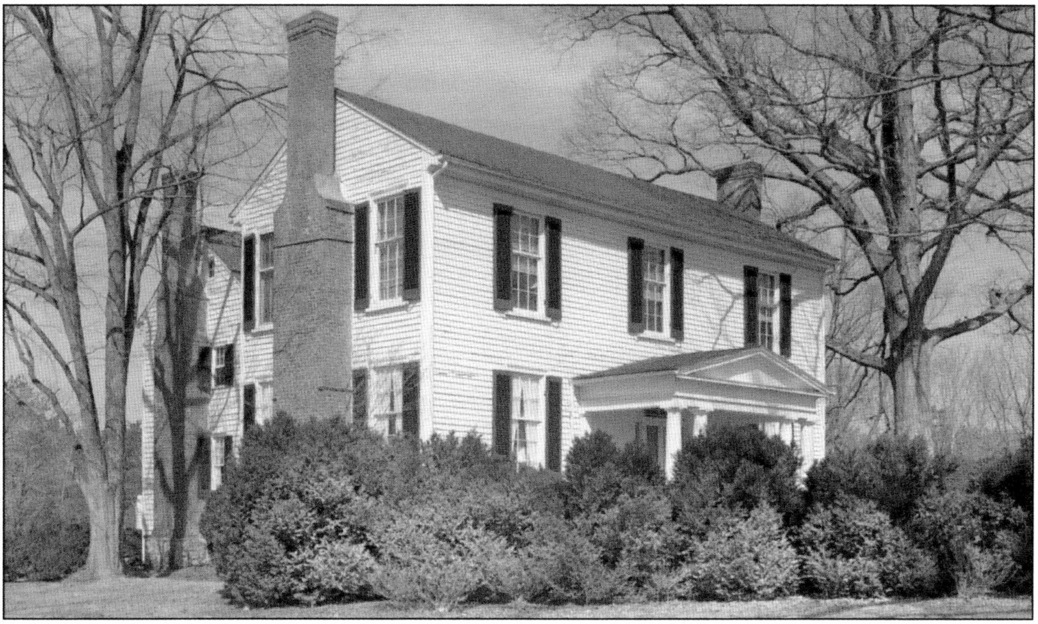

The Williamson House (Melrose) was built near Yanceyville around 1770 and is on the National Register of Historic Places. The building oddly consists of two large houses that were connected. While the structure was built by James Williamson (1752–1806), it is most often associated with his very wealthy son "Royal" George Williamson (1788–1856), who ruled over a vast slave-based plantation. (NCSHPO.)

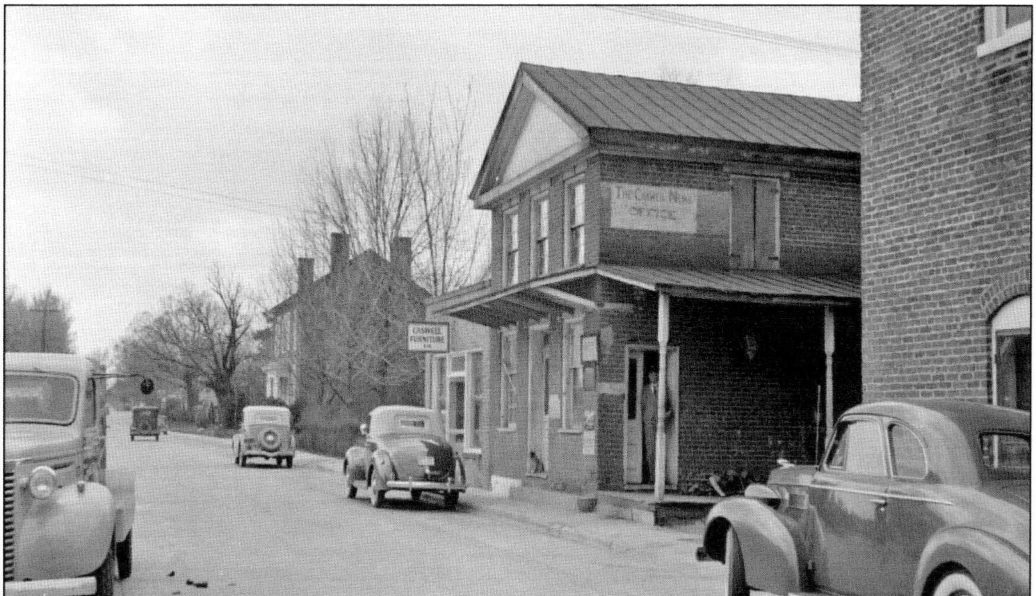

Around 1817, Azariah Graves built an office and storehouse in Yanceyville with living quarters on the second floor. It is the oldest commercial structure in the town. Graves had a large house on his farm east of Yanceyville but apparently used this building for business and as his in-town residence. The structure lies within the Yanceyville Historic District and continues in use. In the background is the old Kerr Hotel (building with three chimneys visible). (Courtesy Library of Congress.)

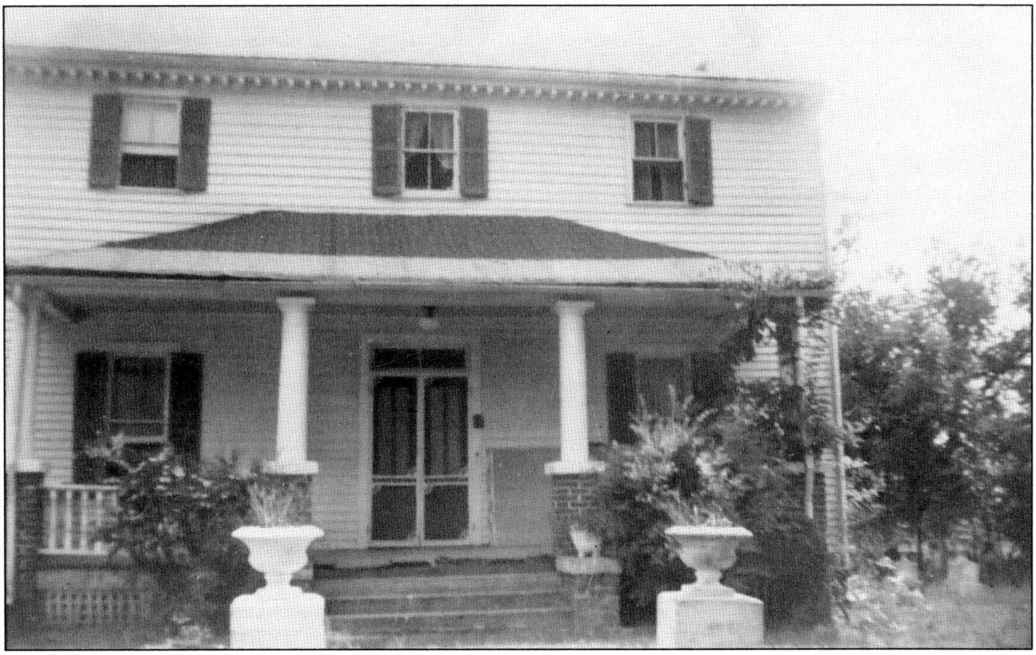

The Graves-Long-Wiggins-Moorefield House was built in 1807 just south of Yanceyville by a member of the Graves family. William Long, a subsequent 19th-century owner, was an agronomist who taught North Carolina tobacco farmers methods of tobacco cultivation (including the use of new plant strains) that greatly increased yield and value. By the 1850s, Long was manufacturing tobacco locally. (Courtesy Frank J. and Mozelle White Moorefield.)

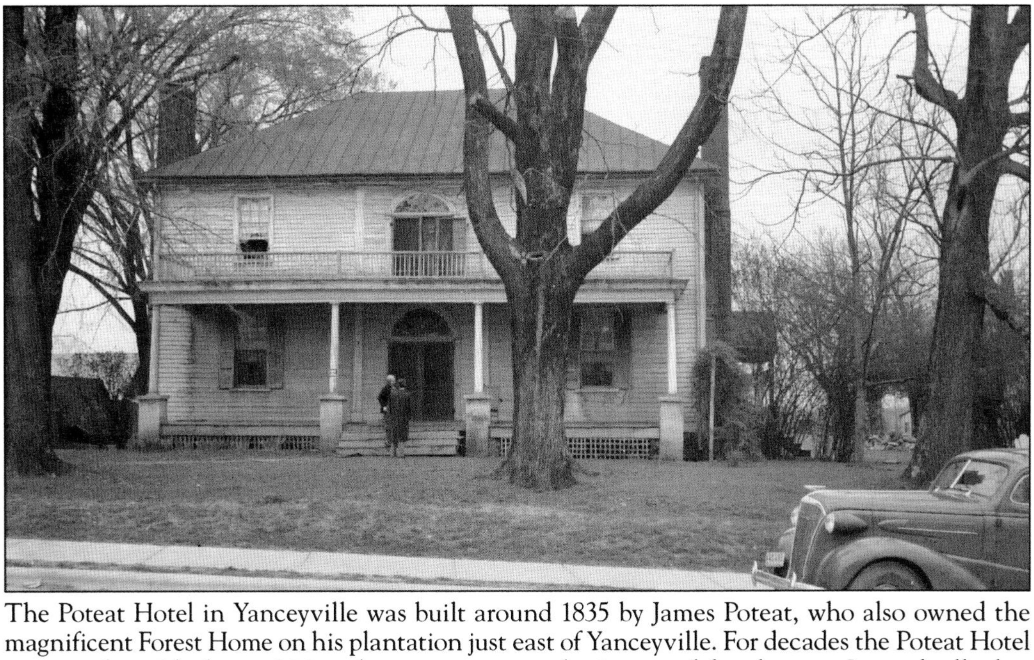

The Poteat Hotel in Yanceyville was built around 1835 by James Poteat, who also owned the magnificent Forest Home on his plantation just east of Yanceyville. For decades the Poteat Hotel was popular with those visiting the county seat on business and for pleasure. Legend tells that when the building was dismantled in the 1950s it provided enough lumber to build several houses. (Courtesy Library of Congress.)

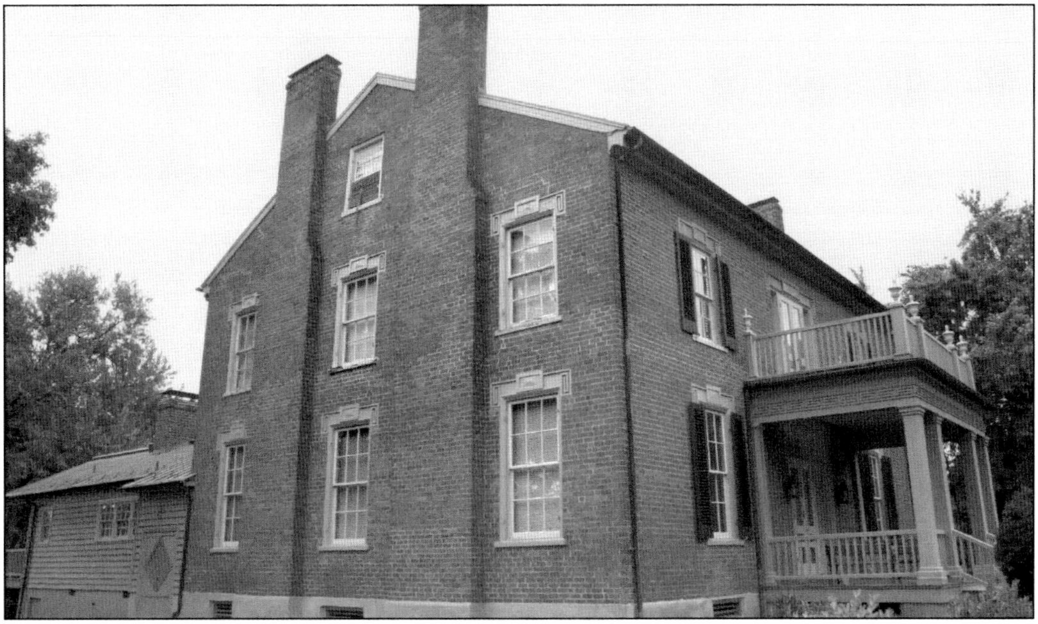

Clarendon Hall in the Yanceyville Historic District was built in 1842 by Thomas Donoho Johnston, who had been conducting business in the town since 1828. In 1852, Johnston was one of the superintendents accepting subscriptions for stock in the new Bank of Yanceyville, of which he soon became president. In 1860, Johnston owned property valued at $161,000 and was the wealthiest man in town. (CCHA Photograph Archives.)

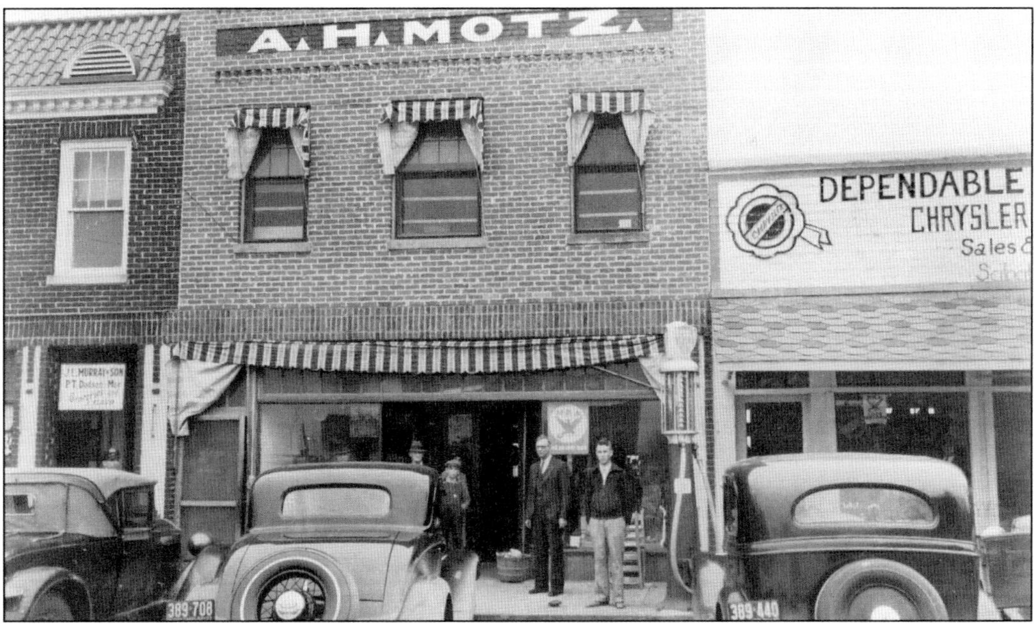

In 1935, the A. H. Motz building was flanked to the left by the E. F. Upchurch building and to the right by a Chrysler automobile dealership. Alexander Hamilton Motz (1885–1973) operated this store on the Yanceyville Square. Earlier he had been a successful merchant in Milton. The A. H. Motz building was designed by Caswell architect J. Frank Moorefield (1885–1962). (Courtesy Yancey Moorefield Smith.)

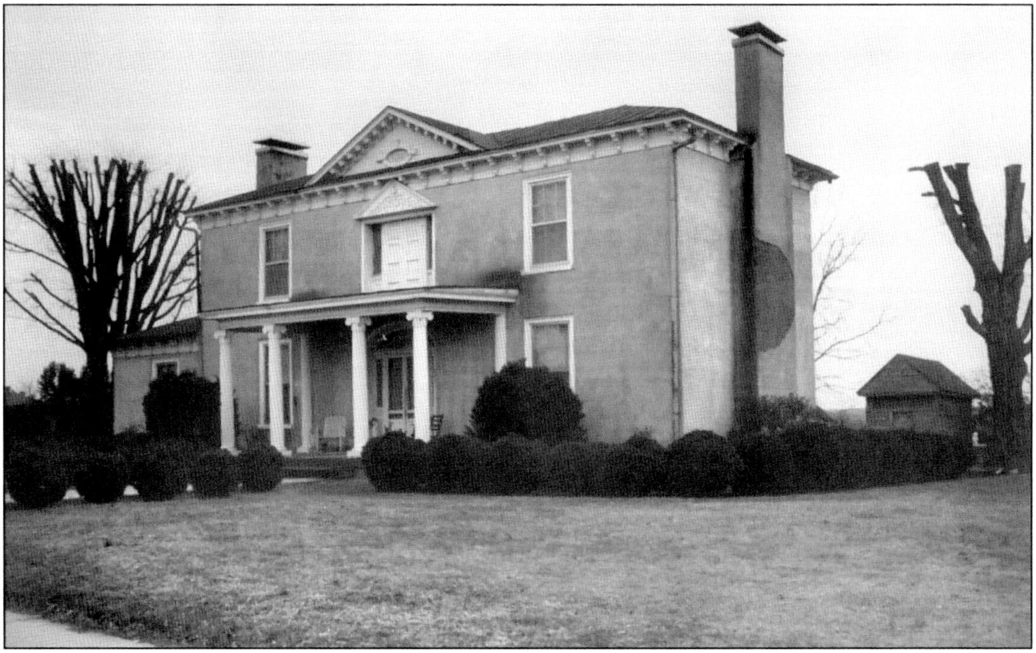

Yanceyville physician Dr. Allen M. Gunn (1807–1884) built his Yanceyville home around 1850. From the building, which resides in the Yanceyville Historic District, he conducted his medical practice and apparently apprenticed many young doctors. Dr. Gunn was a son of Revolutionary War soldier Starling Gunn and cared for the people of Caswell County for over 50 years. (NCSHPO.)

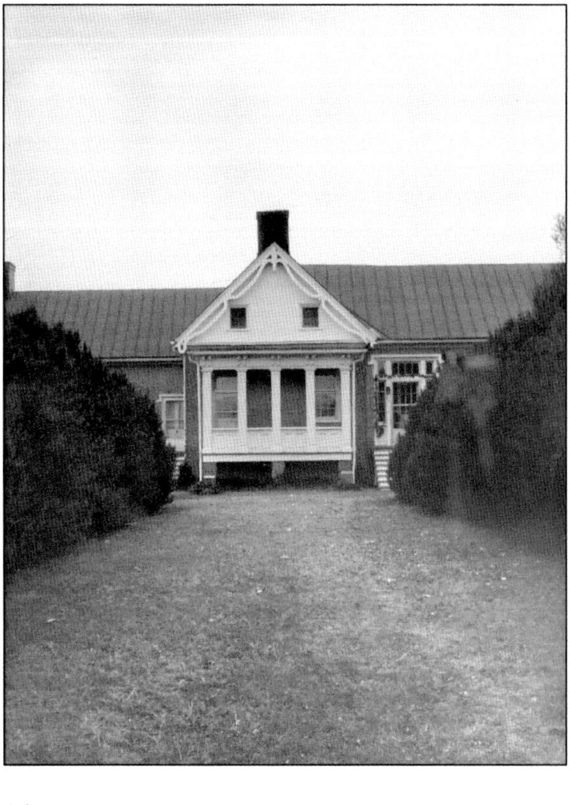

This Yanceyville house was built around 1838 for physician Dr. Nathaniel M. Roan (1803–1879). In addition to a successful medical practice, Dr. Roan was involved in many aspects of public life. His name appears often in the minutes of the county's governing body in connection with road improvement, schools, and charitable efforts. Tragedy struck the family when his son Felix Roan (1837–1891) was killed in a duel. (NCSHPO.)

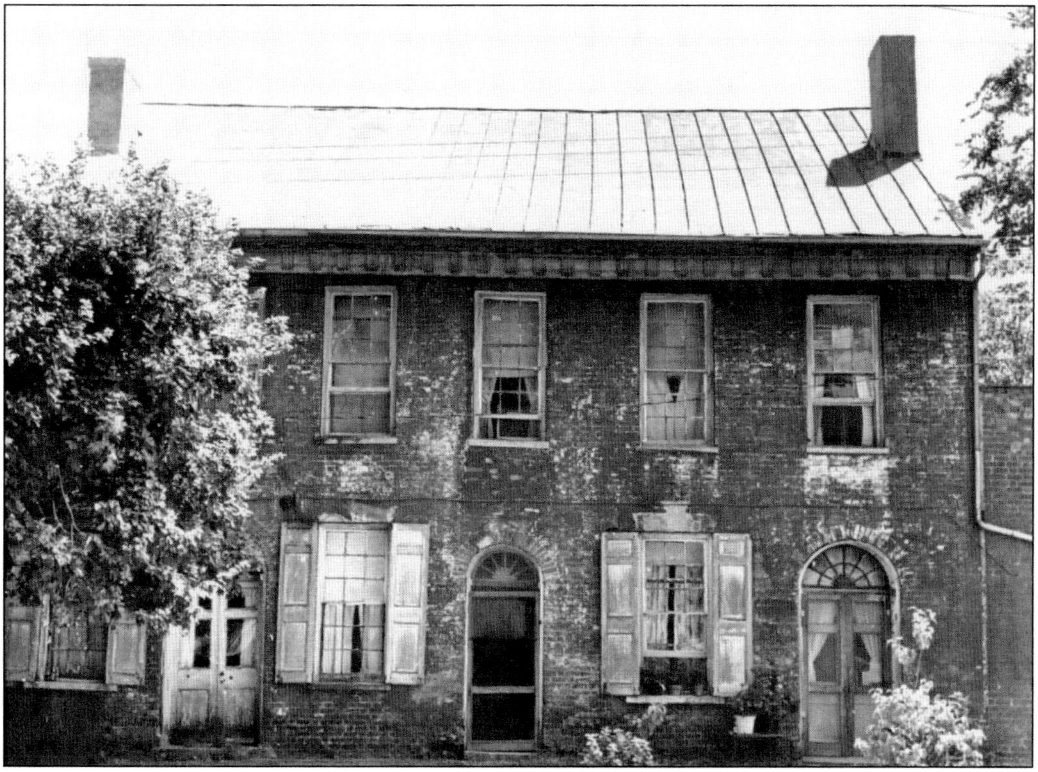

Built around 1818 in Milton, the Union Tavern (also called the Yellow Tavern) is one of Caswell's most important buildings and has been designated a National Historic Landmark, the highest federal designation available. It is one of the finest of the few antebellum hostels remaining in the state. The two-story brick building is best known as the residence and workshop of Thomas Day. The photograph of the exterior dates from 1935 and shows the Federal-style architecture. Note the three main entrances with their sunburst fanlights. The photograph of the interior was also taken in 1935. The stairway shown is thought to be the original method of reaching the second floor. After experiencing a tragic fire, the structure is undergoing a full restoration. (Above, courtesy Houston G. Jones; below, courtesy Library of Congress.)

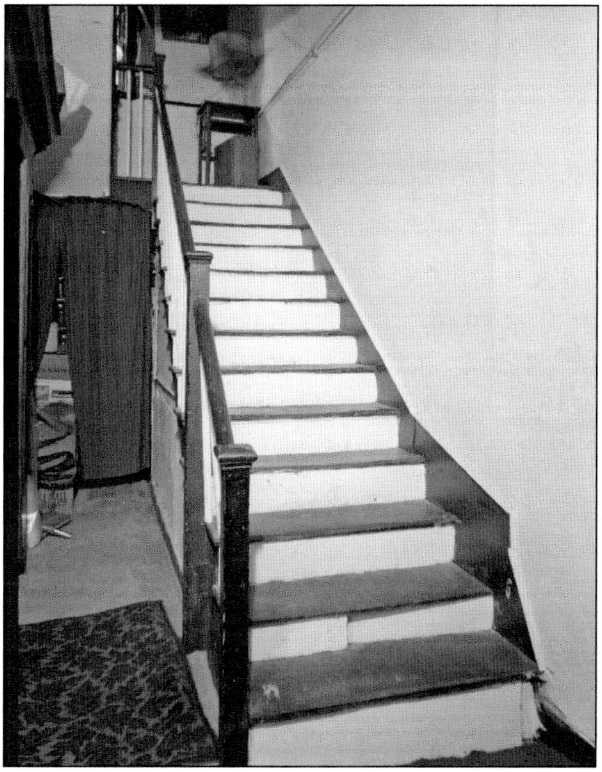

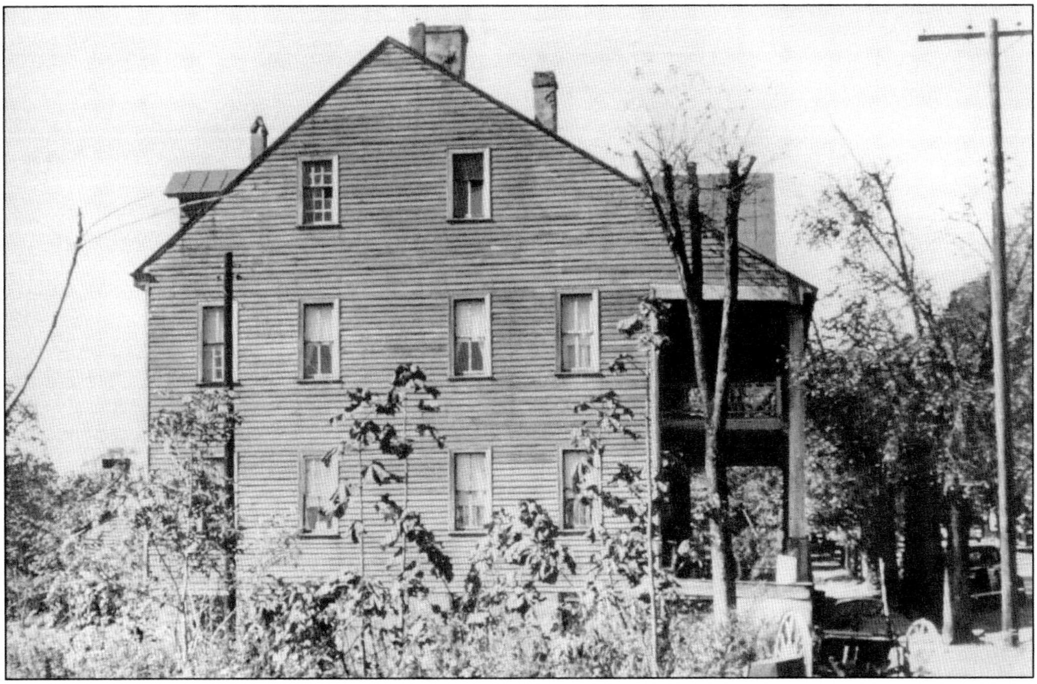

Built around 1826 by Henry Gordon, the 20-room Milton Hotel was the center of Milton social activity for over a century and a local landmark. During its life, the hotel went by several names, including Hotel Caswell and Gordon Hotel. The old building was in its earliest instance a tavern on the coaching lane from Richmond to Raleigh and was famous for its cuisine, especially its hams, fried chicken, biscuits, and desserts. The end came in 1951, when disgruntled striking mill workers from nearby Danville, Virginia, allegedly torched the building to send a message to non-strikers who were living in the hotel. All escaped the fire, including 11 children and an elderly blind man. (Both courtesy Jean Bradsher Scott.)

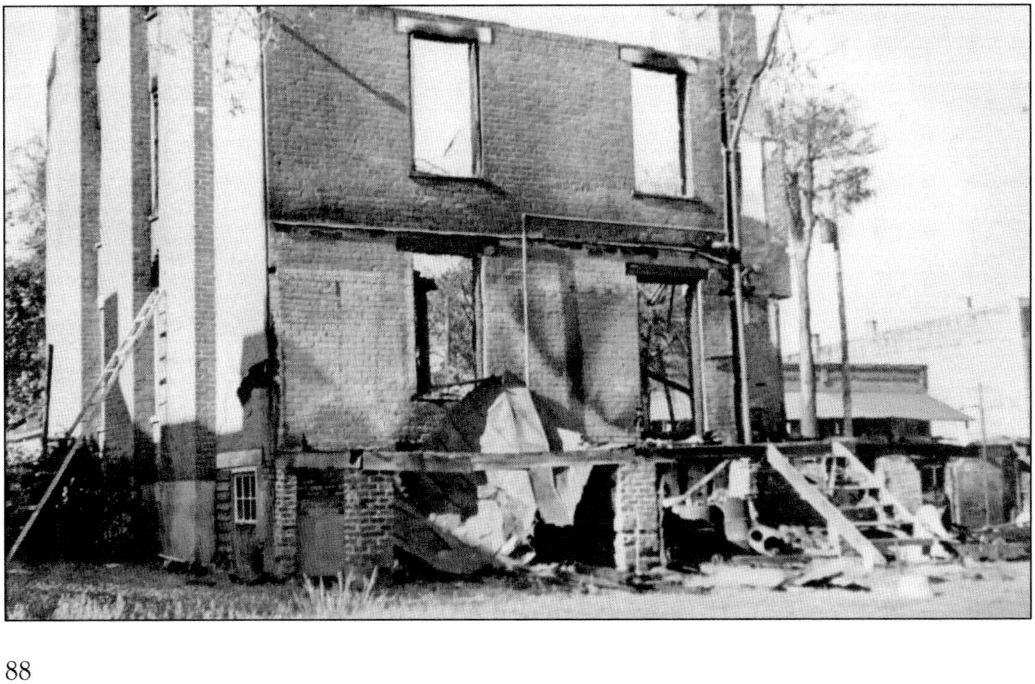

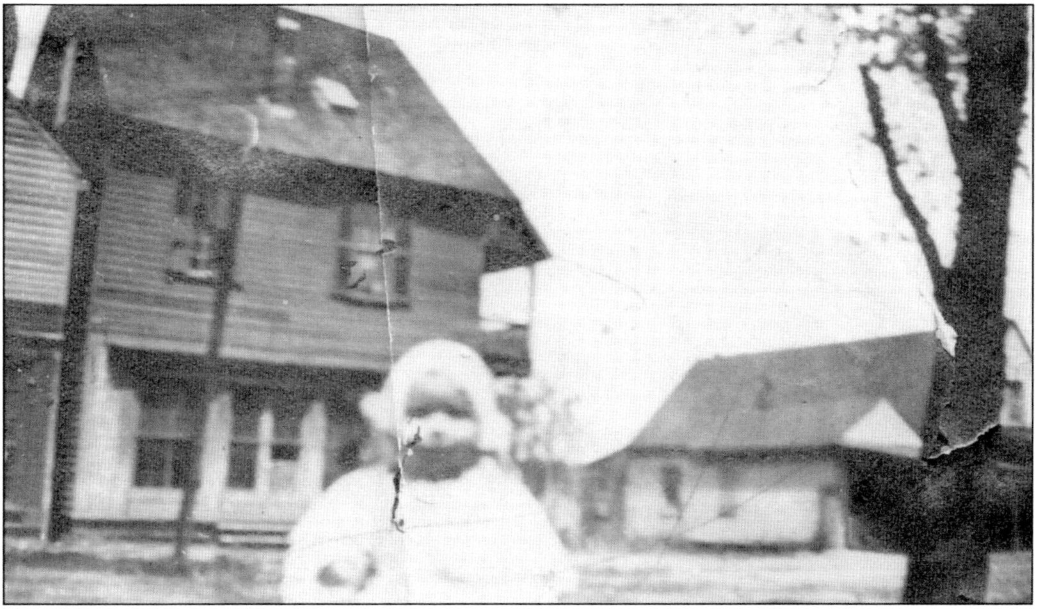

Buildings of three stories were unusual in early Milton, and little is known about the one pictured here other than it was an apartment building constructed in the 1800s that stood on the north side of Broad Street. Seen in the foreground in 1918 is Ella Ray Bradsher. Her family's house was directly across the street from the three-story building. (Courtesy Jean Bradsher Scott.)

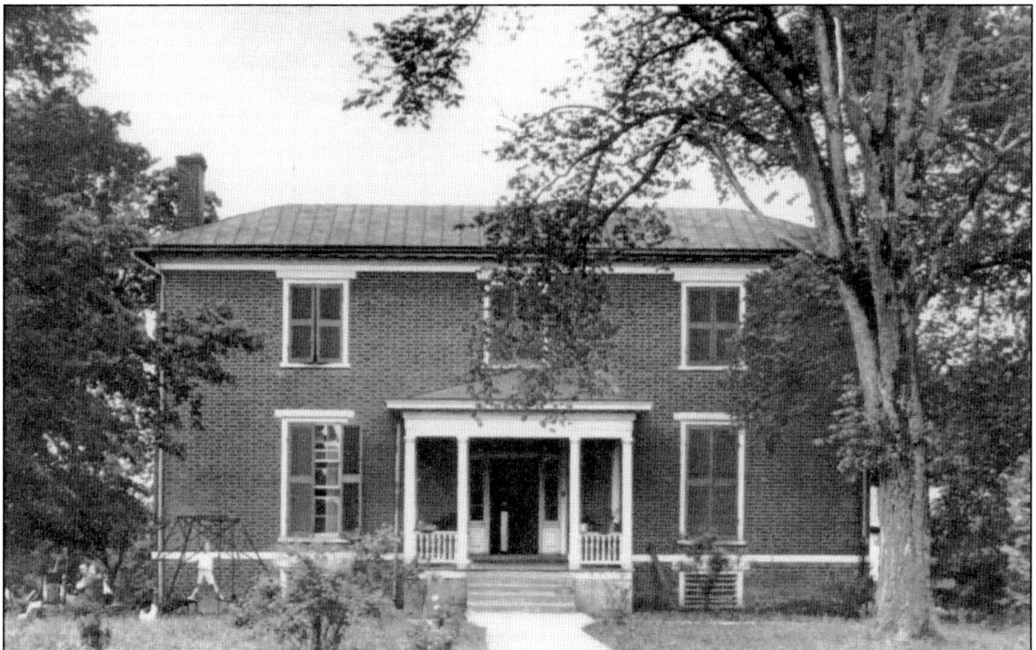

Glenburnie, near Milton, was the ancestral home of Dr. William Lipscomb "Buck" Stamps, M.D. (1816–1896), who graduated from the University of North Carolina and from the University of Pennsylvania School of Medicine. Later owned by the Angle family, the house burned in 1929. The large building included a widow's walk, and the property featured an unusual octagonal brick stable. (Courtesy Lois Angle Love.)

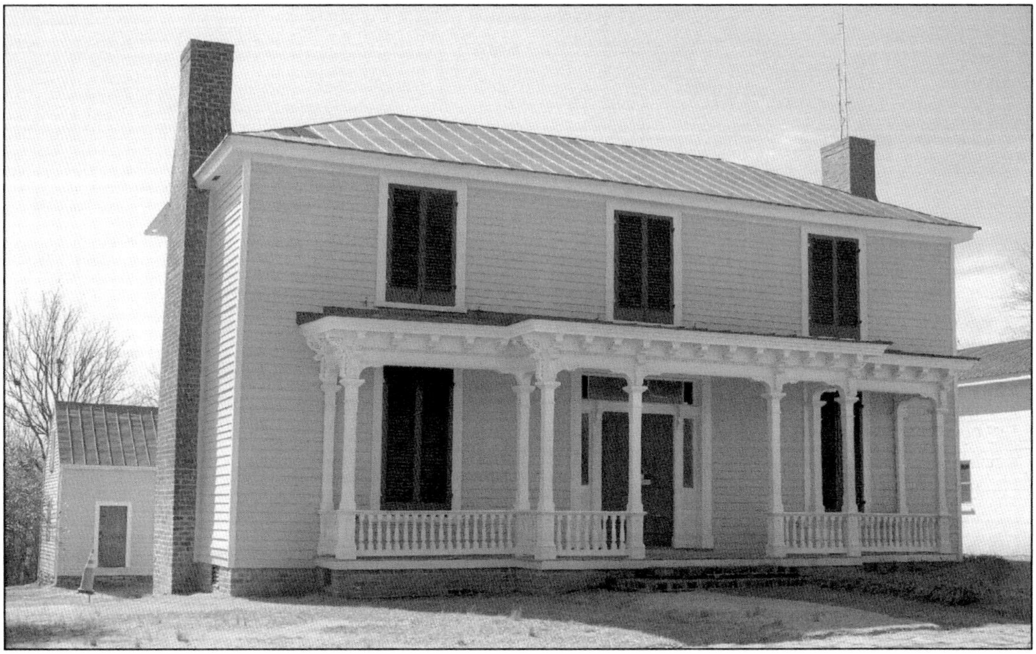

The Friou-Hurdle house was built around 1860 by Jarvis Friou, who moved to Milton in the 1840s and became a successful boot and shoe manufacturer. In 1850, Friou and three employees produced 100 pairs of boots worth $500 and 800 pairs of shoes worth $1,400. He also owned the landmark Milton Hotel. Dr. James Augustus Hurdle, D.D.S., was a subsequent owner of the house. (CCHA Photograph Archives.)

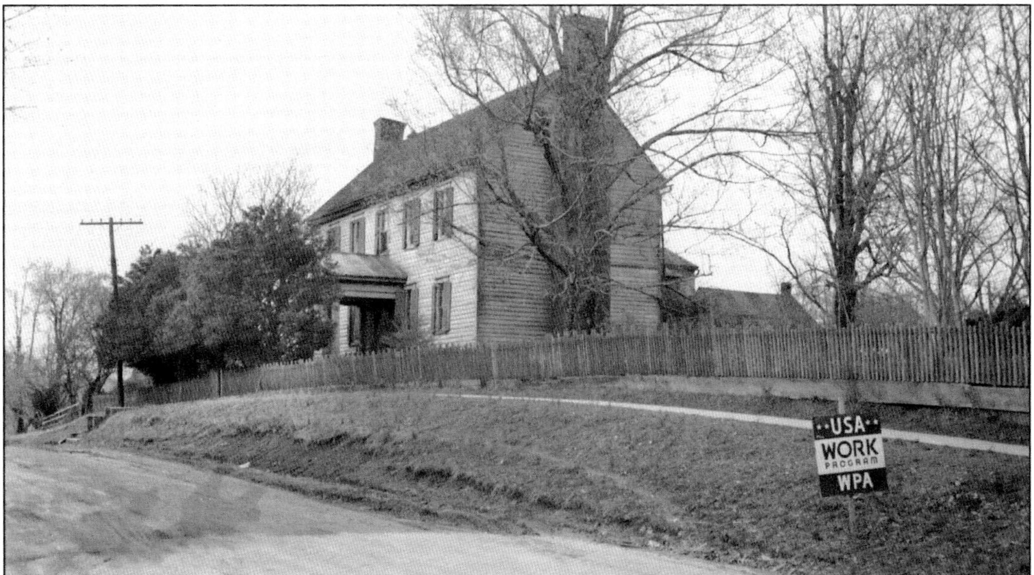

The Clay-Lewis-Irvine House was built in 1820 by Milton land speculator Henry M. Clay, who also owned Clay's Mill and was a trustee of the Milton Male Academy. The second owner was Nicholas Meriwether Lewis (1801–1889), a magistrate who married many couples in the house. Later occupants were the family of John Lewis Irvine (1834–1924), a Civil War veteran who fought with the Milton Blues. (Courtesy Library of Congress.)

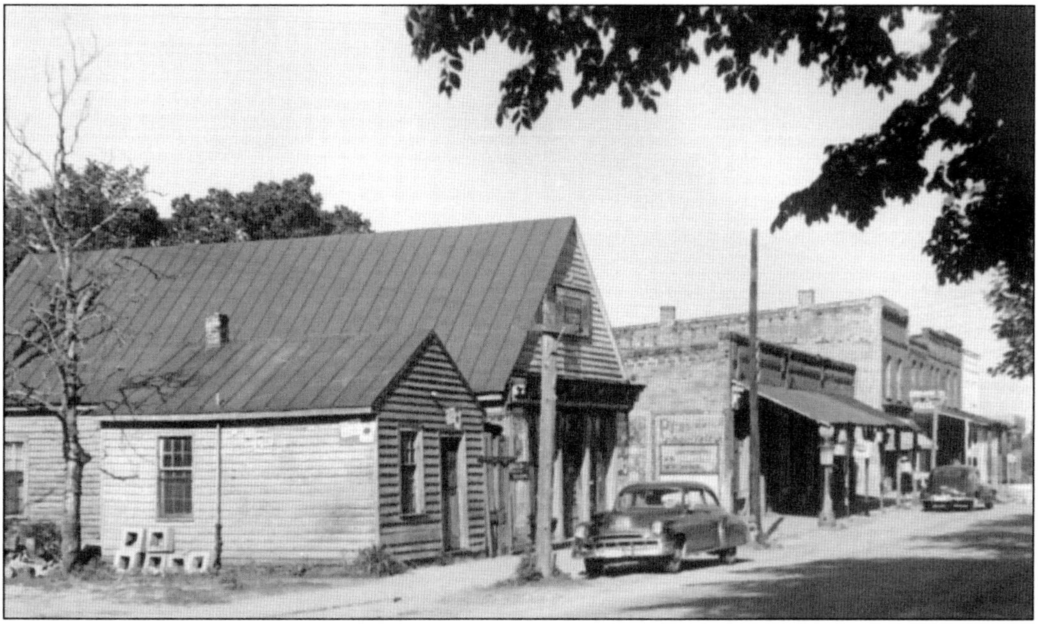

Described as a "museum without walls," the entire town of Milton is listed on the National Register of Historic Places as a Historic District. It is one of the best-preserved antebellum villages in North Carolina and contains structures dating from the early 1800s. Milton was established in 1796 on the Dan River near the mouth of Country Line Creek on land owned by Asa Thomas (1762–1813). The town flourished before the Civil War and was the business and social center of the region. Flat-bottomed bateaux transported goods and materials to and from the town, and mills, factories, and warehouses were constructed. Milton was one of the few towns in Caswell County served by a railroad. However, the Civil War and competition from Danville and Durham resulted in the town's eventual decline. (Both courtesy Jean Bradsher Scott.)

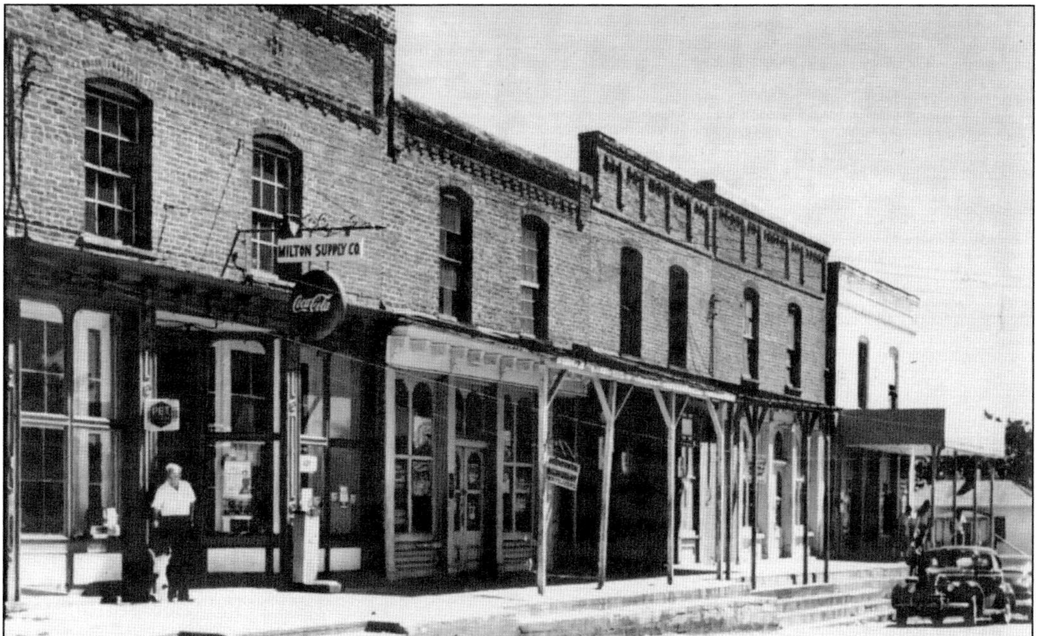

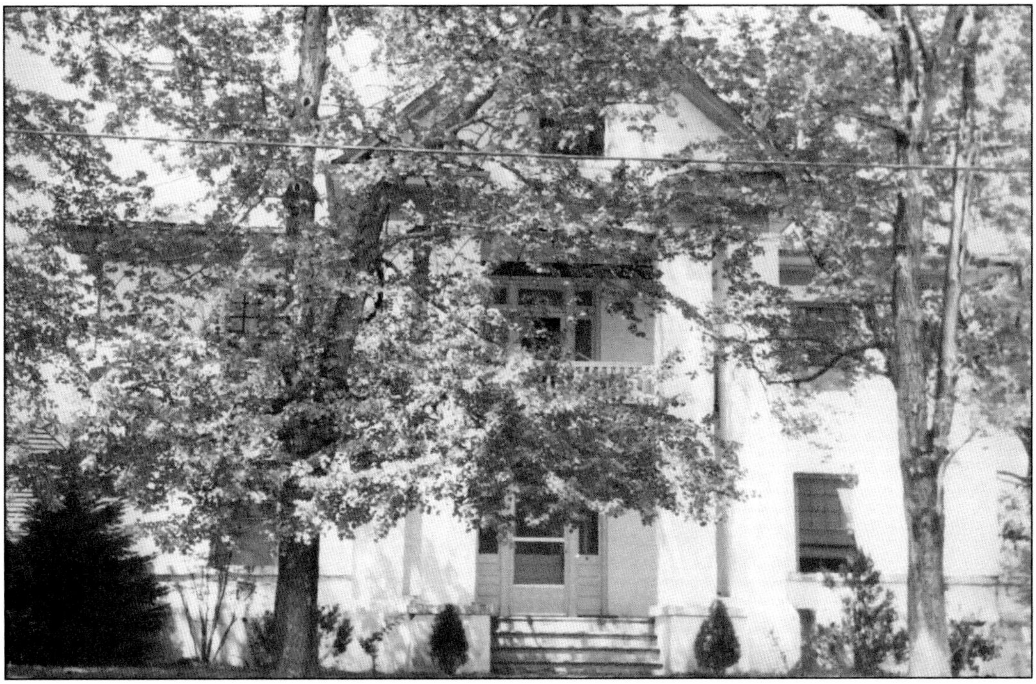

Walter Lea Thomas (1865–1929) built his Milton house around 1910 using the bricks of two antebellum stores that once stood on the site. Thomas's son, Milton merchant Edmund Dixon Thomas (1902–1973), was a subsequent owner, and the house remains in the family. The Thomas Store is nearby. (Courtesy Houston G. Jones.)

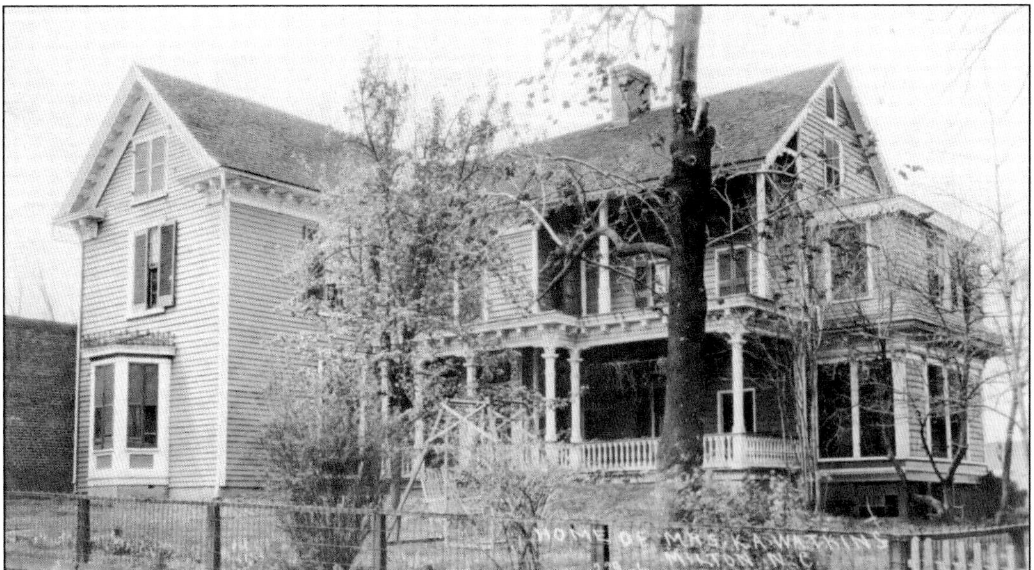

The home of Warner Meriwether Watkins (1843–1894) often was called the most ostentatious house Milton had ever seen. It burned when the Thomas Store next door caught fire. Watkins was a founder of the Farmers Bank at Milton, was involved in several failed attempts to construct railroads in the county, and was president of the board of trustees of the Milton Female Academy. (Courtesy Jean Bradsher Scott.)

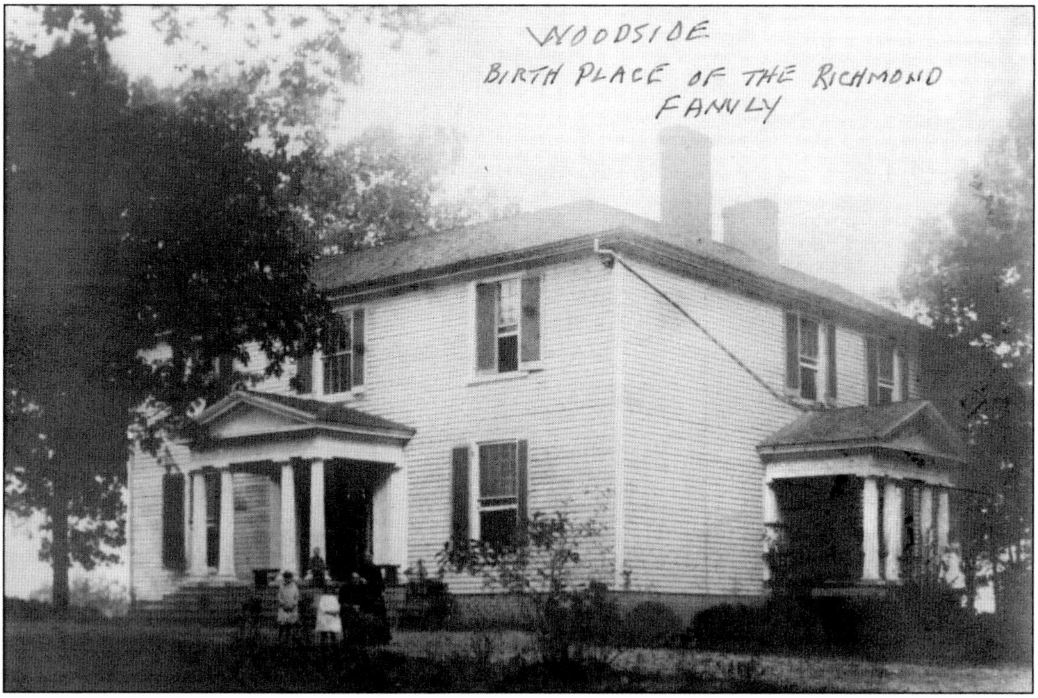

Around 1855, the Richmond-Morton-Holland House, also called Woodside, was built just outside Milton for Caleb Hazard Richmond (1805–1861). The house contains trim by noted craftsman Thomas Day, whose shop was nearby. Born in Woodside was Ellen E. Richmond, who married Civil War brigadier general Stephen Dodson Ramseur, often referred to as Lee's gallant general. The house is listed on the National Register. (CCHA Photograph Archives.)

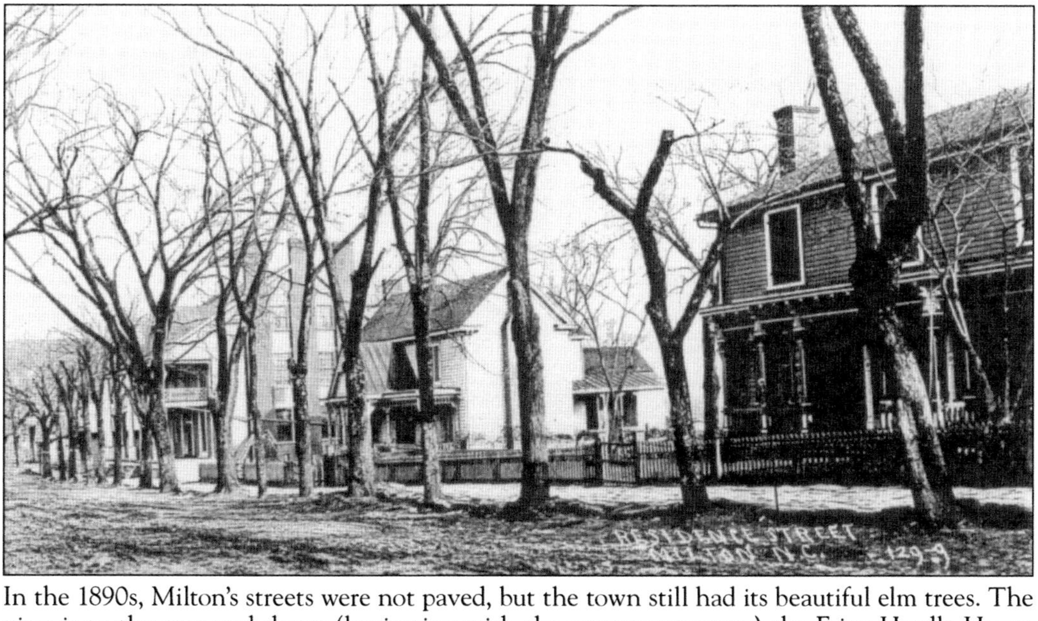

In the 1890s, Milton's streets were not paved, but the town still had its beautiful elm trees. The view is to the east and shows (beginning with the nearest structure) the Friou-Hurdle House (early 19th century), the Jones House (around 1860), and the Milton Hotel with its distinctive three chimneys (around 1826). (CCHA Photograph Archives.)

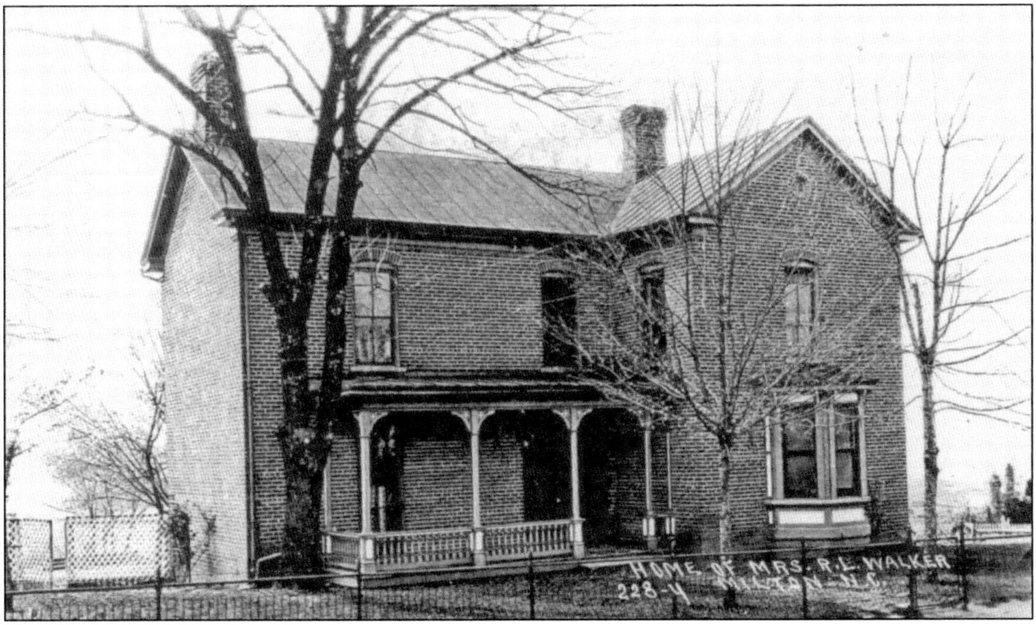

Robert Lewis Walker (1854–1913) built his Milton house around 1880 on a hilltop overlooking the Dan River. He served in both houses of the North Carolina Legislature, was one of the incorporators of the Merchants and Planters Bank of Milton in 1889, and served as the bank's cashier. (CCHA Photograph Archives.)

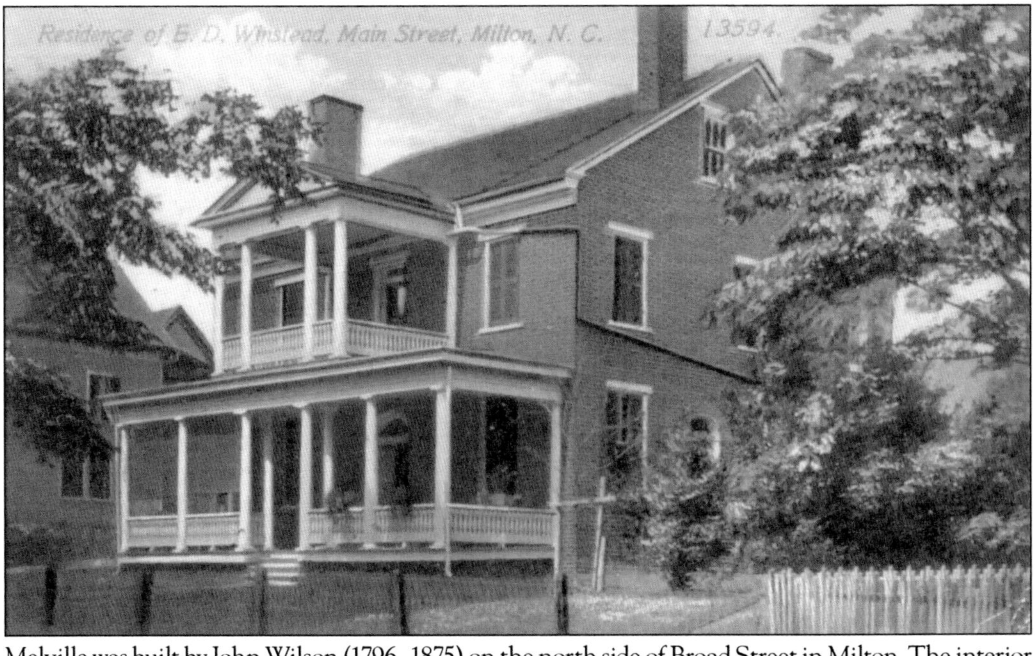

Melville was built by John Wilson (1796–1875) on the north side of Broad Street in Milton. The interior shows the artistry of Thomas Day, whose shop was across the street. Wilson was a wealthy planter and merchant and is buried in Milton's Cedars Cemetery. (CCHA Photograph Archives.)

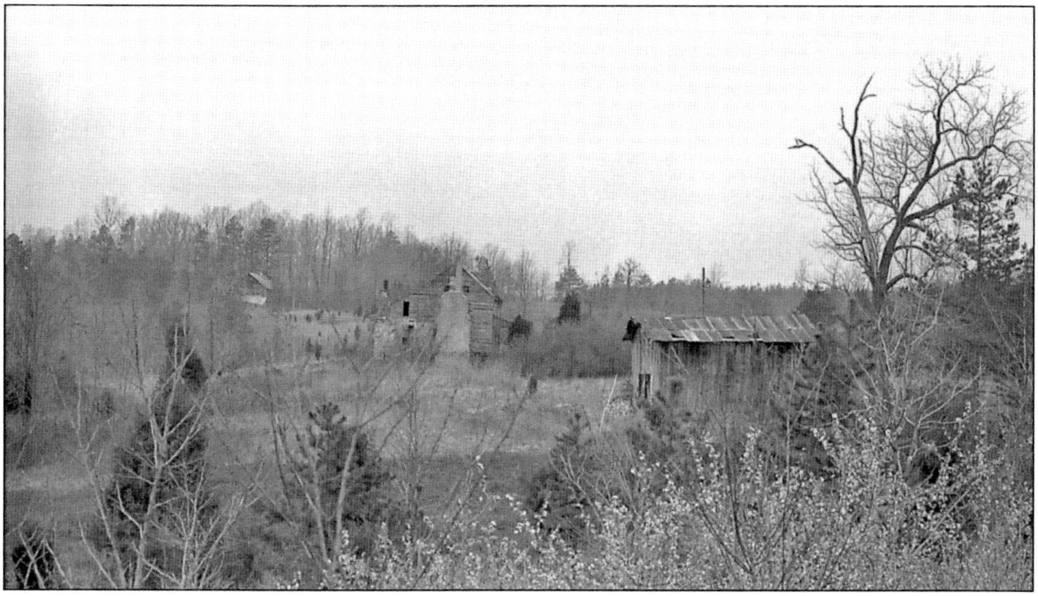

The cabin (with chimneys) on the Slade family farm, while of indeterminate age, is believed to date from the mid-1800s, with many modifications over the years. Legend tells that the Slade slave Stephen, who accidentally discovered the bright-leaf tobacco curing process, lived in his own cabin. Whether this was his cabin has not been confirmed. Some believe it is. Note the tobacco barn in the left background. (NCSHPO.)

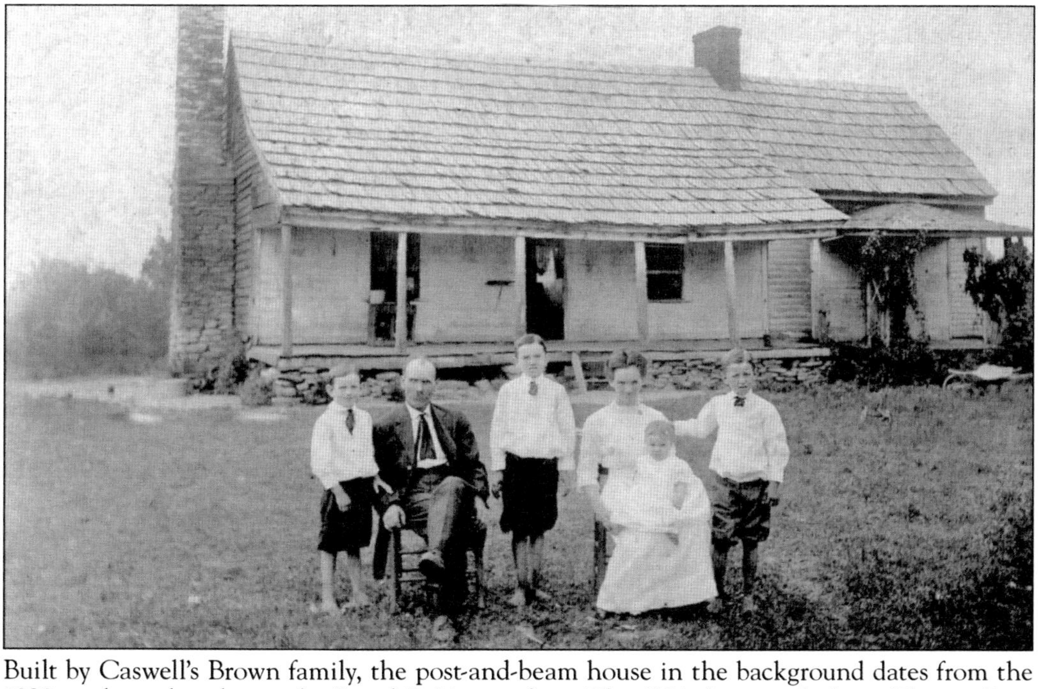

Built by Caswell's Brown family, the post-and-beam house in the background dates from the 1830s and stands today on the David C. Vernon farm. The 1914 photograph shows Thomas Rice (1870–1954), Annie Davis Rice (1879–1974), and their children, Tommy (to his father's right), Billy, Robert, and baby Frances. A member of the Brown family who built the house was a cofounder of the Brown and Williamson Tobacco Corporation. (Courtesy Cyrus and Janice Rice Vernon.)

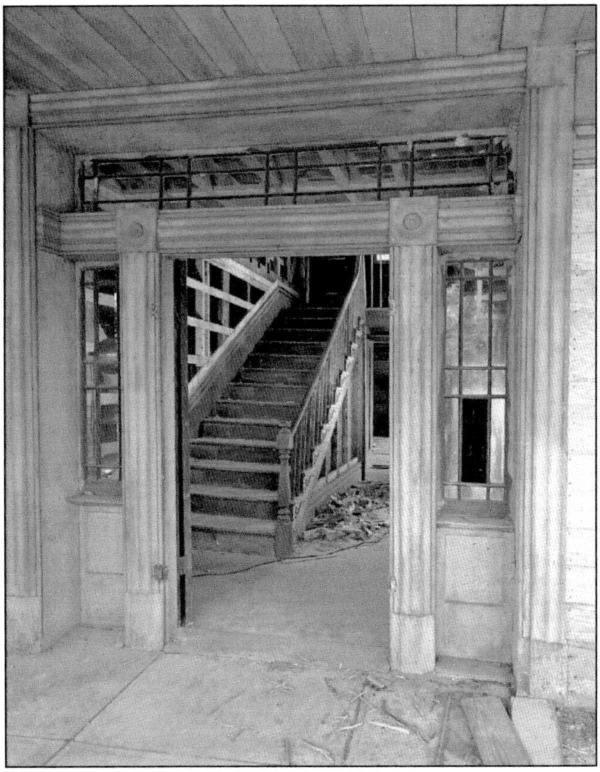

Longwood near Milton, appearing sad after years of neglect, is somewhat representative of Caswell's history. The mansion, once glorious with interior trim by famed cabinetmaker Thomas Day, could no longer be maintained after the Civil War ravaged the county's slave-based tobacco economy. Here restoration has just begun. Today Longwood is one of the best preserved antebellum houses in the county and is on the National Register of Historic Places. (Courtesy NCSHPO.)

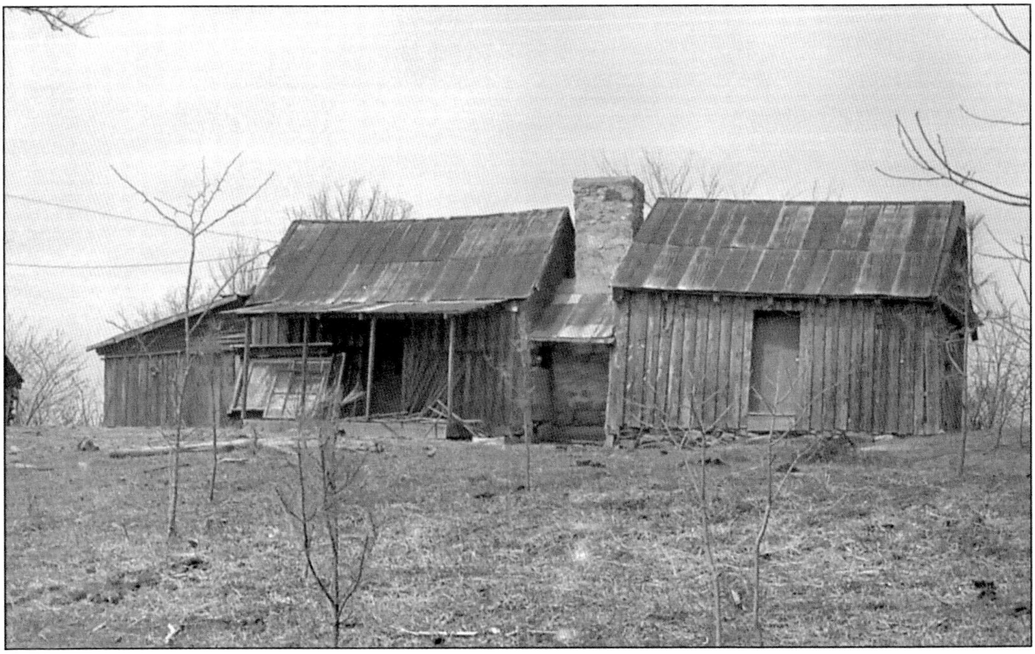

Somewhat crude but interesting, the 1850s log house is one of the few "saddlebag" houses found in the county and probably was used as slave quarters on the farm of a Sidney Lea. There were several planters named Sidney Lea living in Caswell County before the Civil War, and all owned slaves. (NCSHPO.)

Five

Scenes around the County

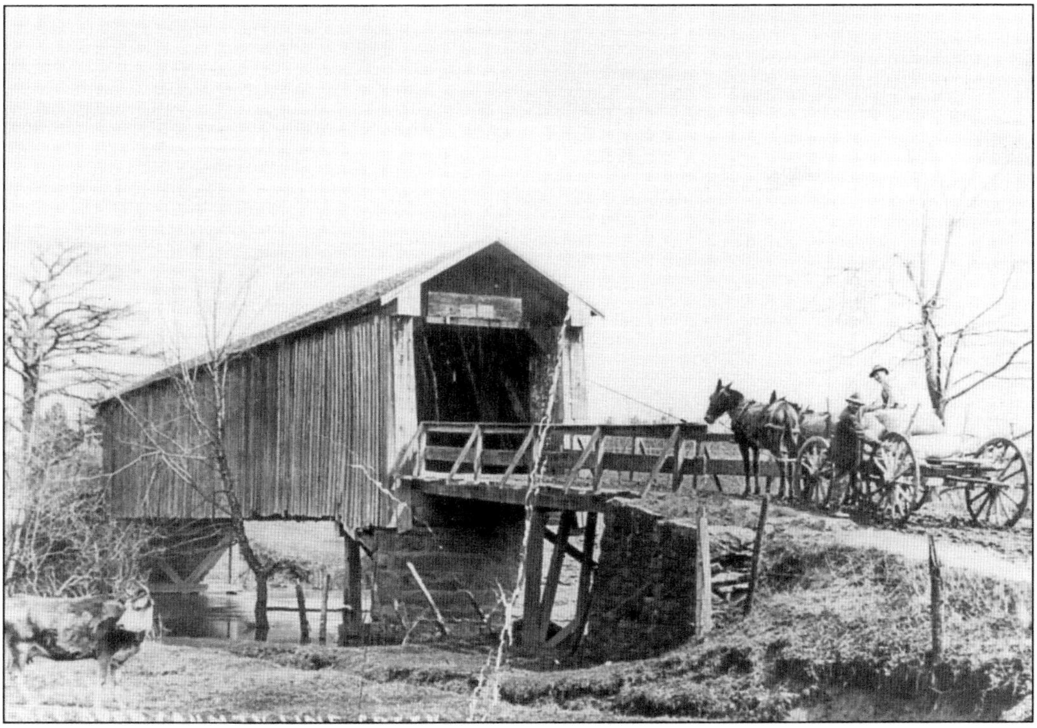

Milton is bordered by two streams, the larger Dan River and Country Line Creek (which empties into Dan River at Milton). In the late 1800s, a covered bridge spanned Country Line Creek on the road that led to Semora. Country Line Creek was so named because it once was thought to be the border between North Carolina and Virginia, which at one time were different "countries." (Courtesy Jean Bradsher Scott.)

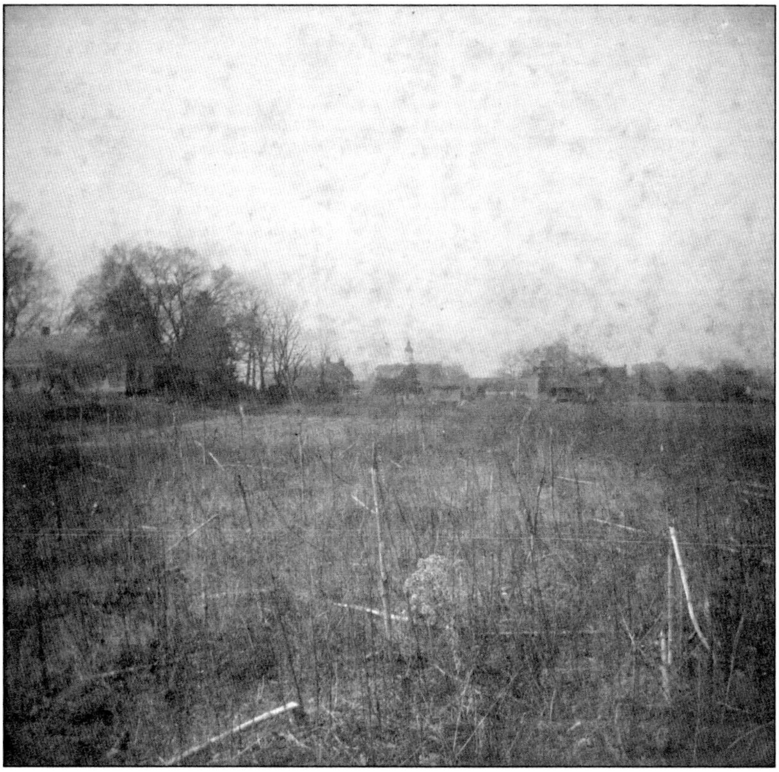

The appearance of the land surrounding the Caswell County Courthouse suggests that this image was captured well before 1900. Whether the view is from the east or west, no improved roads are visible, and the only identifiable building is the courthouse in the distance. The photograph came from the estate of Mary Kerr Motz (1917–2005), whose ancestors had been in Caswell County since the 1700s. (Courtesy Tim Ross.)

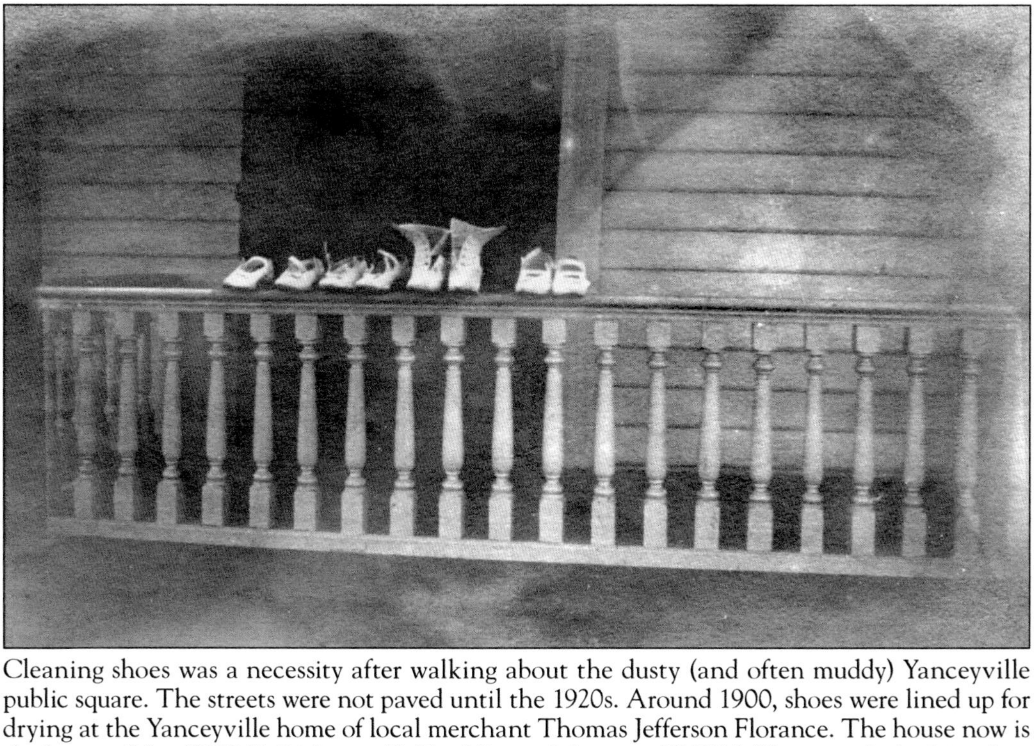

Cleaning shoes was a necessity after walking about the dusty (and often muddy) Yanceyville public square. The streets were not paved until the 1920s. Around 1900, shoes were lined up for drying at the Yanceyville home of local merchant Thomas Jefferson Florance. The house now is the home of the CCHA's Richmond-Miles History Museum. (CCHA Photograph Archives.)

As late as 1939, the small Leasburg community in the far eastern part of Caswell had six stores. One was owned by Lex Darden Sally (1892–1947), who is seen in this early-1900s photograph (seated center). His friend Jesse Carr "Bud" Royster (1892–1979) is without a hat. The identity of the third man is unknown. Note the unusual hatbands. Leasburg was Caswell's first county seat. (Courtesy Karen Wade Avants.)

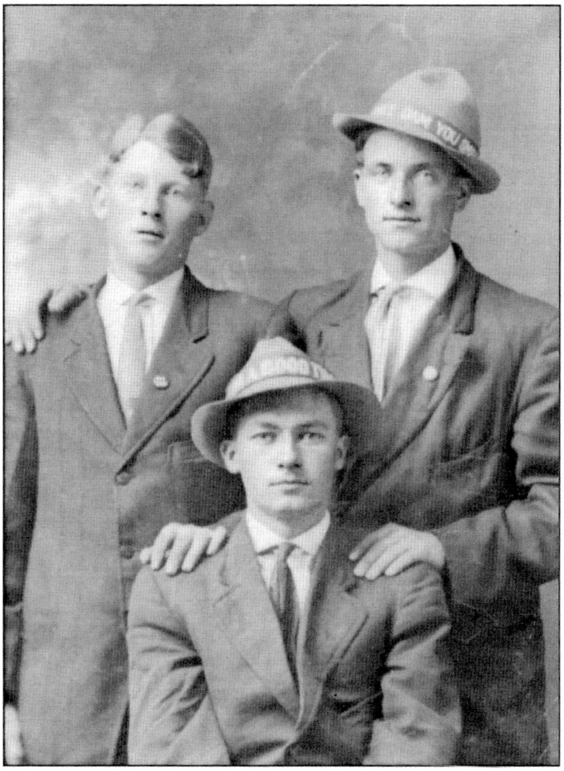

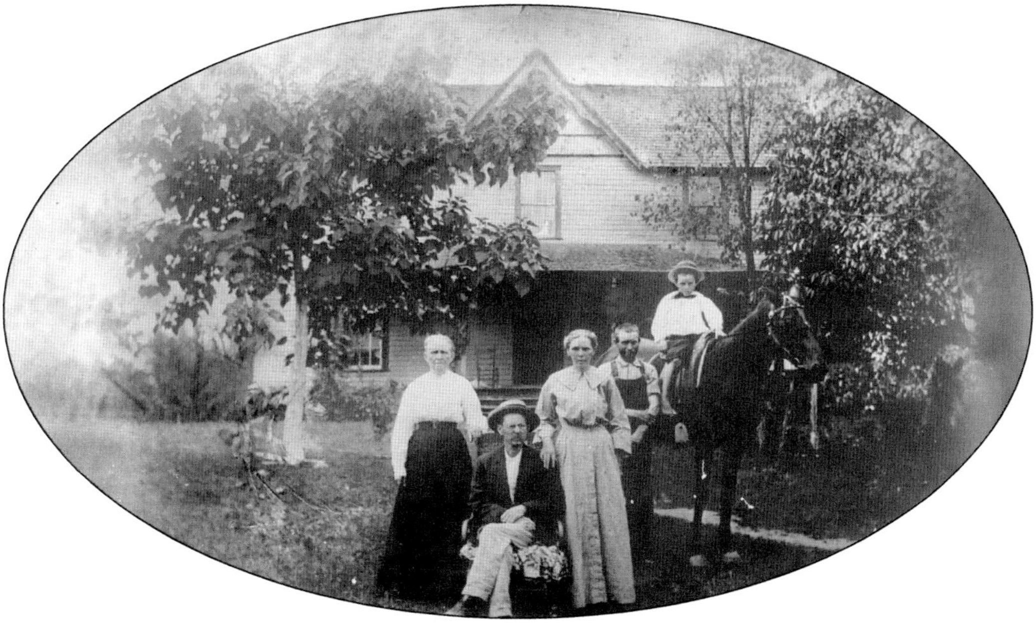

The George Daniel Rice (1860–1919) farm was located near Camp Springs United Methodist Church in southwest Caswell County. Photographed in the early 1900s are, from left to right, Martha Hooper Vincent Rice, George Daniel Rice (seated), Cora Vincent Rice (1876–1952), Joe Totten (a faithful farm worker), and young Stephen Norman Rice (1904–1990) on horseback. (Courtesy Cyrus and Janice Rice Vernon.)

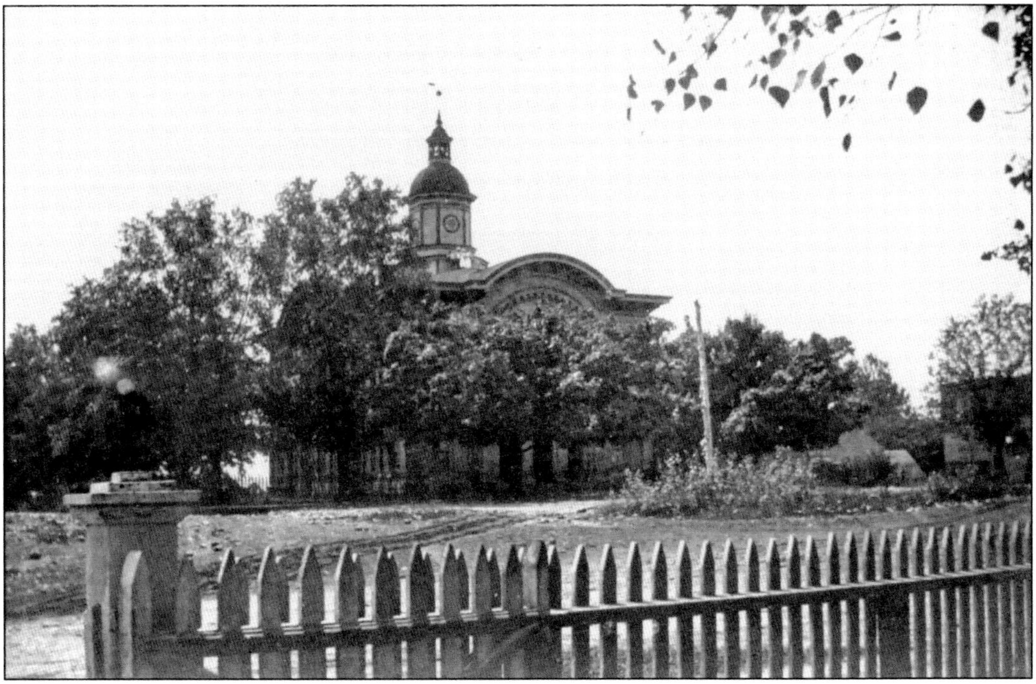

The Caswell County Courthouse roof provided an unparalleled view of Yanceyville and the surrounding countryside. The photograph was taken from the Graves-Florance house across the public square area and shows a group of people on a rooftop excursion. The streets were not paved, and stepping-stone paths radiated from the courthouse to each side of the square. (CCHA Photograph Archives.)

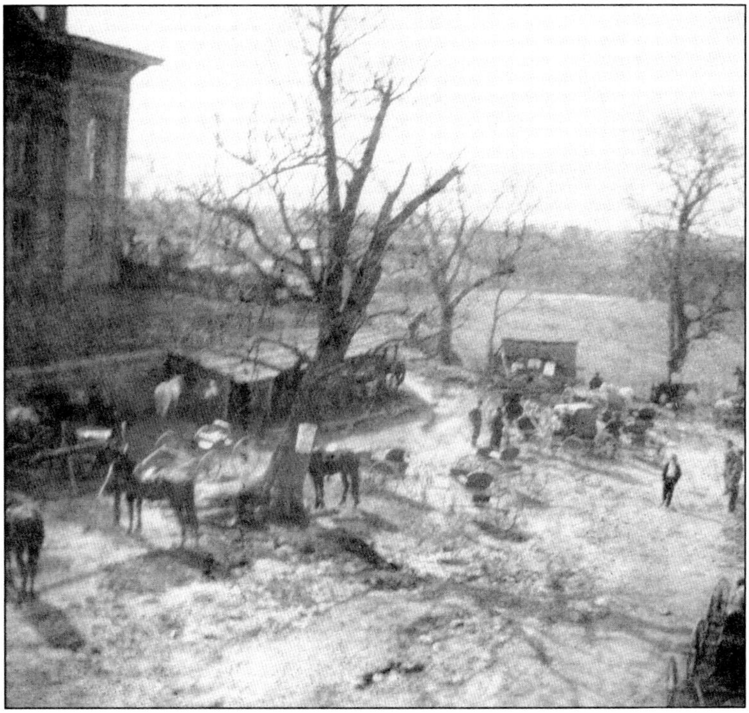

Historians have advised that a stable yard was provided beside the Caswell County Courthouse to meet the needs of those traveling to Yanceyville for county business. The remarkable photograph at left is the only known image and probably dates from before 1900. The view is to the south toward Jail Branch and eventually to Country Line Creek. (Courtesy Tim Ross.)

Outside Henry W. Perry's (1869–1916) Yanceyville drugstore around 1900, people (and a dog) are strolling on the public square. Perry owned the building and operated a pharmacy from the ground floor. For a time, he was the Yanceyville postmaster. Perry married Sallie Willie Graves, a daughter of wealthy Caswell planter Jeremiah Graves Jr. (1835–1901). The building later had several uses, including as an automobile dealership. (Courtesy Tim Ross.)

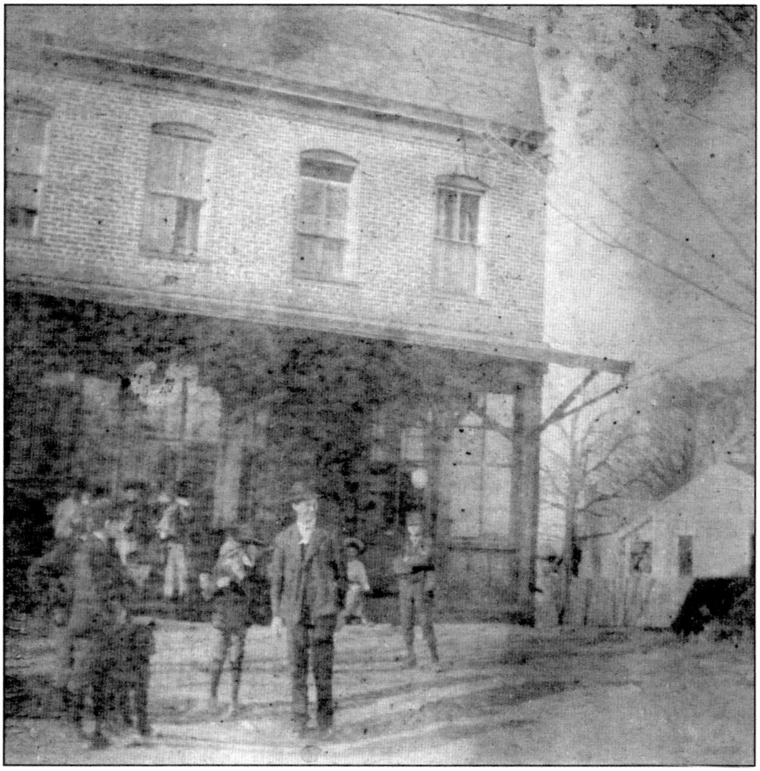

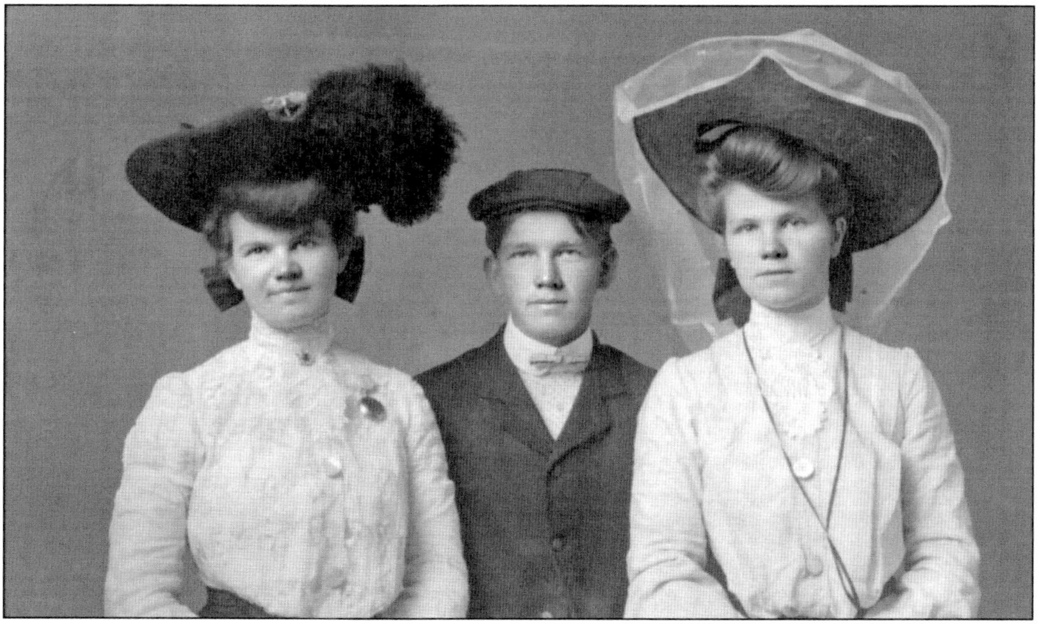

Participating in a 1910 "study in hats" are Caswell residents and siblings, from left to right, Lemma Sue Fowlkes (1883–1974), Robert Jennings Fowlkes (1888–1977), and Jennie Adams Fowlkes (1880–1911). They were children of George Washington Fowlkes (1855–1941) and Betty Jane Johns Fowlkes (1854–1909). Caswell farmer George Washington Fowlkes was married twice, with nine children by each wife. (Courtesy Houston G. Jones.)

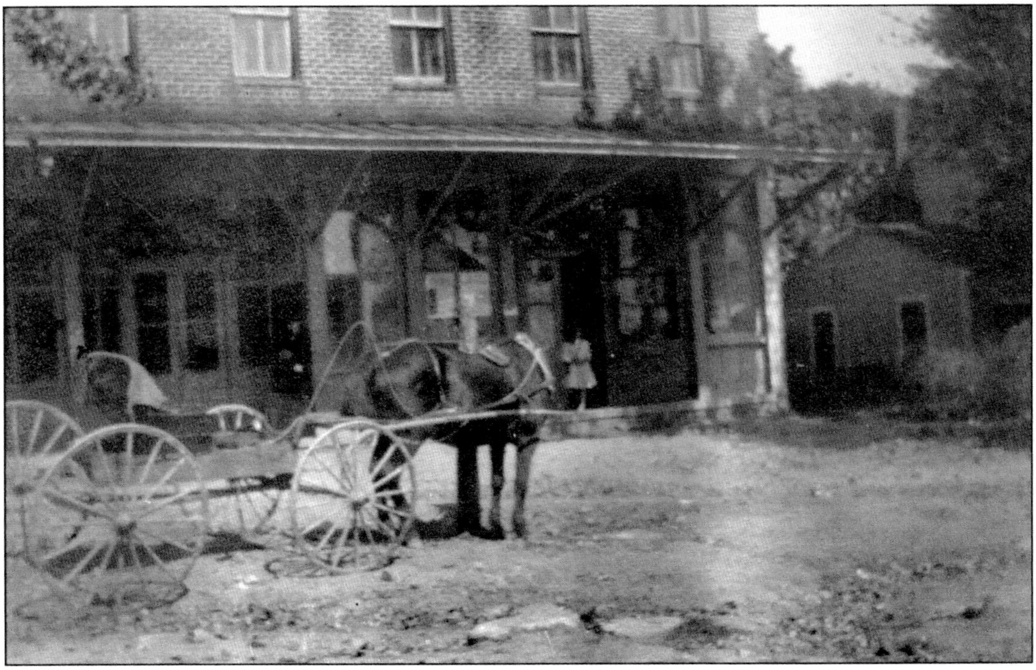

This scene is on the Yanceyville Square in the early 1900s. The horse (tied to the hitching post) and the buggy are in front of a building that was erected in 1894 as a lodge hall, converted (first floor) to a drugstore around 1906, and made into an automobile dealership in 1917. Note the little girl in the doorway. To the right is the Graves-Florance-Gatewood House. (CCHA Photograph Archives.)

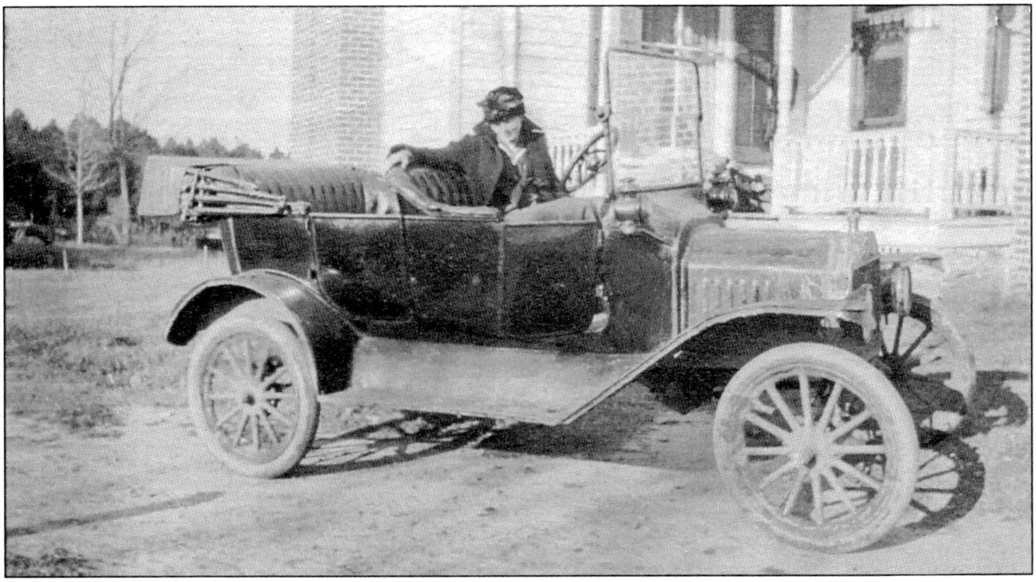

Martha Eliza Hatchett (1896–1993) taught school in Caswell and was affectionately called Miss Marnie. Whether she actually drove this touring car in the 1910s or was just posing is not known. The building is the Bartlett Yancey House, which was owned by her aunt Mat Womack. Miss Marnie married Yanceyville banker Samuel Murphey Bason (1894–1986). Note the car's wooden-spoke wheels. (Courtesy John O. Gunn Estate.)

Sgt. Alvis Lea Florance (1889–1964), in his World War I uniform, is with his mother, Nannie Lea Florance (1869–1939) on the porch of the Graves-Florance House in Yanceyville. Young Florance volunteered for duty, was assigned to the Army Medical Corps, and was headed for front-line service in France when the Armistice was signed. (CCHA Photograph Archives.)

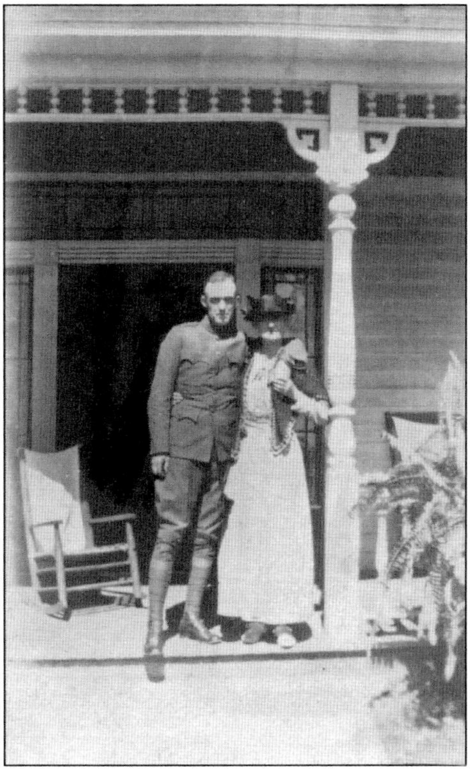

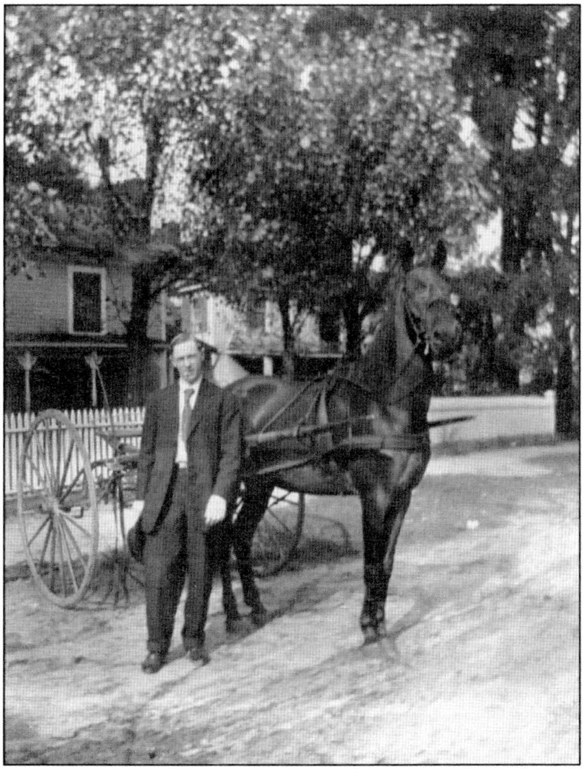

After his World War I service, Alvis Lea Florance returned to work in his father's Yanceyville store. Motor vehicles were available to some, but others preferred the reliable horse and buggy. The Graves-Florance House in the background, built around 1815, was once a girls' school (mid-19th century). Thomas J. Florance (1858–1926), father of Alvis Lea Florance, purchased the house around 1895. (CCHA Photograph Archives.)

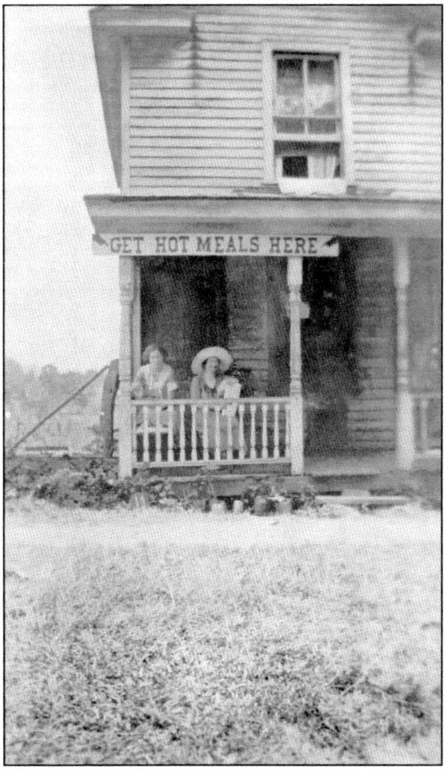

Anna Mae Hooper (1906–1987) and her mother, Erna Wrenn Hooper (1883–1966) (wearing hat), are sitting on the porch of their Yanceyville home in the early 1920s. Meals were offered from this location near the Caswell County Courthouse for a few years until the Hooper family opened a large boardinghouse in another part of town. (Courtesy Louise Moore Atwater Estate.)

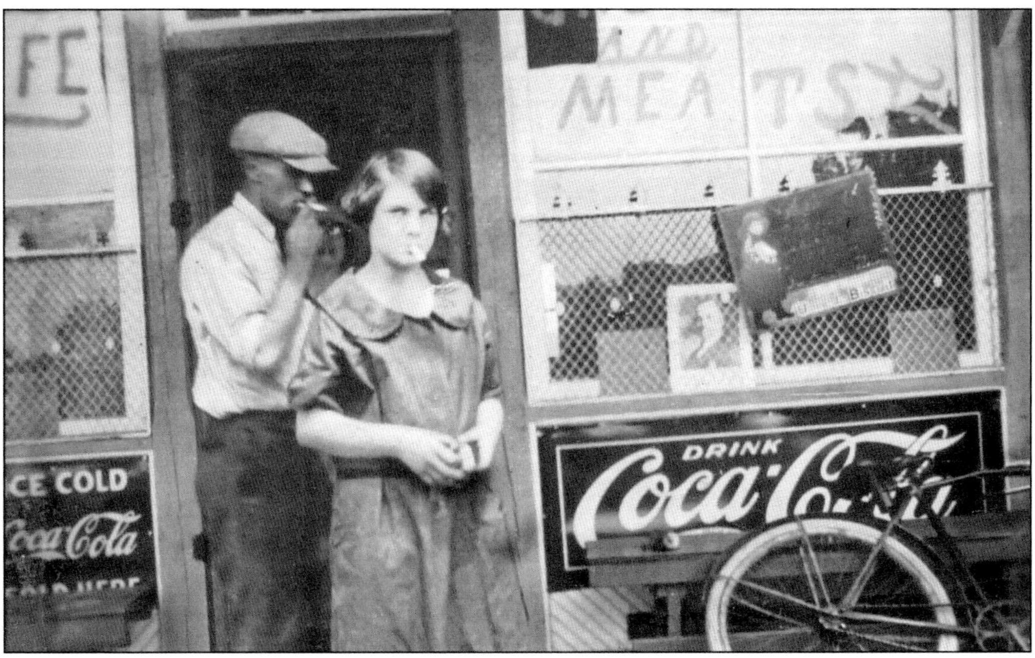

Teenager Elsie Lea Hooper (1910–1994) is pushing the social envelope of the 1920s when she smokes in public outside a store on the Yanceyville Square that specialized in "groceries and meats." The identity of the man, also smoking, is not known. Elsie Hooper would marry Clyde C. Cole (1903–1969), a successful Yanceyville Chevrolet dealer. (Courtesy Louise Moore Atwater Estate.)

Young Thaddeus Cornelius Jones II (1919–1937) displays considerable skill in operating a 1920s wooden-wheeled wheelbarrow. He was a son of Paul Hosier Jones (1896–1952) and Lemma Sue Fowlkes Jones (1883–1974) of Caswell's Locust Hill community. In the background is the Robert Henry Jones (1855–1935) house. (Courtesy Houston G. Jones.)

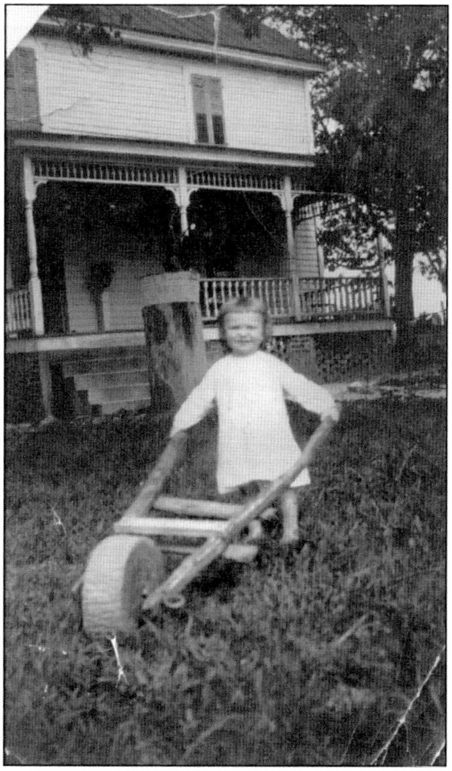

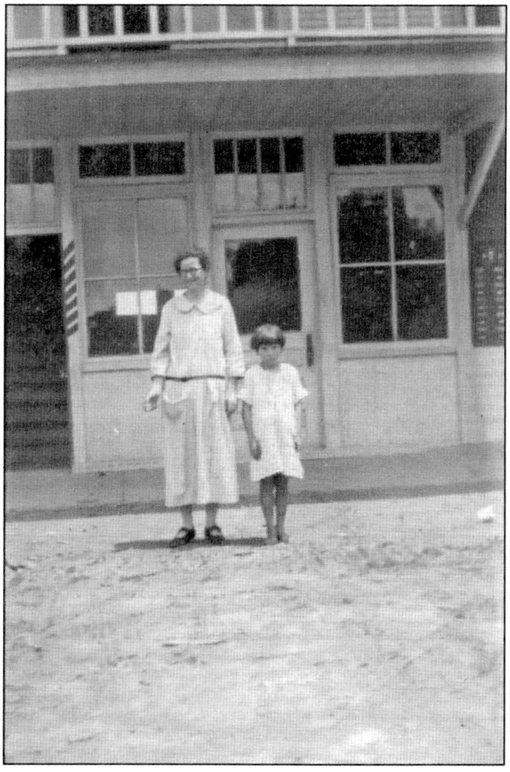

Erna Wrenn Hooper (1883–1966) and her husband, William Melvin "Wid" Hooper (1876–1968), operated a restaurant in Yanceyville and later built a boardinghouse. Wid grew food on his Caswell County farm (now a golf course), and Erna prepared it for use at the restaurant and boardinghouse. The identity of the young girl is not known. Note the barber pole painted on the door frame. (Courtesy Louise Moore Atwater Estate.)

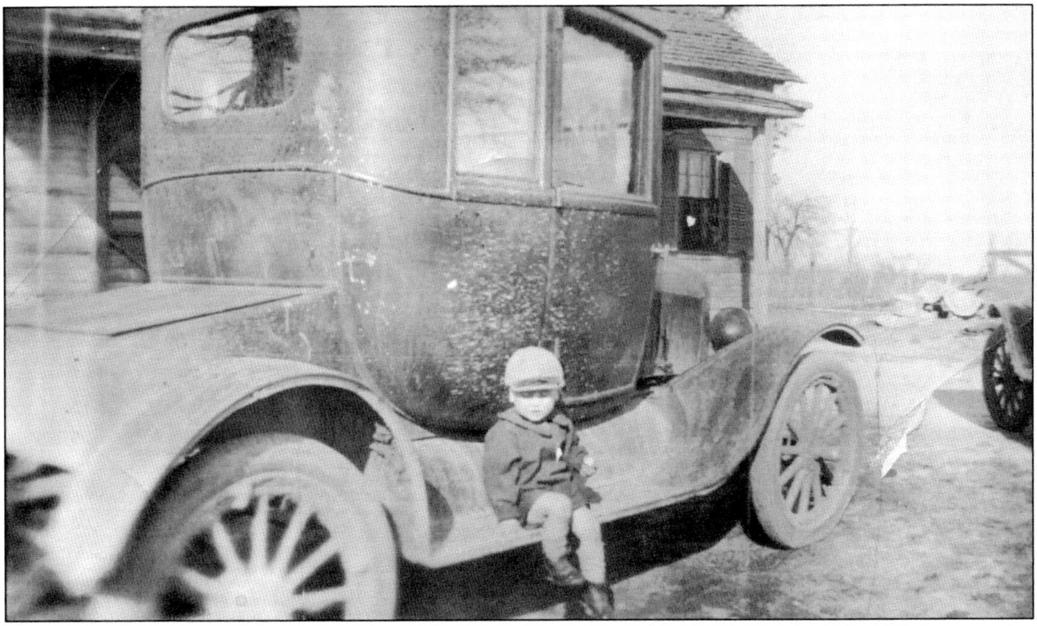

Too young to drive but old enough to ride, young James Basley "Jimmy" Harrelson Jr. sits on the running board of this vintage motorcar around 1928. Jimmy Harrelson, a World War II veteran, is a son of Caswell farmer and grocer James Basley Harrelson (1902–1976) and Addie Louise Jones Harrelson (1905–1974). The location was the Thaddeus Cornelius Jones house in Locust Hill. (Courtesy Houston G. Jones.)

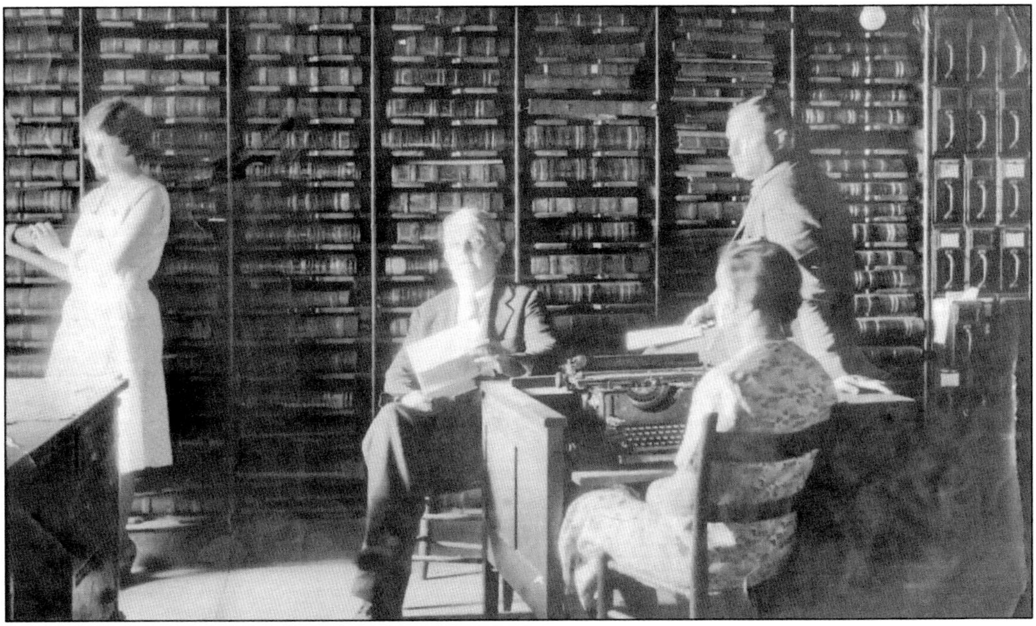

Responsible for the smooth operation of the Superior Court in Yanceyville and for its records, the Clerk of Court's Office in the 1930s was a busy place. From left to right are Ruth Anderson, Clerk of Court George A. Anderson (served 1926–1934), Mary Slade Anderson (at typewriter), and Sheriff John Yancey Gatewood (1893–1954). The two ladies were daughters of Clerk Anderson. (CCHA Photograph Archives.)

In the 1930s, the public well in Yanceyville still worked. In 1852, William Lockhart was paid $195 to dig the well. A pump was added in 1853. In 1855, Joseph J. Yarbro provided a new pump. In 1856, Thomas B. Atkins was paid $51 for replacing the pump. In 1860, Atkins repaired the well. In 1869, A. A. Mitchell was paid $65 for a new pump. (North Carolina Collection.)

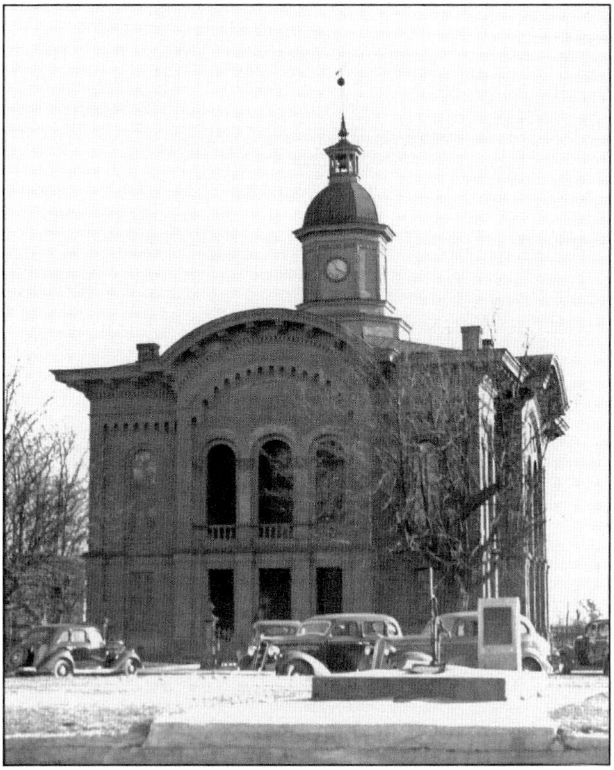

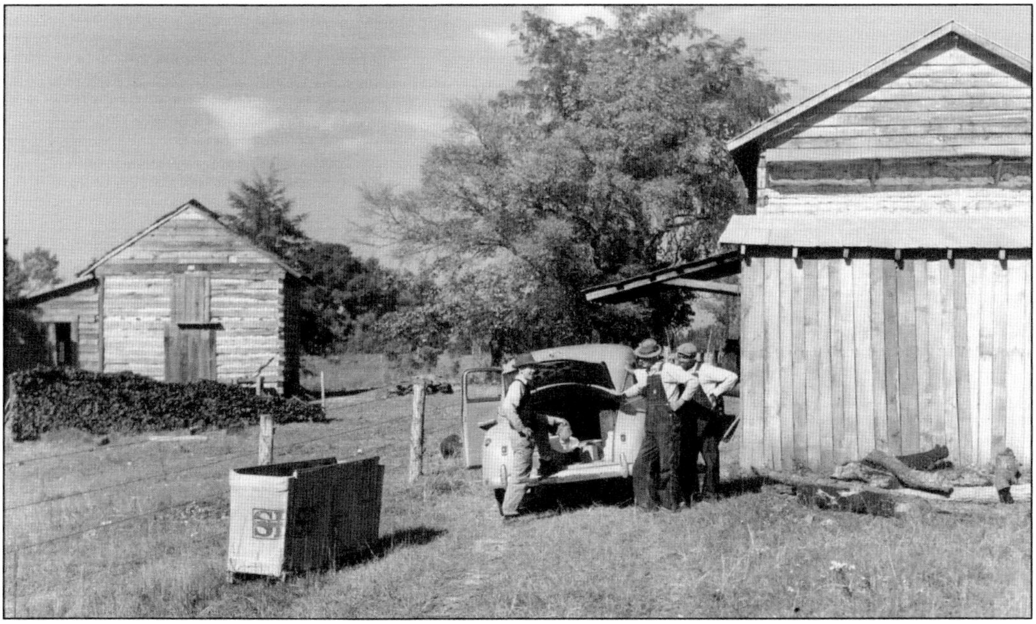

During the 1930s, Caswell farmers who did not raise their own beef often purchased it from a traveling meat peddler. When a cow was killed, the meat was cut up, placed in the trunk of a car (along with a scale), and driven from farm to farm. The customer selected the desired cut, which was weighed and wrapped in newspaper. Here a transaction is in progress. (Courtesy Library of Congress.)

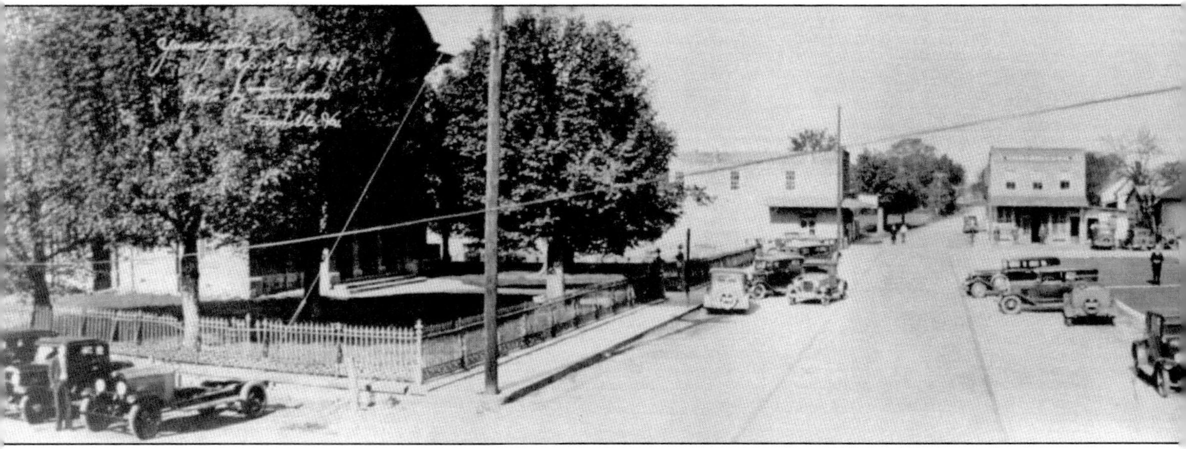

The Yanceyville Square anchors the business district as it looked on April 28, 1931. The buildings are, clockwise from left: the Caswell County Courthouse (behind trees); Neal's department store (became the Caswell Theater); W. N. Harrelson's store (became Watlington's); building that once was the post office; W. H. Hooper's store (Masonic lodge upstairs); Bank of Yanceyville (four white columns); Yanceyville Drug Co.; Florance building; and the Crowell Auto Co. In

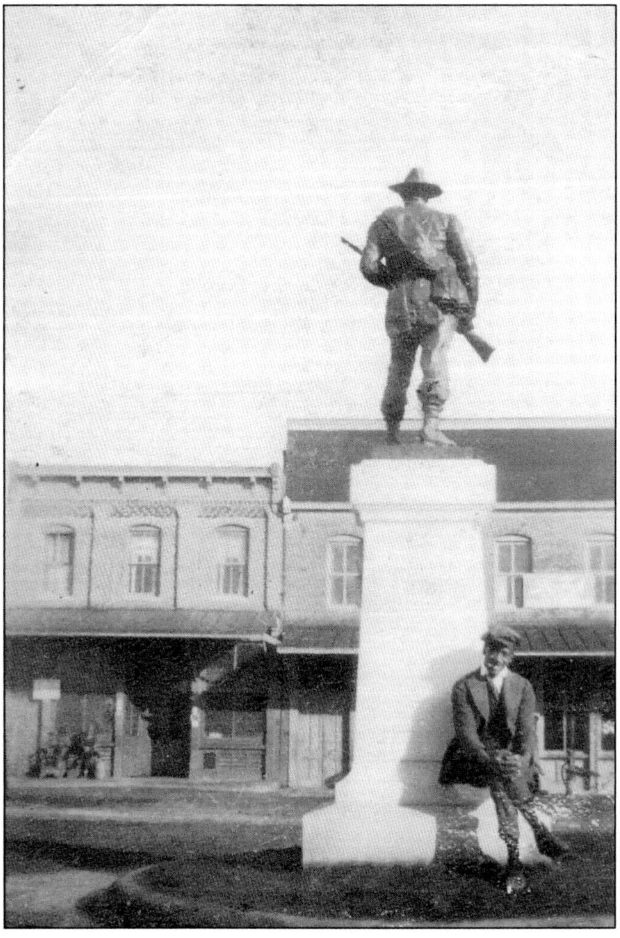

The base of the monument on the Yanceyville Square serves as a convenient seat for this local resident, taking his ease in the morning sun. The monument was erected in 1921 through the efforts of the Caswell County chapter of the United Daughters of the Confederacy. Both this photograph and the one opposite are contemporaneous with the panoramic view above. (Courtesy Helen Little).

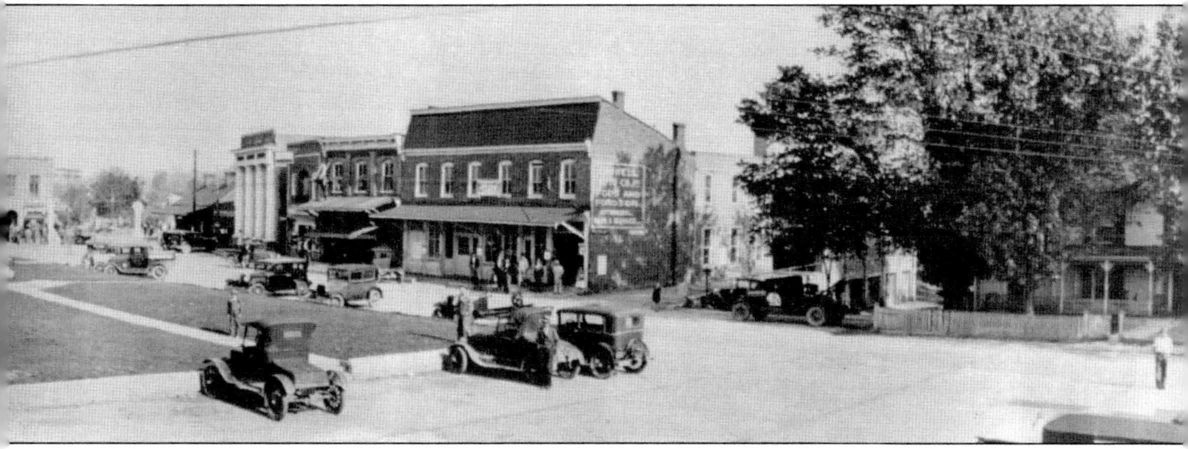

the center of the square proper is the Confederate monument (statue of a Confederate soldier facing north). Note the people turned toward the photographer, indicating this was no candid shot. While difficult to see, one man is standing outside a second-story window of the Florance building. It was Ashley Yarbrough (1888–1958), whose wife-to-be worked inside as a telephone operator. (Courtesy Ryland Lee Farmer.)

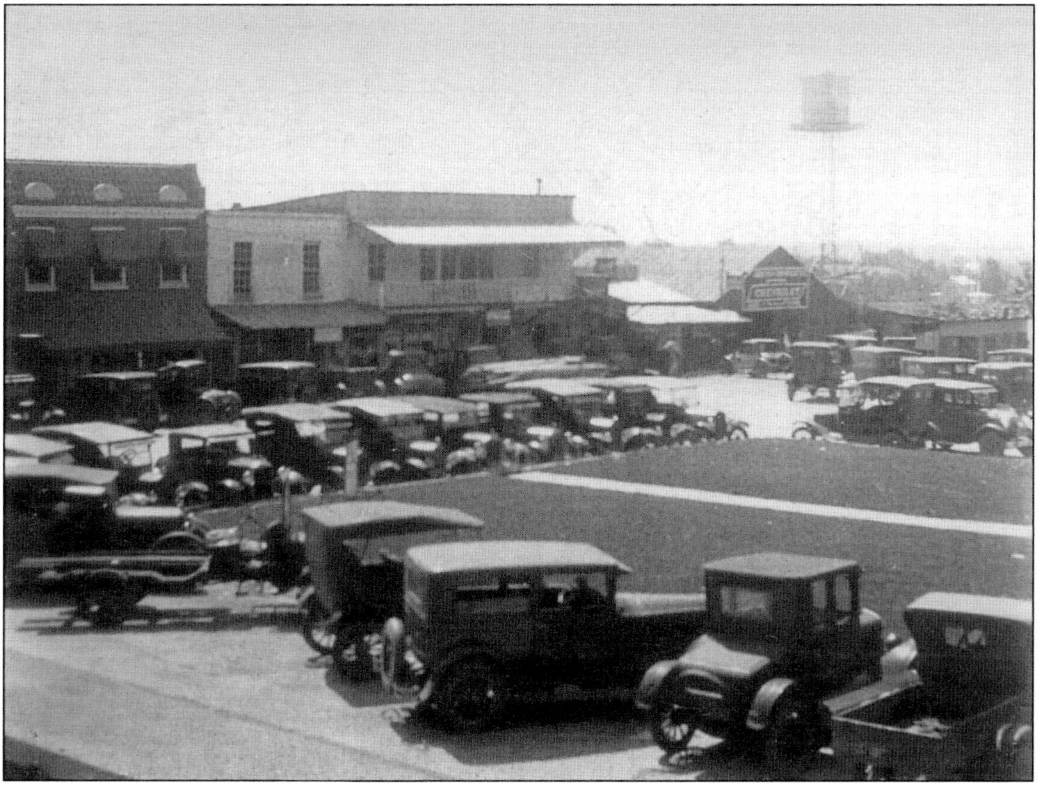

This view of the east side of the square is taken from the second floor of the Florance building opposite the courthouse. The panoramic photograph above was taken from the roof or upper floor of one of these buildings, probably one of the two-story white buildings. In the 1920s and 1930s, cars parked "head on" to the square. Today parking around the square is greatly restricted because of car size and the need for driving space. (Courtesy Helen Little)

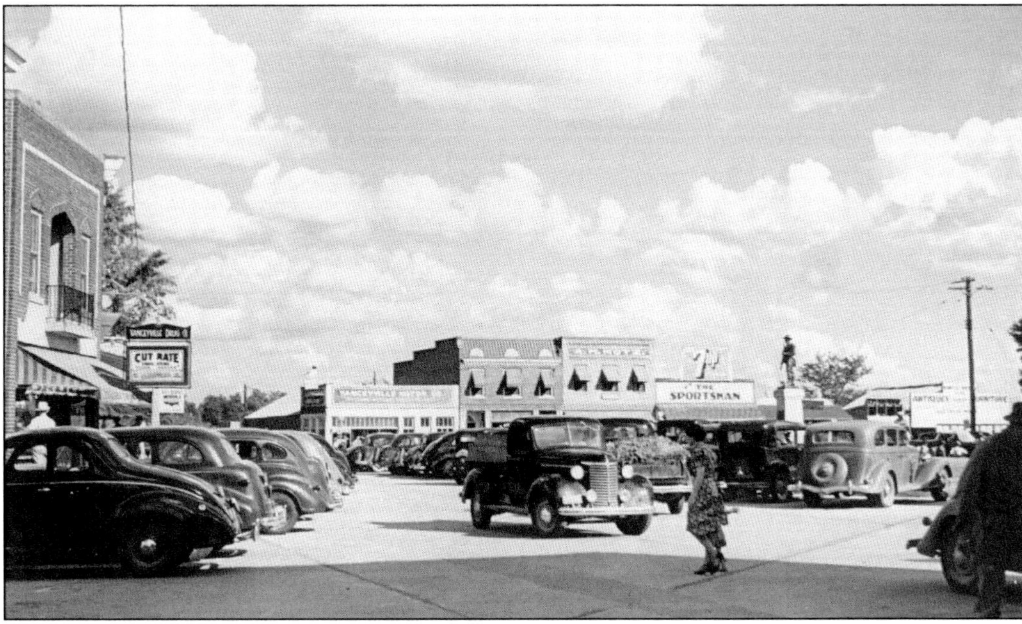

Saturdays in 1938 brought people to Yanceyville for shopping, and few parking spaces were available. On the left is the Yanceyville Drug Co. building with its upstairs apartment and balcony. Farther around the square are John A. Massey's Yanceyville Motor Co., the Upchurch Building, the A. H. Motz Building, and the Sportsman Bar. The Confederate monument watches over the town. (Courtesy Library of Congress.)

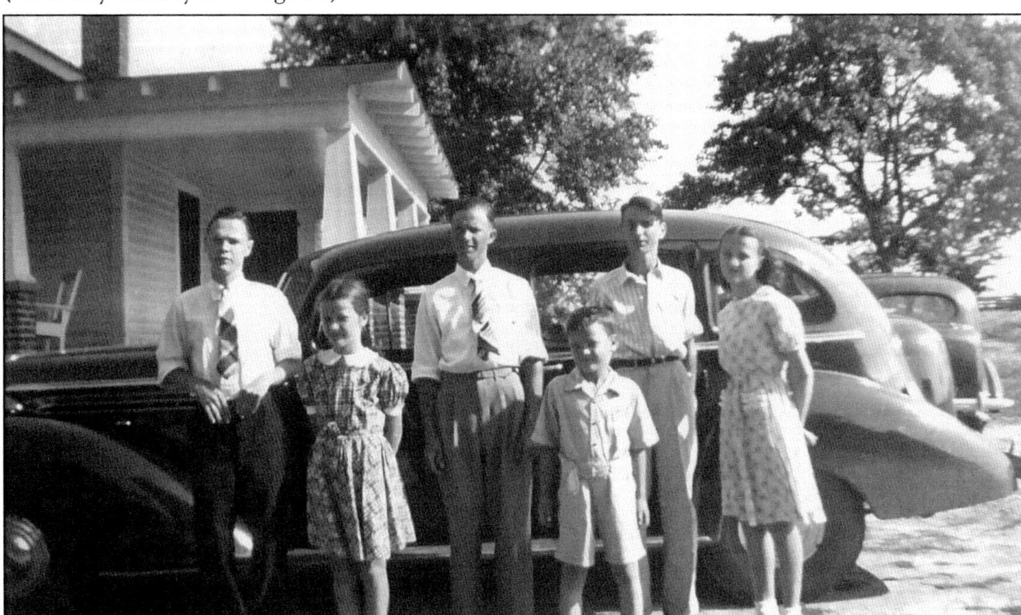

Robert Weldon Davis (1886–1971) and Annie Dora Zimmerman Davis (1889–1972) were the parents of 13 children. Around 1940, several of their children were at the Davis farmhouse near Hamer between Milton and Yanceyville. Robert Weldon Davis was a farmer and bridge builder. His ancestor, John Boswell Davis (1756–1841), was a friend of Francis Asbury, one of the first American Methodist bishops. (Courtesy Tom Oliver.)

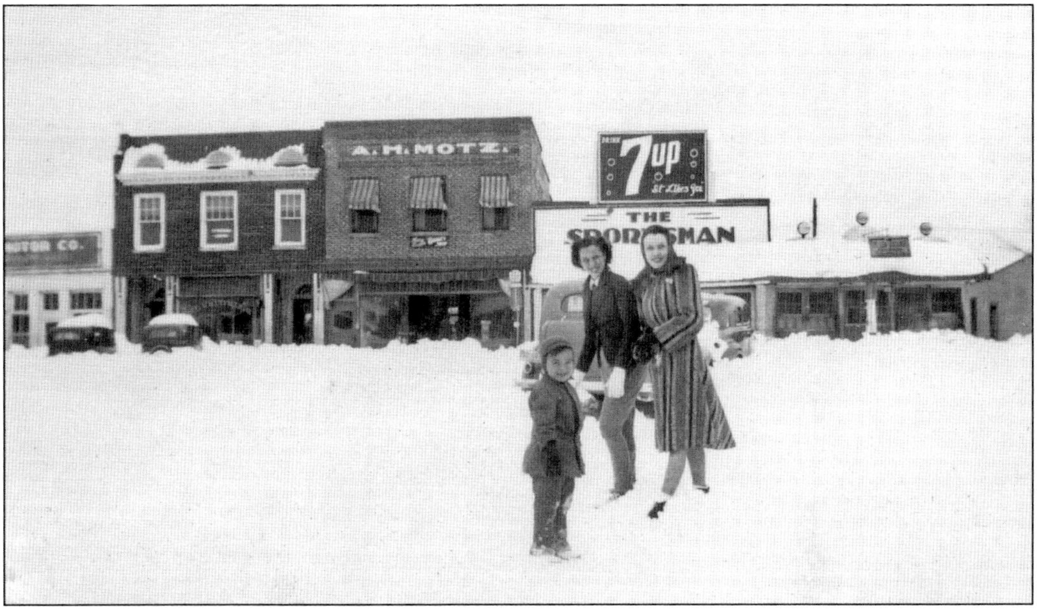

In January 1940, Caswell County experienced a record-setting blizzard. Snow fell heavily for almost 24 hours, a rarity for the region. Plows struggled to open main roads, and the local Civilian Conservation Corps camp did much of the work clearing snow around the Yanceyville Square. Radio broadcasts across the area warned motorists to avoid Caswell County as it had the most snow, and travel was difficult if not impossible. The photograph above shows the Yanceyville Square looking east before the streets were totally cleared. The image below shows the Kerr family venturing from their Yanceyville house. They are, from left to right, Eliza Katharine Kerr (1921–1997), Albert Yancey Kerr (1878–1942), Mary Frances Kerr, and George Yancey Kerr (1925–1986). The Kerr house, built around 1845, once was a hotel. (Above, courtesy Louise Moore Atwater Estate; below, courtesy Katherine Hunter Cooper Estate.)

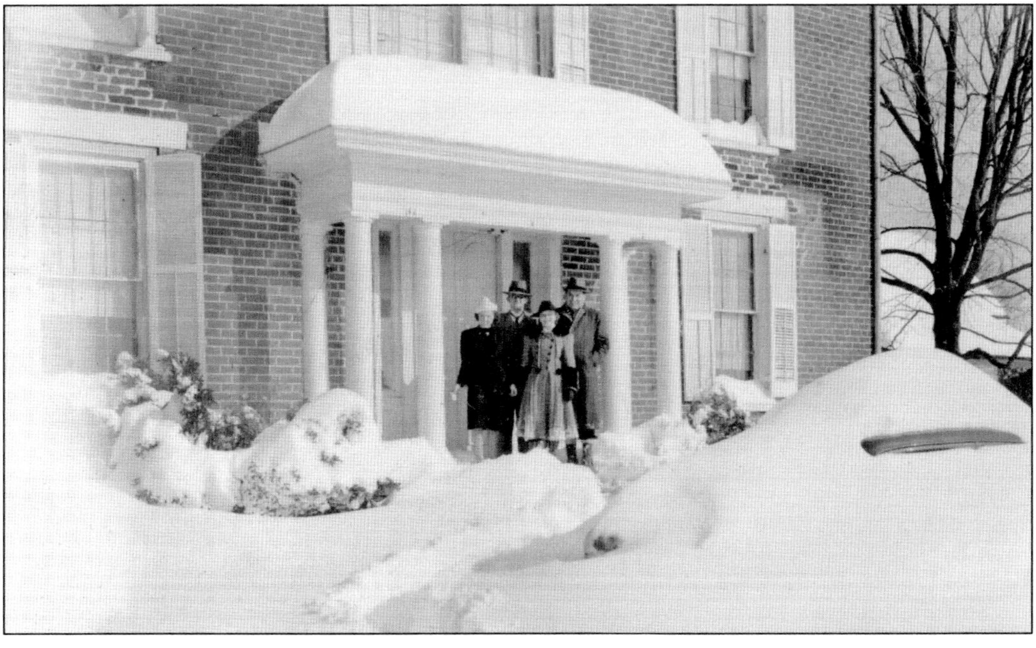

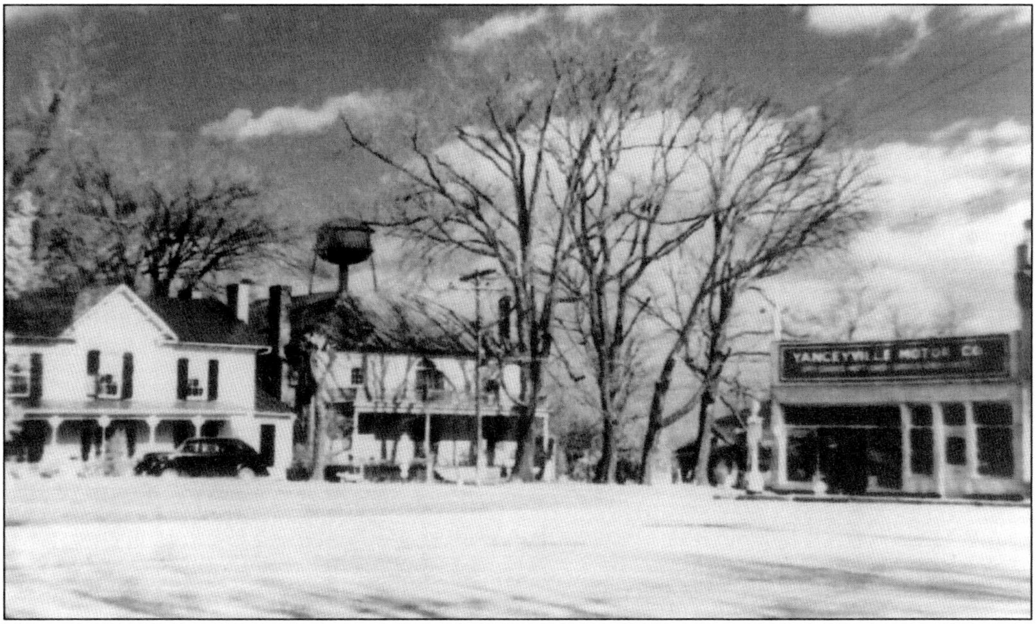

The northeast corner of the Yanceyville Square in the early 1940s shows the Graves-Florance-Gatewood House on the left, with the Poteat Hotel next, followed by the Yanceyville Motor Co. building on the right. Beyond the Yanceyville Motor Co. building, barely visible, is the Hooper Boarding House, which was operated by Erna Mae Wrenn Hooper. (Courtesy Ann McGuire Harvey.)

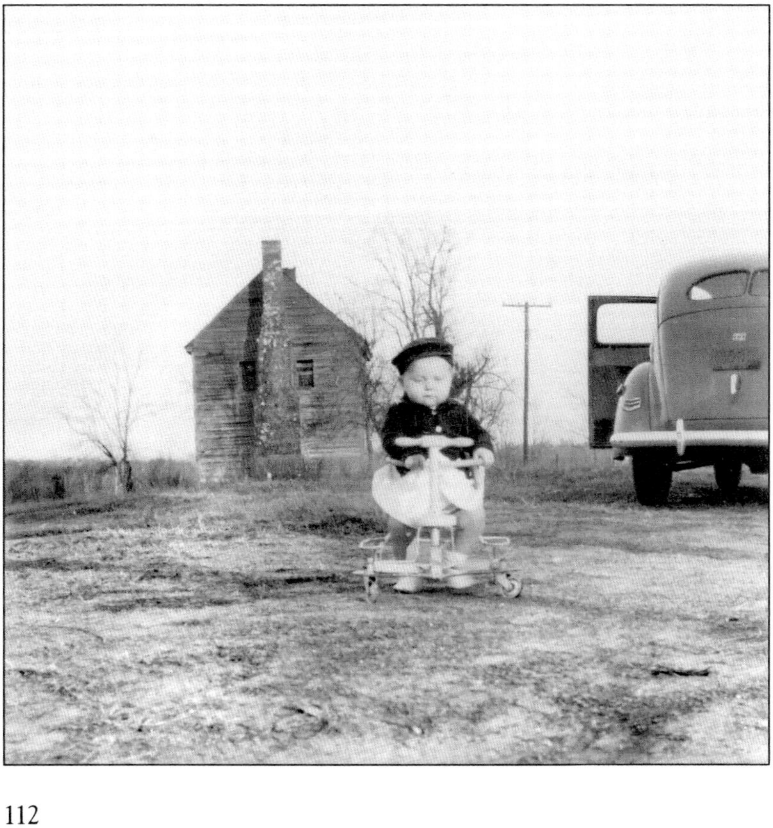

The Old Leasburg Tavern, seen behind young Raymond Y. Allen Jr. in the 1940s, stood for over 150 years and was a convenient resting place for travelers on the stagecoach route that ran nearby. The historic structure, later referred to as the Lex Sally House, was dismantled in the 1970s. (Mildred Wade Henderson.)

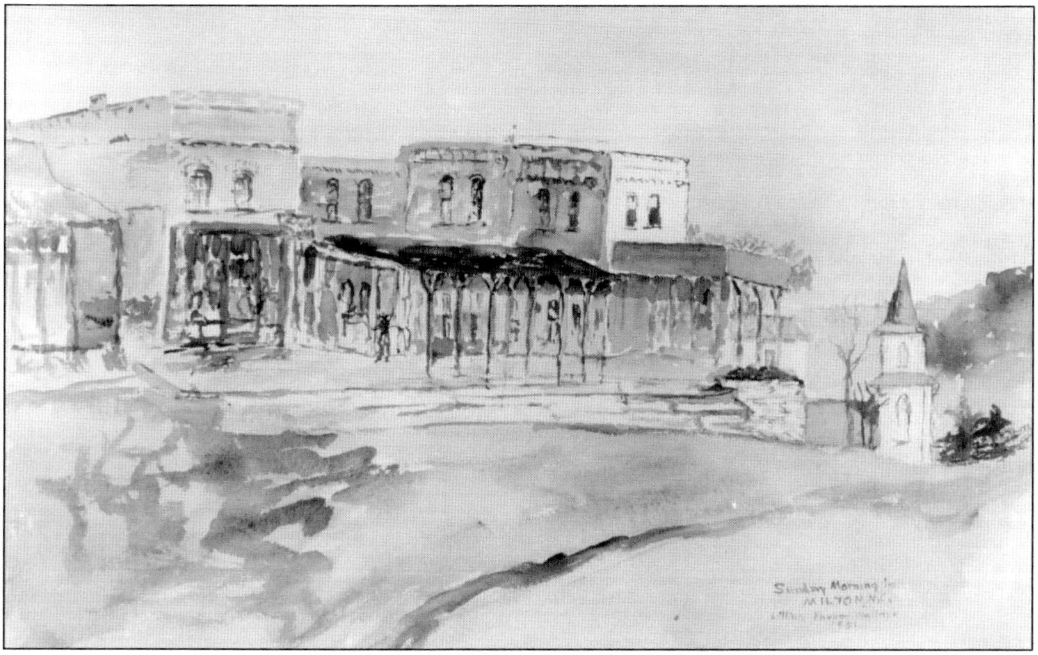

Sunday Morning in Milton is a 1951 watercolor of the Milton business district by Dr. Lillian Parker Wallace (1890–1971). The original was donated to the North Carolina Collection at the University of North Carolina. In addition to being an accomplished artist, Lillian Parker Wallace was a history professor at Meredith College in Raleigh, North Carolina. (Courtesy Houston G. Jones.)

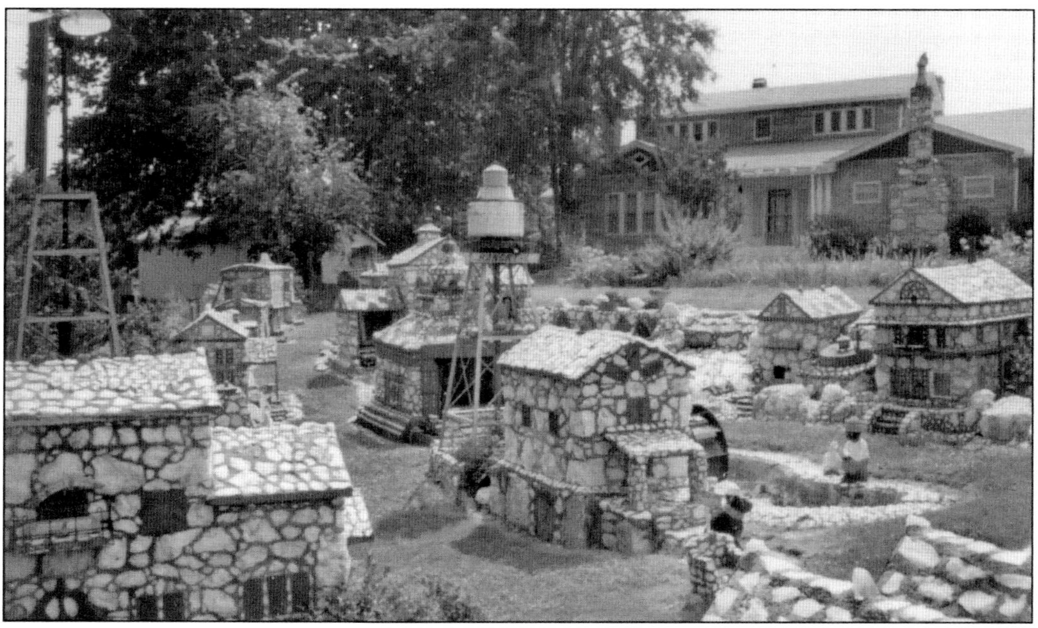

World War I veteran Henry Lafayette Warren (1892–1977) built Shangri-La Village beside his home and service station in Prospect Hill. The remarkable miniature village, constructed of white flint rock, stands 3 to 4 feet high and includes a church, mill, theater, silo, house, garage, and rock retaining walls. Warren worked on Shangri-La until his death at 84. His home is in the background. (Courtesy Nelson and Cindi Straughn.)

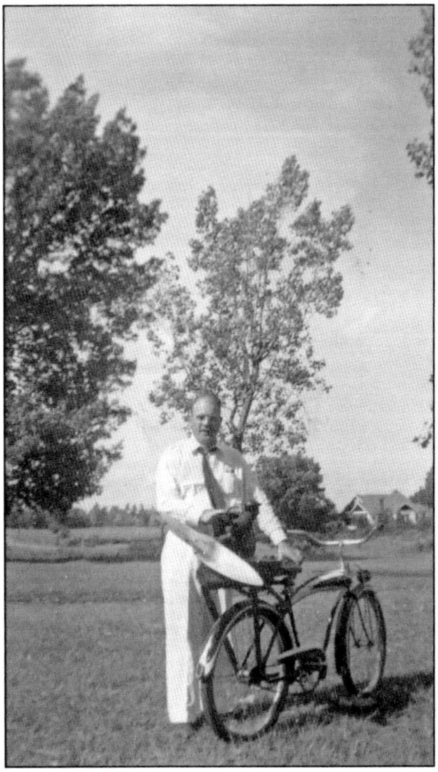

Not only was Dr. Ludolphus Graham Page (1902–1970) a much-loved and respected Caswell County dentist, he was a pilot who had an airport in his backyard and an inventor. He designed and built a propeller-powered bicycle and proved it operational. On his property, Dr. Page also constructed a fallout shelter and an underground hangar for his airplane. (Courtesy Dr. Graham Allison Page.)

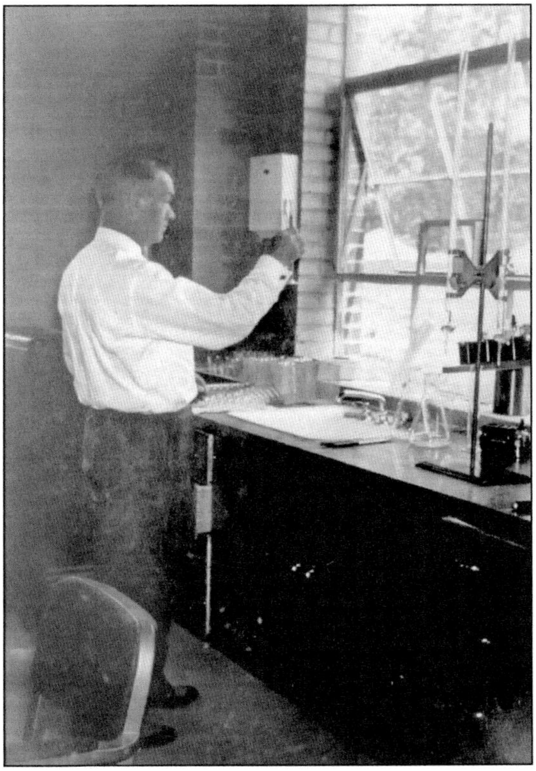

Until 1953, Yanceyville relied on deep wells for its municipal water supply. That year a new reservoir and water-treatment facility were completed and commissioned. The lake and plant were constructed at a cost of $122,000, which was financed through bonds. Plant manager William Laroy Gunn (1910–1984) is testing water quality in the facility's laboratory. He was superintendent of the Yanceyville Sanitary District for 38 years. (Courtesy Ann Gunn Everitt.)

Flanked by students Bertie Lou Wyrick (left) and Annie Bell Dunevant (right), Principal Millard Quentin Plumblee (1906–1987) prepares to depart on the 1954 Anderson High School trip to Washington, D.C. M. Q. Plumblee was Anderson's principal for over 30 years (1931–1962). In 1962, the high school students and faculty were consolidated with Bartlett Yancey High School in Yanceyville. Plumblee was principal at that school from 1962 to 1970. (Courtesy Gordon Plumblee.)

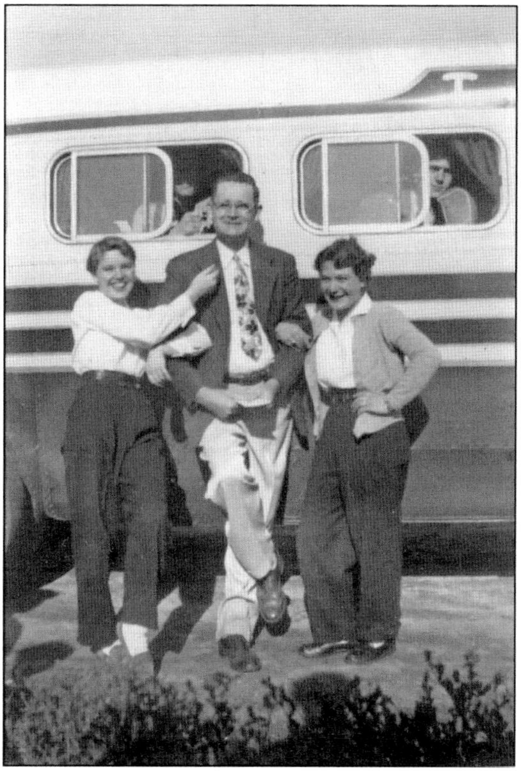

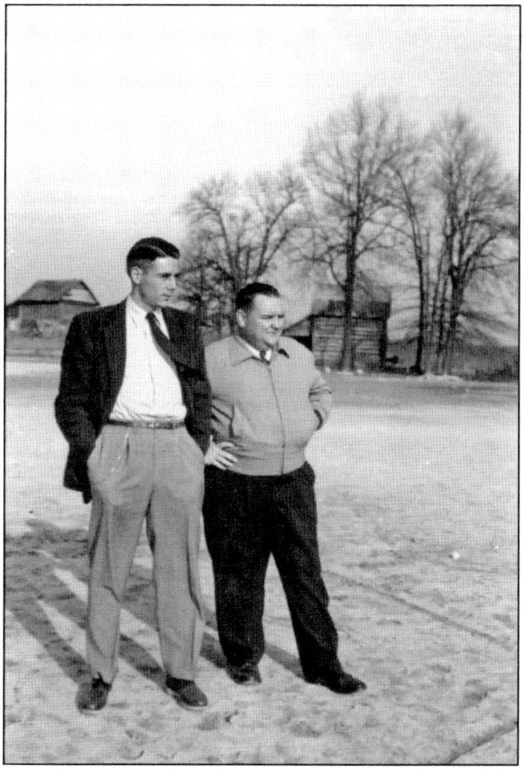

Bartlett Yancey High School teachers Bill Niven (left) and Ralph Eugene Sadler (1919–1981) coached the school's 1953 six-man football team, which practiced and played games on the old athletic field (showing very little grass). Niven became the high school's principal. Sadler coached, taught agriculture, and was instrumental in founding the school's nationally recognized Future Farmers of America chapter. Note the tobacco barns in the background. (Courtesy Ann Gunn Everitt.)

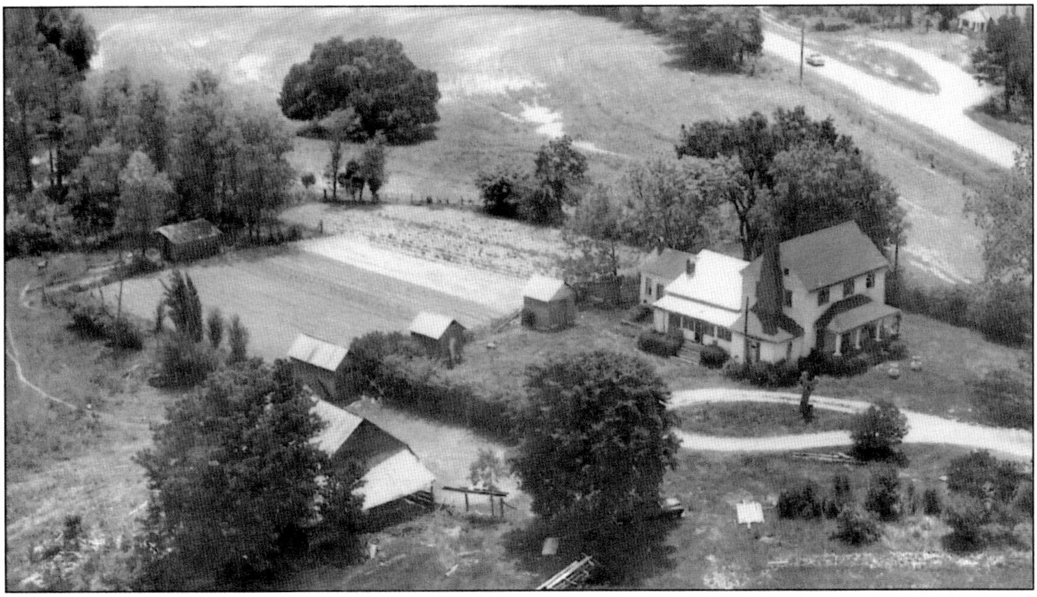

The Arthur William Moorefield tobacco farm south of Yanceyville, pictured in the 1960s, was anchored by the 1807 house and outbuildings typical of the 1800s, including a barn, corncrib, smokehouse, and chicken coop. The grove of trees in the upper left shaded a large slave cemetery. The house was one of the first in the county to have electricity, which was generator-created. (Courtesy Frank J. and Mozelle White Moorefield.)

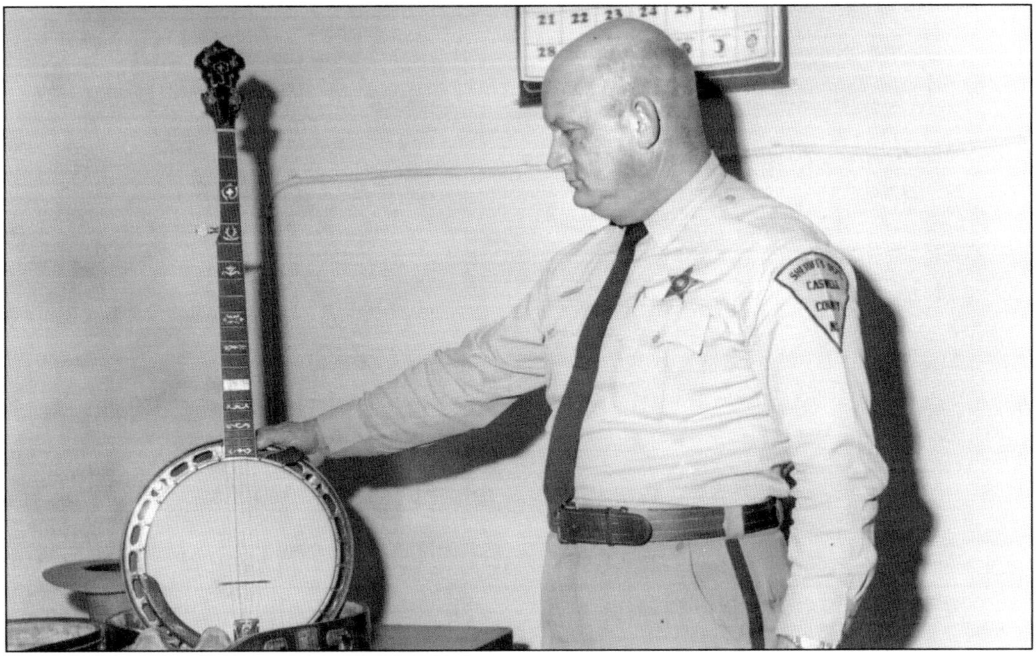

What Caswell County sheriff Bobby E. Poteat is doing with this banjo in the 1960s is not known. Poteat was sheriff for 12 years (1966–1978) and was the 42nd high sheriff of Caswell County since 1777. The county's first sheriff was David Shelton (*c.* 1734–*c.* 1800). For over a century, the sheriff's office was in the old Caswell County Courthouse, built in 1861. (CCHA Photograph Archives.)

Six

Entertainment, Events, and Sports

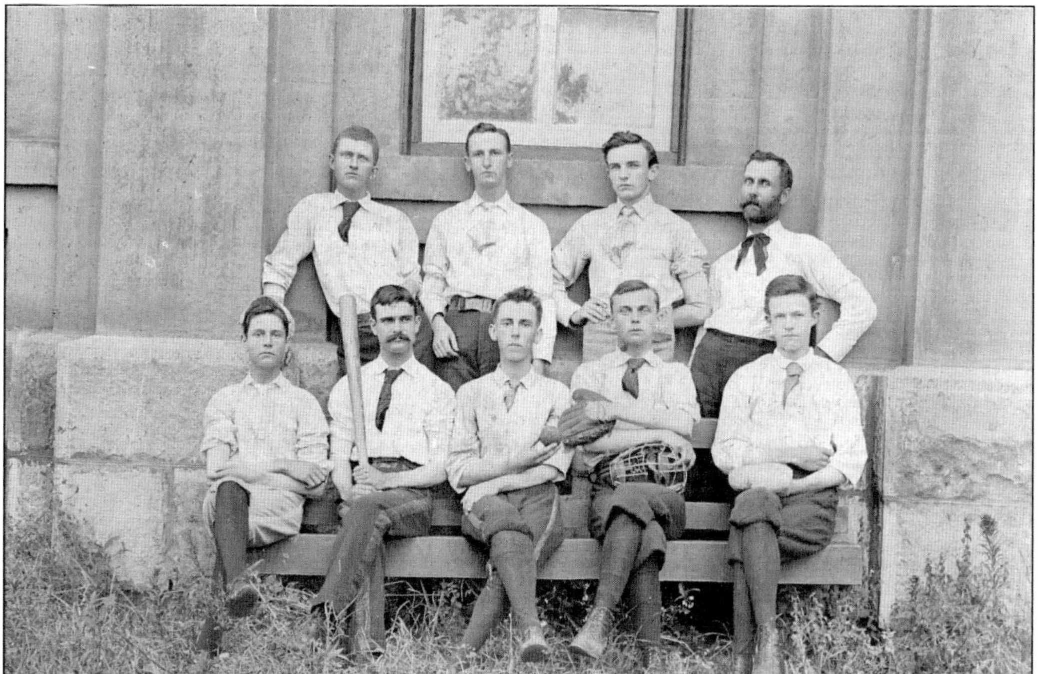

The members of the 1890s Yanceyville baseball team are, from left to right, (first row) Steve Richmond, Pomp Richmond (with bat), Nat Graves (ball in hand; could be the pitcher), Bob Roan (apparently the catcher), and A. Yancey Kerr; (second row) Jim Slade, John Graves, John H. Kerr, and B. S. Graves (coach). (CCHA Photograph Archives.)

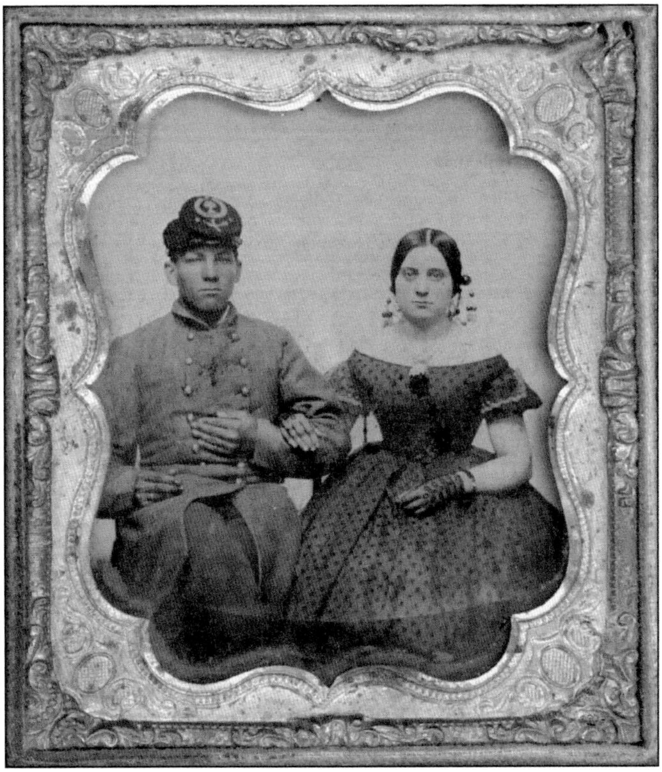

The Civil War ended Caswell's boom era. Felden Lewis Hodges (born 1845) served in the Confederate cavalry and survived the conflict. His older brother George was killed. Hodges is in uniform, probably on the day of his marriage to Henrietta Harrelson two months before the war ended in 1865. The veteran was married three times and left a large family in Caswell County. (Courtesy James Y. and Nettie Dameron Blackwell.)

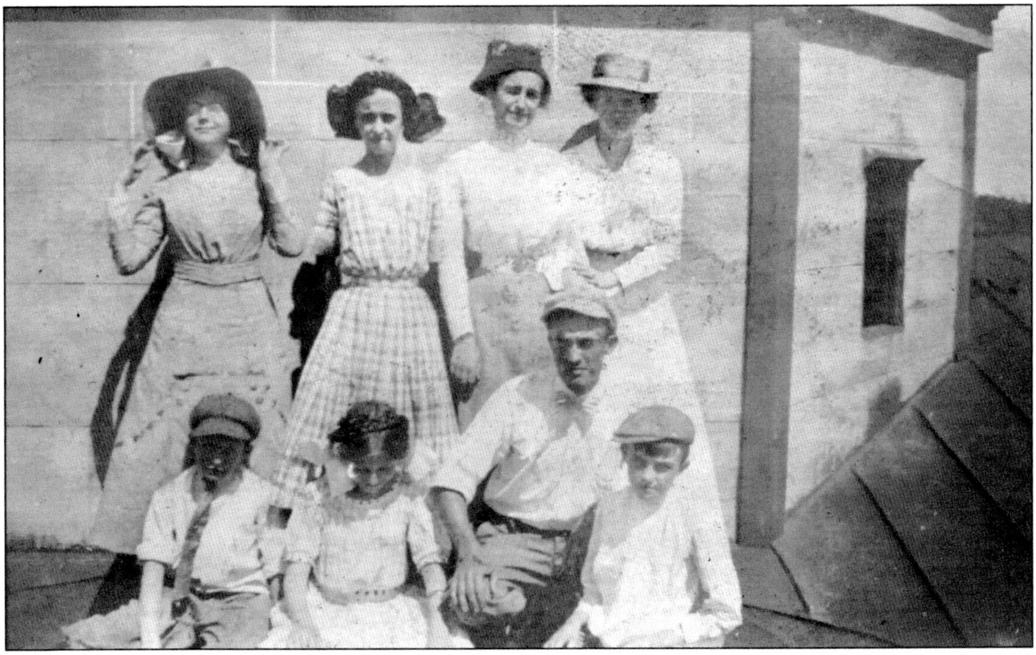

As the Caswell County Courthouse was the tallest structure in the area, excursions onto the roof to take in the vistas were a popular pastime. Access was gained through the bell tower cupola after negotiating a narrow catwalk in the dark attic. Around 1900, unidentified but well-dressed roof walkers are taking in the sights. (CCHA Photograph Archives.)

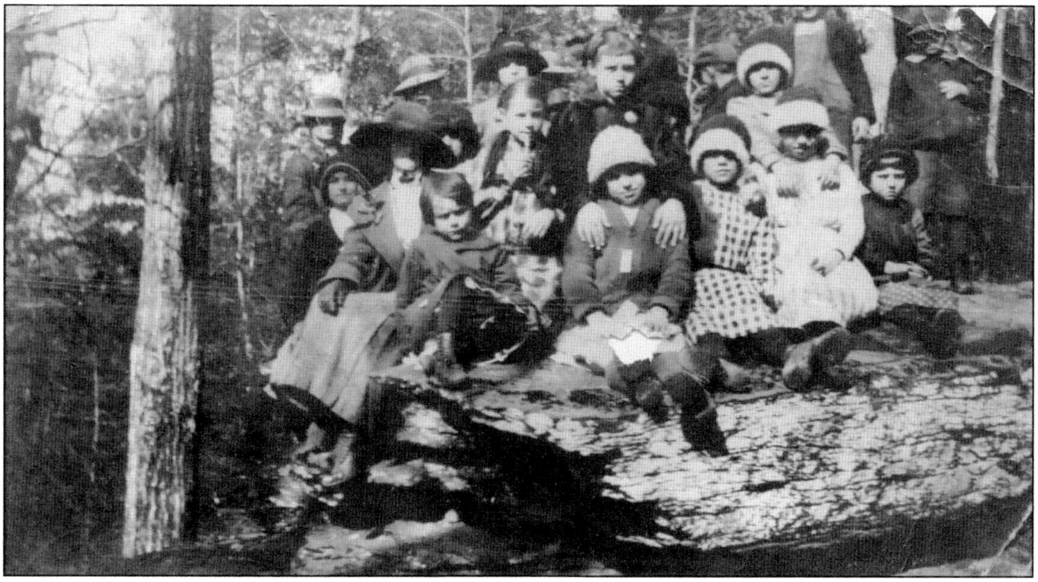

Tradition teaches that Indian Rock, northwest of Yanceyville on a tributary of Moon Creek, was used as a fortress by Native Americans. Many arrowheads have been found nearby as well as stone blades and scrapers. In 1915, schoolteacher Virginia Badgett Daniel took her class on a field trip to the outcropping. (Courtesy Houston G. Jones.)

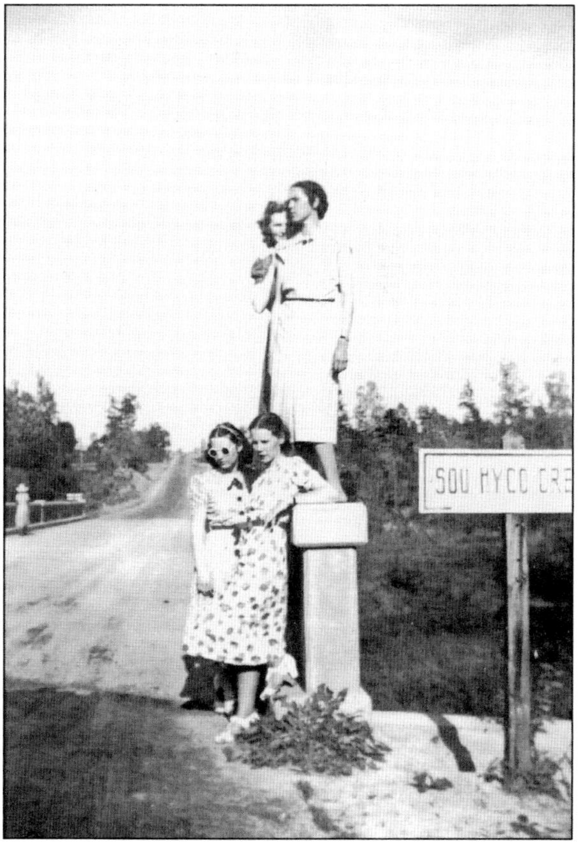

The South Hyco Creek bridge is the setting in 1939 for these young Caswell County ladies who are celebrating high school graduation in a somewhat unusual manner. The girl in front on the bridge railing is Mildred Wade Henderson of Leasburg. Behind her is Sarah Virginia Newman. On the bridge (without sunglasses) is Sarah Jane Womack. (Courtesy Karen Wade Avants.)

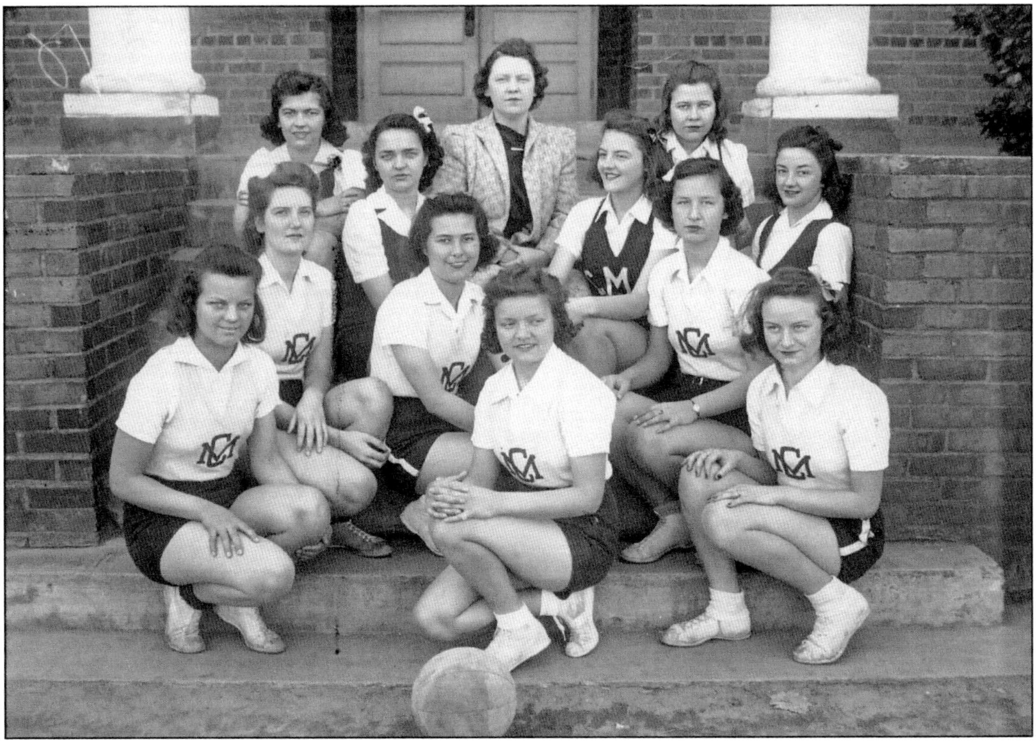

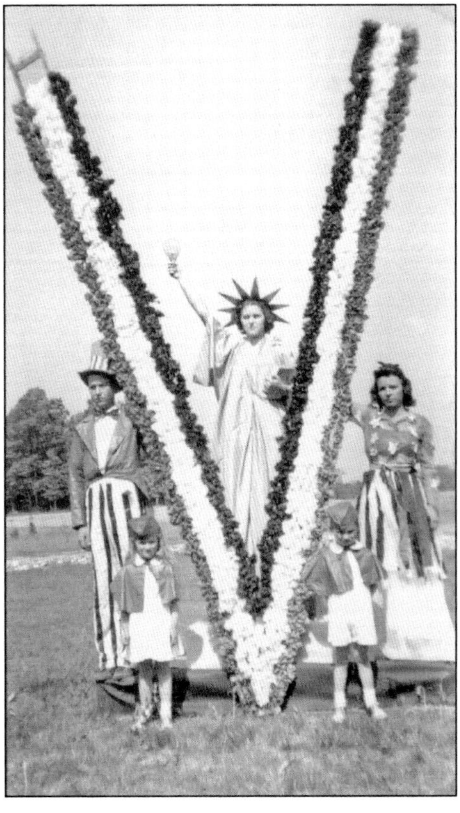

Ruby Claire Neighbors Hodges (1911–2006), at center in back, was a much-loved teacher and coached the 1941 Cobb Memorial High School girls' basketball team. Ruby ended her career teaching at Caswell's Piedmont Academy. She believed knowledge could be found outside the usual classroom experience and encouraged woodworking, cooking, skits, and other extracurricular activities. Many elementary students drove their first nail in her class. (Courtesy Houston G. Jones.)

This "V for Victory" tableau was staged by the Prospect Hill High School senior class as part of its graduation celebration (Class Night) in April 1942. Because the United States was in the throes of World War II, the class chose a patriotic theme to show support for the troops. (Courtesy Nelson and Cindi Straughn.)

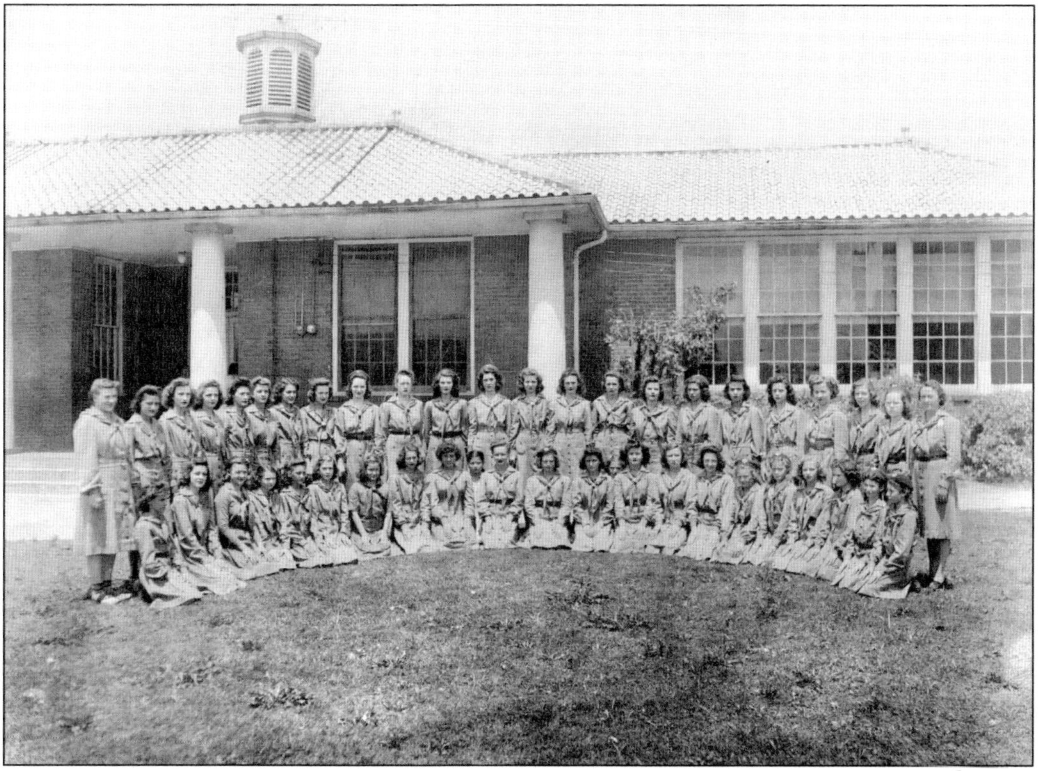

The Girl Scouts was a popular activity in the 1940s, as is evidenced by this gathering of the Yanceyville Girl Scout Troop at the Bartlett Yancey Elementary School. To the far right is troop leader Pattie Griffin Gunn (1895–1956). Sixth from the right among the kneeling girls is famous artist Maud Florance Gatewood. (Courtesy Pattie Griffin Gunn Estate.)

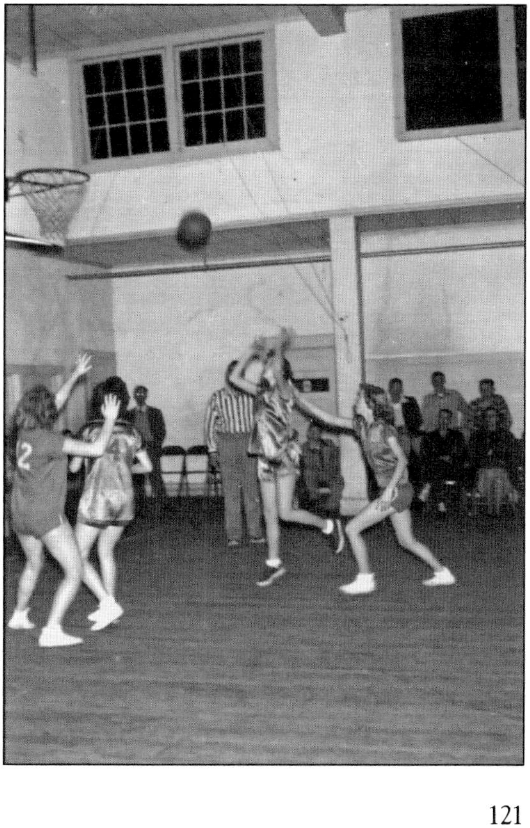

In the early 1950s, girls' basketball was much different than today. Each team had six players, with offensive and defensive squads on separate sides of the court. The Bartlett Yancey High School girls' team played in the old auditorium that doubled as a gymnasium. The man in the far corner in glasses and a sweater vest is teacher Norman Stroupe Upchurch (1904–1989). (Courtesy Ann Gunn Everitt.)

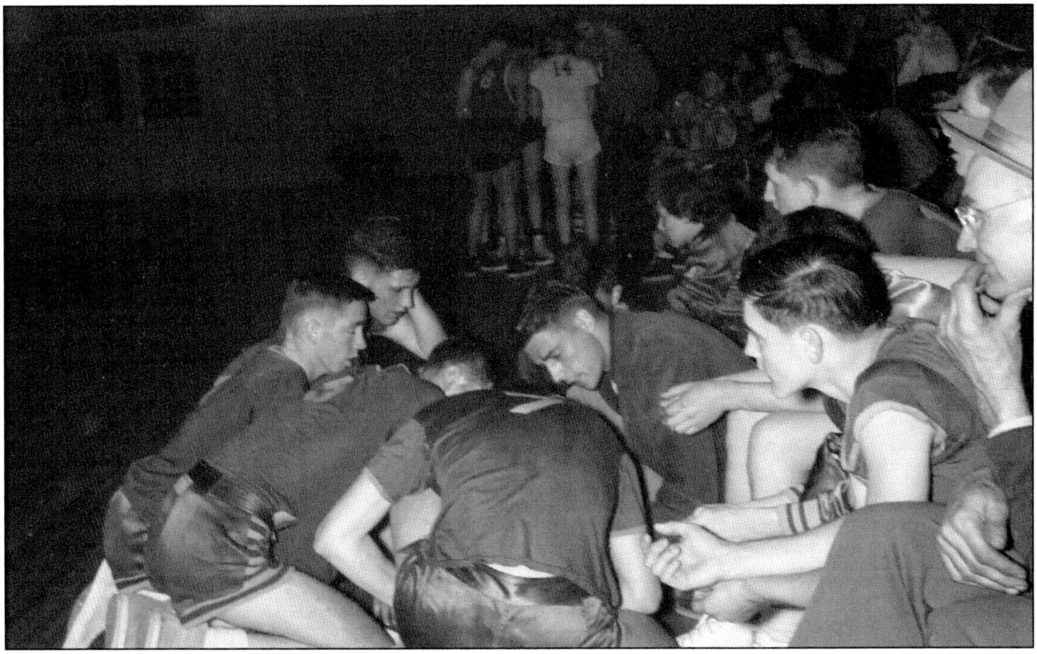

A popular sport at most small rural schools, basketball often attracted as much community support as football. The 1952–1953 Bartlett Yancey High School basketball team played in the old auditorium in Yanceyville. In the center is coach Bill Niven, at far left is player Duke Foster, and closest to the camera at right is player Billy Gwynn. (Courtesy Ann Gunn Everitt.)

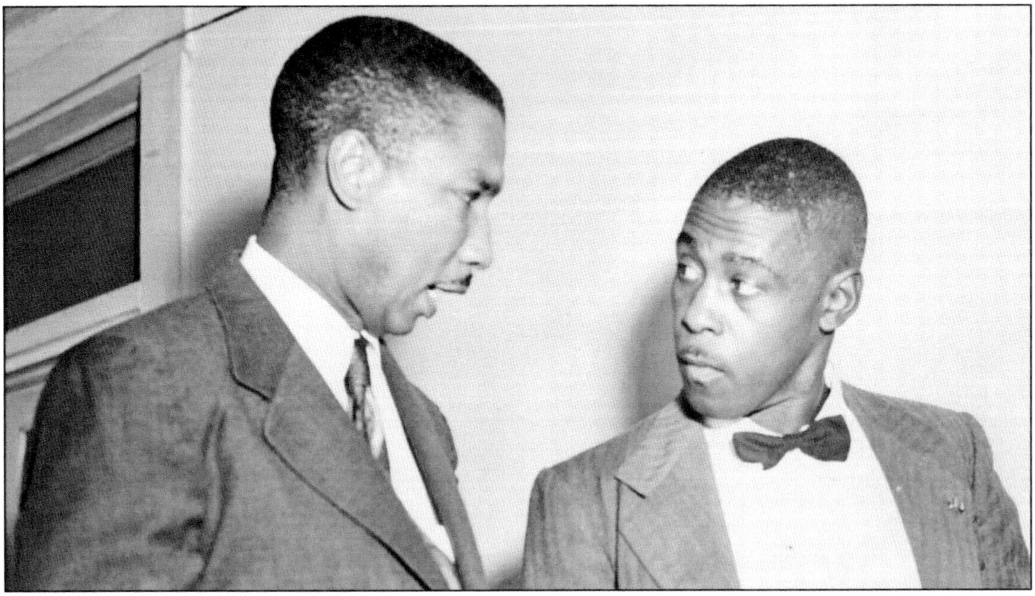

In 1951, Caswell farmer Matt Ingram (left) was convicted in a Yanceyville court of assault on a white female by "leering" from 50 feet. Ingram prevailed on appeal. White Yanceyville lawyer Ernest Frederick Upchurch (1877–1960) represented Ingram, knowing that his action would not be popular with the local white community. Lawyer Robert H. Carter (right) was later provided by the NAACP. The case attracted national attention. (©CORBIS/Bettmann, donated by Corbis-Bettmann.)

In 1962, the Fultz Quads sent this Christmas card to Dr. Ludolphus Graham Page, D.D.S. Dr. Page was the sisters' dentist when they lived in Caswell County. Born in 1946, the girls became famous as the first known black identical quadruplets. The quads represented Pet Milk for many years. Their early schooling was in Yanceyville. (Courtesy Catherine Fultz Griffin.)

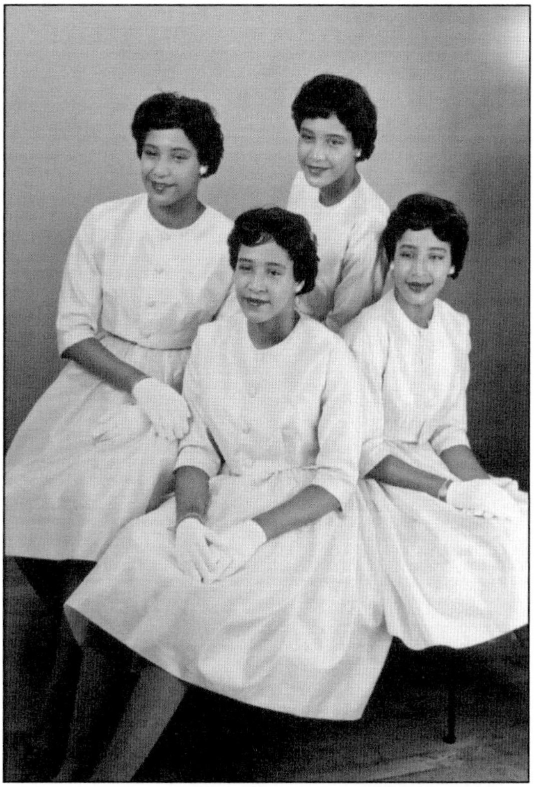

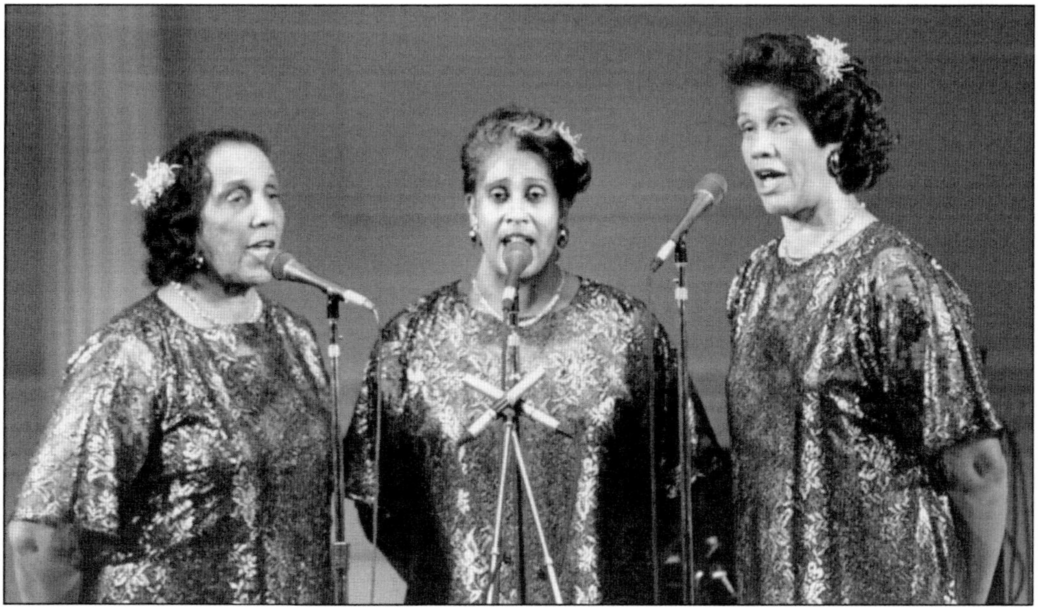

The Badgett sisters of Caswell County won a North Carolina Folk Heritage Award in 1990 for singing spirituals, hymns, and gospel songs in the jubilee style, a form of unaccompanied close harmony learned from their father, Cortelyou Odell Badgett (1905–1978). Their albums include *Just A Little While to Stay Here* and *The Voice that Refused to Die*. Badgett Sisters Parkway in Caswell County was named in their honor. (Courtesy Connie Badgett Steadman.)

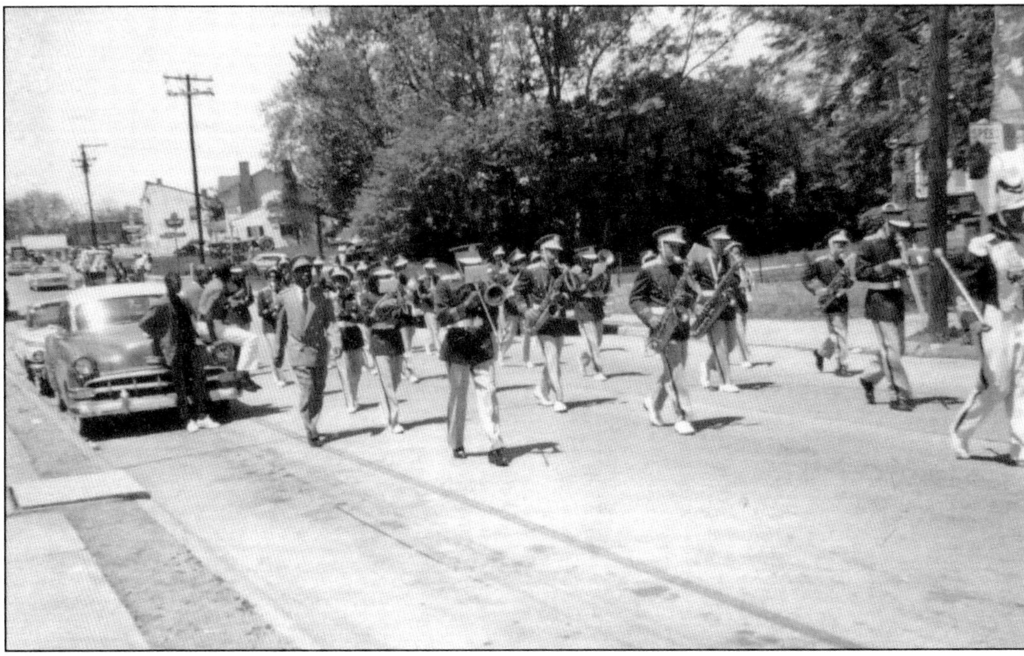

In the early 1960s, Caswell County schools remained segregated. The black Caswell County High School in Yanceyville had an excellent marching band. The white Bartlett Yancey High School had no music department and no band, marching or otherwise. The buildings of the central square area of Yanceyville are seen in the background. (Courtesy Helen Little.)

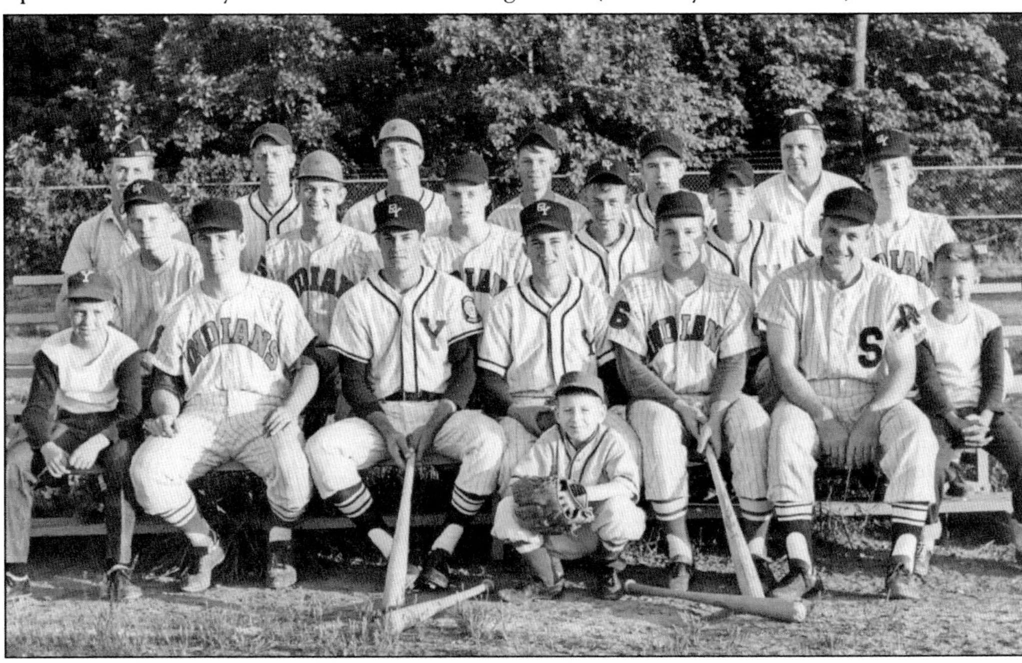

American Legion baseball was a popular summer activity in Caswell County. The 1965 team was coached by Neal Watlington, who played major league baseball for 12 years. The American Legion representatives (with American Legion caps) are Charles Edward Guthrie (1918–2005) at left and Hoyt Ray Moore at right. (Courtesy John O. Gunn Estate.)

Bibliography

Anderson, George A. *Caswell County in the World War 1917–1918*. Raleigh, NC: Edwards and Broughton Printing Co., 1921.

Barfield, Rodney D., and Patricia M. Marshall. *Thomas Day, African American Furniture Maker*. Raleigh: North Carolina Office of Archives and History, 2005.

Bottoms, Timothy S. *From a Needle to an Anvil: The Connally General Store and Leasburg, Caswell County, North Carolina*. Master's Thesis, University of North Carolina at Greensboro: 1991.

Brittain, Joan T. *Laurence Stallings*. Boston: Twayne Publishing, 1975.

Brown, Deborah F. *Dead-End Road*. Bloomington, IN: AuthorHouse, 2004.

Bumgarner, Matthew. *Kirk's Raiders: A Notorious Band of Scoundrels and Thieves*. Shelby, NC: Westmoreland Printers, 2000.

Graves, Louise, comp. *Graves: Twelve Generations, Some Descendants and Kin*. Dallas: self published, 1977.

Hall, Randal L. *William Louis Poteat: A Leader of the Progressive-Era South*. Lexington, KY: University Press of Kentucky, 2000.

Jones, Houston G. *Bedford Brown: State Rights Unionist*. Carrollton, GA: West Georgia College, 1955.

Little-Stokes, Ruth, and Tony P. Wrenn. *An Inventory of Historic Architecture Caswell County North Carolina*. Waynesville, NC: Don Mills, Inc, 1979.

Malone, Bartlett Yancey. *Whipt 'Em Everytime*. Jackson, TN: McCowat-Mercer Press, Inc., 1960.

Motley, Charles B. *Milton, North Carolina: Sidelights of History*. Self published, 1976.

———. *Carolina Communities*. Radford, VA: Commonwealth Press Inc., 1995.

Plumblee, Millard Quentin. *At the Foot of the Hill: The Pattillo Family and Allied Lines*. Charlotte, NC: Delmar Printing and Binding, 1987.

———. *From Rabbit Shuffle to Collins Hill, Stories of Southern Caswell County, North Carolina*. Burlington, NC: Full Service Printing, 1984.

Powell, William S. *When the Past Refused to Die: A History of Caswell County, North Carolina, 1777–1977*. Durham, NC: Moore Publishing Company, 1977.

Rotary Club, Yanceyville, North Carolina, comp. *Wheel Tracks: Biographical Sketches (1942–1943)*. Yanceyville, NC: Service Publication of the Yanceyville North Carolina Rotary Club, 1943.

Scott, Jean Bradsher, comp. *In the Beginning: The Churches of Caswell County*. Yanceyville, NC: Caswell Parish Inc., 1998.

Veterans of Foreign Wars Post No. 7316, *Service Record Book of Men and Women of Yanceyville, N. C., and Community*. Self published, 1948.

Walker, Vanessa Siddle. *Their Highest Potential*. Chapel Hill, NC: University of North Carolina Press, 1996.

Whitlow, Jeannine D., ed. *The Heritage of Caswell County North Carolina*. Winston-Salem, NC: Hunter Publishing Company, 1985.

INDEX

Caswell County Historical Association

The Caswell County Historical Association, Inc., (CCHA) was established in 1956 in Yanceyville, North Carolina, and operates as a nonprofit organization. The goals of the CCHA are to promote the study of local history and genealogy, to collect and interpret historical artifacts, and to preserve local historical structures. The CCHA owns and operates the Richmond-Miles History Museum in Yanceyville, which is located in the historic Graves-Florance-Gatewood House on the Square.

This book is the fourth in a series that explores and celebrates the history of Caswell County and its people. The first three were, in order of publication:

Powell, William S. *When the Past Refused to Die: A History of Caswell County, North Carolina, 1777–1977.* Durham, NC: Moore Publishing Company, 1992.

Little-Stokes, Ruth, and Tony P. Wrenn. *An Inventory of Historic Architecture, Caswell County, North Carolina.* Waynesville, NC: Don Mills, Inc., 1979.

Whitlow, Jeannine D., ed. *The Heritage of Caswell County, North Carolina.* Winston-Salem, NC: Hunter Publishing Company, 1985.

The CCHA also has a significant internet presence:

Caswell County Historical Association Web site:
www.rootsweb.ancestry.com/~nccha/

Caswell County Family Tree:
http://wc.rootsweb.ancestry.com/cgi-bin/igm.cgi?db=caswellcounty

Caswell County Historical Association Web log:
http://nccha.blogspot.com/

Caswell County Photograph Collection:
www.flickr.com/photos/nccha/

Caswell County Historical Association Message Board:
http://groups.yahoo.com/group/nccha/

The following are additional Web sites to which the CCHA is a major contributor:

Caswell County Cemetery Census:
http://cemeterycensus.com/nc/casw/

Caswell County, North Carolina, GenWeb Web site:
www.rootsweb.ancestry.com/~nccaswel/index.htm